EVALUATION IN EDUCATION

EVALUATION IN EDUCATION

Foundations of
Competency Assessment
and Program Review

—— *Third Edition* ——

RICHARD M. WOLF

New York
Westport, Connecticut
London

Copyright Acknowledgment

The author and publisher gratefully acknowledge permission to
reprint material from:

C. E. Beeby, 1938. *The Intermediate School of New Zealand*. Wellington,
N.Z.: New Zealand Council for Educational Research.

Library of Congress Cataloging-in-Publication Data

Wolf, Richard M.
    Evaluation in education : foundations of competency assessment and
program review / Richard M. Wolf — 3rd ed.
        p. cm.
    Includes bibliographical references and index.
    ISBN 0-275-93616-3
    1. Educational evaluation. 2. Educational surveys.
    3. Educational tests and measurements—Evaluation. I. Title.
LB2822.75.W65 1990
379.1'54—dc20   90-44606

Library of Congress Catalog Card Number: 90-44606
ISBN: 0-275-93616-3

First published in 1990

Praeger Publishers, One Madison Avenue, New York, NY 10010
An imprint of Greenwood Publishing Group, Inc.

Printed in the United States of America

The paper used in this book complies with the
Permanent Paper Standard issued by the National
Information Standards Organization (Z39.48-1984).

10 9 8 7 6 5 4 3 2 1

To Marie

CONTENTS

FIGURES AND TABLES

PREFACE

The preparation of a new edition of a book is a test of the durability of one's ideas. When I began writing the first edition of this book almost fifteen years ago, I was trying to address issues in the field of evaluation as I saw them then. I recognized that the field was in its early stages of development and was likely to change considerably over time. Of course, I had no idea how the field would change. Accordingly, I decided to take as nondoctrinaire an approach to evaluation as I could. In my case, this meant identifying questions that might be asked when undertaking an evaluation study and the kinds of information one would need in order to answer those questions. In contrast, a number of writers at that time were staking out various ideological positions in evaluation. Some, for example, regarded true experiments as the only way to estimate the effects of educational programs while others regarded evaluation as nothing more than a fact-gathering enterprise for administrators. I felt that such strong positions were unwarranted in a fledgling field.

My sense now is that my initial decision was not only prudent but also wise. The basic questions that must be addressed when conducting an evaluation study and the classes of information needed to answer those questions have not changed in the intervening years. Furthermore, the absence of a specific doctrine has enabled me to avoid getting entangled in useless arguments. Thus, the present edition should be seen more as an extension and refinement of some basic ideas than as a wholly new work. Of course, there is new material here—even a new chapter. But this should be seen as additional layers on the same structure.

While the basic views presented in this book have not changed, the field of evaluation has. It has gone from its infancy to become an established field. This is reflected throughout this edition, but especially in chapter fourteen. There is much that one can point to with pride in the field, and some of this is described in that chapter. But there are some dark clouds on the horizon.

There is a growing debate in the social sciences about method. For most of the past half century, the social sciences have attempted to develop objective measurement procedures to be used in as scientifically rigorous a way as possible. The collection of views, approaches, and the like that have traditionally been used come under the general heading of "positivism." There is, of course, much more to positivism than this, but it can suffice for now. Various people have expressed dissatisfaction with positivism for a number of reasons and have sought other ways of gaining knowledge in the social sciences. The debate is often referred to as quantitative vs. qualitative approaches to evaluation and research. This is an overly terse summarization of the debate. Much more is involved than simply a difference in techniques and procedures. In fact, what is at stake are the basic ways of knowing in the behavioral sciences. Some aspects of this debate are presented in chapter fourteen. It's hardly a beginning, however. The interested reader is referred to the references listed at the end of that chapter. The reason for mentioning the debate in the preface is to alert the reader to an issue that will occupy the field for some time to come. However, it should not be viewed as an impediment to the conduct of evaluation studies for two reasons. First, the approach advocated throughout this book includes the use of both quantitative and qualitative techniques and procedures. Second, it is possible to plan and carry out evaluation studies without reference to "pure" paradigms. The consensus of practicing evaluation workers is that one can be effective and successful in the field without having to use ideologically pure paradigms. The eclecticism of the approach advocated here is its serviceability.

Some years ago I eagerly awaited the publication of a book that I had admired considerably in its first and second editions. Alas, the third edition was a terrible disappointment. While it contained fresh and interesting material, it was clearly lacking something. After some reflection, I discovered what was lacking. The author used the third edition to build on material presented in the first and second editions. This was a grave mistake since it was unrealistic to expect people to read, at the very least, the second edition before tackling the third. It is unfortunate that this was reflected in generally unfavorable reviews and poor sales.

I vowed not to commit the same error. Accordingly, this edition does not depend on having read either of the previous editions of this book. For those who have read previous editions, I apologize for a fair amount of repetition and hope that you find the new material worthwhile. For people who have not read either of the previous editions, you will find everything I have to say about evaluation at this time in this book.

EVALUATION IN EDUCATION

— 1 —

THE NATURE OF EDUCATIONAL
EVALUATION

INTRODUCTION

Any work that sets out to deal with a relatively new aspect of education is obliged to furnish the reader with a definition, description, and discussion of that aspect. This is particularly true of the burgeoning field of educational evaluation where there is considerable confusion. This confusion stems partly from the fact that many of the techniques and procedures used in evaluating educational enterprises are rather technical, and educators are often not knowledgeable about such matters. A more basic reason for the confusion, however, is that different authors have different notions of what educational evaluation is or should be. These dissimilar views sometimes stem from the training and background of the writers, the particular professional concerns with different aspects of the educational process, from specific subject-matter concerns, from differences in temperament, and even from differing episte-mological views. A consequence of all this is that a reader unfamiliar with the field is often exposed to writings that not only differ but are even contradic-tory. Such writings are not just expressions of honest differences about what evaluation is and how it should be carried out. Often they are reflections of deep philosophical conflicts about what evaluation is or should be. At other times, they reflect a confusion that often attends the development of a rela-tively new field of inquiry.

One goal of this book is to reduce the confusion about what evaluation is and is not, how it should be organized and carried out, how the results of eval-uation studies should be reported, and how they can be used. There is no in-tent, however, to shield the reader from honest differences that exist within the field. These can and should be exposed and discussed. However, it is not necessary or even desirable to deal with a number of highly idiosyncratic views regarding educational evaluation. Rather, the emphasis here is on the presentation of a conceptualization of educational evaluation that attempts to be comprehensive, coherent, sensible, and practical. It combines features emphasized by a number of writers in the field but attempts to weld them into a unified view of educational evaluation. It sometimes sacrifices the private concerns of writers when these might interfere with the basic ideas of evaluation. The critical reader can deal with the subtleties, complexities, and differences that exist at the frontiers of evaluation once the basic ideas are learned.

TOWARD A DEFINITION OF EVALUATION

There are a number of definitions of educational evaluation. They differ in level of abstraction and often reflect the specific concerns of the person who formulated them. At the most general level, evaluation has been defined as "a formal appraisal of the quality of educational phenomena" (Popham, 1988). This definition, unfortunately, does not help very much since it is left to the reader to determine what the terms "formal appraisal" and "quality" mean. A somewhat more elaborate definition was provided by L. J. Cronbach who defined evaluation as the "collection and use of information to make decisions about an educational program" (Cronbach, 1963). By "educational program" Cronbach meant anything ranging from a set of instructional materials and activities, distributed on a national level, to the educational experiences of a single learner. The context of Cronbach's remarks, however, were the curricula that were developed in the late 1950s and early 1960s that were intended to upgrade the quality of instruction and learning in various subject-matter areas. Cronbach's concern was with the testing and modification of the new courses that emerged from various study groups and educational laboratories. It was his belief that only by extensive information-gathering activities in actual classroom situations would it be possible to determine where and how programs were succeeding and failing so that modifications could be made on as sound a basis as possible. Cronbach's article suggested various kinds of information that could be sought in an evaluation enterprise and how these could be analyzed and used in decision making for the purposes of course improvement. His article went on to discuss a number of other issues in evaluation, some of which will be taken up later.

It is Cronbach's definition of evaluation that is of interest here. It is composed of two elements. The first, "the collection and use of information," puts equal emphasis on collection and use of information. The idea is that decisions are to be made on the basis of information, not on impressions or beliefs about how an educational program is supposed to function. In his article, Cronbach clearly stated that the kind of information he was primarily interested in was information relating to learner performance. Specifically, Cronbach wanted to find out what changes a course or curriculum produced in learners, what kinds of questions learners could answer after having studied a particular subject for a period of time, what kinds of problems they could solve, and what kinds of issues they could deal with. Cronbach asserted that this kind of information could provide the basis for sound decision making. The second element of Cronbach's definition, "to make decisions,'" denotes an action orientation. Evaluation should lead to action, as opposed to conclusions not acted on. While he does not say so specifically, he implies that evaluation activity that does not contribute to the decision-making process is a waste of time and money. Evaluation, according to Cronbach, must contribute to the decision-making process, notably to course improvement, if it is to have any justification in education.

This definition of evaluation, emphasizing the collection and use of information about learner performance for purposes of making sound decisions about educational programs, is a distinct improvement on the "formal appraisal of the quality of educational phenomena" definition, but it still does not go far enough in saying what evaluation is. A more extended definition, supplied by C. E. Beeby, describes evaluation as "the systematic collection and interpretation of evidence, leading, as part of the process, to a judgment of value with a view to action" (Beeby, 1978). This definition has four key elements. First, the use of the term "systematic" implies that what information is needed will be defined with some degree of precision and that efforts to secure such information will be planful. This does not mean that only information that can be gathered through the use of standard tests and other related measures will be obtained. Information gathered by means of observational procedures, questionnaires, and interviews can also contribute to an evaluation enterprise. The important point is that however information is gathered it should be acquired in a systematic way. This does not exclude, a priori, any kind of information. The second element in Beeby's definition, "interpretation of evidence," introduces a critical consideration sometimes overlooked in evaluation. The mere collection of evidence does not, by itself, constitute evaluation work. Yet uninterpreted evidence is often presented to indicate the presence (or absence) of quality in an educational venture. High dropout rates, for example, are frequently cited as indications of the failure of educational programs. Doubtless, high dropout rates are indicators of failure in some cases, but not all. There may be very good reasons why people drop out of educational programs. Personal problems, acceptance into educational programs, and landing a good job are reasons for dropping out that may in no way reflect on a program being studied. In some cases, dropping out of an educational program may indicate that the program has been quite successful. For example, a few years ago, the director of a community college program that was training people for positions in the computer field observed that almost two-thirds of each entering class failed to complete the two-year program. Closer examination revealed that the great majority of "dropouts" had left the program at the end of the first year to take well paying jobs in the computer department of various companies (usually ones they had worked in while receiving their training). The personnel officers and supervisors of these companies felt that the one year of training was not only more than adequate for entry- and second-level positions but provided the foundation on which to acquire the additional specialized knowledge and skill required for further advancement. Under such circumstances, a two-thirds dropout rate before program completion was no indication of a program failure or deficiency. In was, in fact, a strong indicator of success.

Clearly, information gathered in connection with the evaluation of an educational program must be interpreted with great care. If the evaluation worker[1] cannot make such interpretations himself, he or she must enlist the aid of others who can, otherwise, the information might be seriously misleading. In the above example, the problem of interpretation was relatively simple. Dropout statistics are easily gathered, and one can usually have confidence in the numbers. More complex situations arise when one uses various tests, scales, or observational and self-report devices such as questionnaires. In these situations the interpretation of evaluation information can be extremely difficult. Unfortunately, the interpretation of information has too often been neglected. Specific mention of it in a definition is welcome since it focuses attention on this critical aspect of the evaluation process.

The third element of Beeby's definition, "judgment of value," takes evaluation far beyond the level of mere description of what is happening in an educational enterprise. It casts the evaluation worker, or the group of persons responsible for conducting the evaluation, in a role that not only permits but requires that judgments about the worth of an educational endeavor be made. Evaluation not only involves gathering and interpreting information about how well an educational program is succeeding in reaching its goals, but judgments about the goals themselves. It involves questions about how well a program is helping to meet larger educational and social goals. Given Beeby's definition, an evaluation worker who does not make a judgment of value, or who, for political or other reasons avoids making a judgment, is not an evaluation worker in the full sense of the term. Whoever does make such a judgment after the systematic groundwork has been laid is completing an evaluation.

Lest the reader get the mistaken impression that the evaluation worker has great power in education, a distinction needs to be made between two types of judgments. The first is the judgment of value of the enterprise being evaluated. This is the type described above and is clearly within the scope of the evaluation worker's professional function. The second type of judgment is taken in light of the first and, along with other relevant factors, is the decision on future policy and action. This is clearly the domain of administrators, governing boards, and other policymakers. If these decision makers make both kinds of judgments, they are taking over an essential part of the professional evaluation function. This is to be avoided.

An illustration may be given. Several years ago I was involved in the evaluation of a program for disadvantaged junior high-school students held on Saturday mornings at a local school. Expectations with regard to student performance were more than fulfilled. There was a high degree of enthusiasm among students and teachers. Also, parents were pleased that their children were constructively occupied. The program, while voluntary, was consistently well attended. All in all, the program was highly successful, and the evaluation report clearly communicated this. The most difficult task in preparing the evaluation report was identifying suggestions for ways to improve the program.

Unfortunately, the program was terminated at the end of the year. The reason given was that it was too expensive. Opening a public school on Saturday morning required additional outlays for heating and light, custodial salaries, and insurance as well as for an administrator, required for legal reasons. When these additional costs and, one suspects, inconveniences were taken into account, it was decided that the program, although highly successful, could no longer be justified. The situation, however, was one in which the evaluation workers fulfilled their professional function and the administrators fulfilled theirs. The fact that the decision about future policy was inconsistent with the judgment of the program's value must be accepted as one of those unhappy situations in which other institutional factors had a determining influence on future action.

It is also possible that a decision might be made to retain a marginally effective program. It may be that the political or public value of a program is deemed important enough to continue it, despite a low level of effectiveness. It is also possible that funds may be available to operate a program of marginal quality that might not be available for other more worthwhile endeavors. It is the decision maker's job to determine whether to fund it or not. The point remains: the evaluation workers, or those charged with the evaluation of a program, should render a value judgment; it is the responsibility of decision makers to decide on future policy and action. Each has an area of responsibility, and each must be respected within their domain. This must be understood at the outset. If it is not, there is danger that evaluation workers may become frustrated or cynical when they learn that policy decisions have been made contrary to what results of their evaluation suggest.

The last element of Beeby's definition, "with a view to action," introduces the distinction between an undertaking that results in a judgment of value with no specific reference to action and one that is deliberately undertaken for the sake of future action. The same distinction is made by Cronbach and Suppes although the terms "conclusion-oriented" and "decision-oriented" were used (1969). Educational evaluation is clearly decision-oriented. It is intended to lead to better policies and practices in education. If this intention is in any way lacking, an evaluation enterprise should probably be dropped, since evaluation workers should be able to use their time to better advantage.

So far no mention has been made about what kinds of action might be undertaken as the result of an evaluation study. The range is considerable. A conscious decision to make no changes could result from a carefully conducted evaluation study, or a decision to abolish a program altogether, although the latter case is not very likely. In fact, I do not know of a single instance where a decision to terminate a program was based solely on the results of an evaluation study. Between these extremes, modifications in content, organization, and time allocation could occur, as well decisions about additions, deletions, and revisions in instructional materials, learning activities, and criteria for staff selection. Such decisions come under the general heading of course improvement and are discussed in some detail by Cronbach (1963). M. Scriven used the term "formative evaluation" to characterize many of these kinds of decisions (1967). In contrast, decisions about which of several alternative programs to select for adoption or whether to retain or eliminate a particular program are "summative"' in nature, to use Scriven's terminology. Scriven's distinction between formative and summative evaluation has achieved a fair measure of popular acceptance although the number of clearly summative studies is small. The basic idea is that evaluation studies are undertaken with the intention that some action will be taken as a result.

DIFFERENCES BETWEEN EVALUATION, MEASUREMENT, RESEARCH, AND LEARNER APPRAISAL

Beeby's definition of evaluation goes some distance toward specifying what evaluation is. However, in order to function effectively, a definition must not only say what something is, it should also say what it is not. This is particularly important with regard to evaluation. Three activities that are related to evaluation are measurement, research, and learner appraisal. Evaluation shares some similarities with each. The differences, however, are considerable and need to be examined so that evaluation can be brought more sharply into focus.

Evaluation and Measurement

Measurement is the act or process of measuring. It is essentially an amoral process in that there is no value placed on what is being measured. Measurements of physical properties of objects such as length and mass do not imply that they have value; they are simply attributes of interest. Similarly, in the behavioral sciences, the measurement of psychological characteristics such as word knowledge, neuroticism, attitudes toward various phenomena, problem solving, and mechanical reasoning does not in itself confer value on these characteristics.

In evaluation, quite the opposite is the case. The major attributes studied are chosen precisely because they represent educational values. Objectives are educational values. They define what we seek to develop in learners as a result of exposing them to a set of educational experiences. They can include achievements, attitudes toward what is learned, self-esteem, and a host of other prized outcomes. Such outcomes are not merely of interest; they are educational values. Thus, while evaluation and measurement specialists often engage in similar acts, such as systematically gathering information about learner performance, there is a fundamental difference between the two in the value that is placed on what is being measured.

A second important distinction between evaluation and measurement inheres in the object of attention of each. By tradition and history, measurement is undertaken to compare individuals with regard to some characteristic. For example, two learners may be compared with regard to their reading comprehension. This is accomplished by administering the same reading comprehension test to the two learners and seeing how many questions each has answered correctly. Since they have been given the same test, a basis for comparison exists. This is the traditional measurement approach. In evaluation, on the other hand, it is often neither necessary nor even desirable to make such comparisons between individual learners. What is of interest is the effectiveness of a program. In such a situation, there is no requirement that the learners be presented with the same set of questions. In fact, under some circumstances, it may be prudent to have them answer entirely different sets of questions. The resulting information can then be combined with that obtained from other learners and summarized in order to describe the performance for the entire group. Such a procedure introduces efficiency into the process of information gathering and will be discussed in more detail later. The point to be made here is that evaluation and measurement are typically directed toward different ends: evaluation toward describing effects of *treatments*; measurement toward description and comparison of *individuals*. In evaluation, it is not necessary that different learners respond to the same questions or tasks.

Learner Appraisal

Closely related to the notion of measurement is learner appraisal. Appraising the proficiencies of learners for purposes of diagnosis, classification, marking, and grading is usually considered the prerogative of teachers. The introduction of systematic evaluation procedures has been viewed in some cases as an intrusion on this traditional teacher function. Nothing could be further from the truth. Evaluation is directed toward judging the worth of a total program and, sometimes, toward judging the effectiveness of a program for particular groups of learners. It is not an external testing program that is intended to supplant teacher responsibility for learner appraisal. In fact, it is, more often than not, simply not possible to do so. For example, if in the course of evaluating a program, it is decided that different groups of learners will answer different sets of questions, the resulting evaluative information will contribute absolutely nothing to the process of learner appraisal. Measurements of individual learner proficiencies will still have to be made to fulfill the appraisal function. Thus, teachers need not fear that systematic evaluation of educational programs will intrude on the appraisal role of their professional function. Quite the opposite may occur. (Teachers wishing to use evaluative information to assist them in appraising learner performance may find themselves frustrated when they learn that evaluative information does not help them in this regard.)

Evaluation and Research

Although evaluation and research share a number of common characteristics, there are some notable differences. Research typically aims at producing new knowledge that may have no specific reference to any practical decision, while evaluation is deliberately undertaken as a guide to action. This distinction is highlighted in the last phrase of Beeby's definition of evaluation, "with a view to action." Any distinction based on motivation is obviously fragile, and one operation can shade into another, but in practice there is usually a marked difference in content, presentation, and often method between research inspired by scholarly interest or an academic requirement, and an investigation undertaken with a definite practical problem in mind. To be sure, scholarly research has often led to highly practical payoffs—the work of atomic physicists in the 1930s is a dramatic case in point. A basic difference in motivation, however, remains.

A more basic distinction between evaluation and research lies in the generalizability of results produced by each type of activity. Research is concerned with the production of knowledge that is as generalizable as possible. For example, a research worker may undertake an investigation to determine the relationship between student aspiration and achievement. The study will be designed and carried out in such a way as to ensure results that are as generalizable as possible. They will be obtained over a wide geographical area, apply to a broad range of ages, and be as true in several years as now. Generalizability of results is critical in research. Little or no interest may be attached to knowledge that is specific to a particular sample of individuals, in a single location, studied at a particular point in time. In fact, if a researcher's results cannot be duplicated elsewhere, they are apt to be dismissed. In their now famous chapter on designs for research in teaching, D. T. Campbell and J. Stanley drew attention to the notion of generalizability when they discussed threats to the integrity of various designs under two broad headings—internal validity and external validity (1963). External validity was their term for generalizability.

Evaluation, in contrast, seeks to produce knowledge specific to a particular setting. Evaluation workers, concerned with the evaluation of a reading improvement program for third graders in a single school or school district, will direct their efforts toward ascertaining the effectiveness of the program in that locality. The resulting evaluative information should have high local relevance for teachers and administrators in that school district. The results may have no scientific relevance for any other school in any other locality; well-intentioned educators, interested in such a program, will have to determine its effectiveness elsewhere in a separate study.

The fact that evaluation does not produce generalizable knowledge has produced an interesting phenomenon in the United States and elsewhere. Scholarly journals typically report the results of research studies, but rarely, if ever, publish the results of evaluation studies. The justification for such policy is that evaluation studies seldom produce knowledge that is sufficiently general in nature to warrant widespread dissemination. Thus, typical practice is for an evaluation enterprise to produce a few copies of a report for local consumption. Educators in other localities may often fail to learn of successful programs that are going on elsewhere, unless they communicate with persons from those places at professional meetings. The situation is being remedied somewhat by the publication of a few journals devoted to evaluation work. *Educational Evaluation Policy and Analysis*, *Evaluation Review*, and *Evaluation in Education*, for example, occasionally report the results of evaluation studies although the focus is primarily on general issues in evaluation and methodological matters.

Another important distinction between evaluation and research lies in the area of method. In research there are fairly well-developed canons, principles, procedures, and techniques for the conduct of studies, which have been explicated in various works (Campbell and Stanley, 1966; Kaplan, 1964; Kerlinger, 1986). These methods ensure the production of dependable and generalizable knowledge. While the methods of research frequently serve as a guide to evaluation endeavors, there are a number of occasions when such methods are neither necessary nor practicable. Evaluation is not research, and the methods of the latter do not need to dictate the activities of the former. In fact, classical research is often inappropriate for evaluation studies. This issue will be taken up in detail in chapter nine.

Some writers assert that any evaluative effort must rigorously employ the methods of experimental research and that anything less is apt to be a waste of time and money. This is an extreme position. While research methods are often useful in planning evaluation studies, they should not be worn as a straitjacket. Meaningful evaluative activity can be pursued that does not follow a classical research model. For example, a program intended to train people in a particular set of skills, such as welding, could be undertaken with a single select group of learners and their proficiency assessed at the conclusion of the training program. Such an enterprise would violate most, if not all, of the precepts of scientific research, for example, lack of randomization, absence of a control group, etc. However, it might yield highly pertinent evaluative information that could be used for a variety of purposes. An inability to follow research prescriptions for the design and conduct of studies need not be fatal for evaluation work. There are occasions when departures from a strict research orientation are necessary and appropriate. Substantial and important work can be done in evaluation that does not require the use of formal research methods. One must, of course, be extremely careful. A number of specific considerations in the design and conduct of evaluation studies will be presented in chapter nine.

The previous discussion was intended to introduce the reader to the concept of educational evaluation. Definitions of educational evaluation were presented and discussed, and evaluation was briefly contrasted with measurement, learner appraisal, and research. But definition and contrast can only go so far. In a way, the remainder of this book is an elaborate attempt to convey the nature of educational evaluation, and what it entails. Before proceeding to a more systematic and detailed examination, some background material needs to be presented so that educational evaluation may be seen in a larger context.

THE ROLE OF EVALUATION IN THE EDUCATIONAL PROCESS

The prominence given to educational evaluation can be traced to the mid-1960s. The United States Congress passed the Elementary and Secondary Education Act of 1965 (ESEA), which provided plentiful funding for the improvement of educational programs. This was by far the most ambitious piece of educational legislation ever passed by the federal government and provided substantial amounts of money for local educational agencies and universities. The ESEA also contained a requirement that programs funded under Titles I and III of the act be evaluated annually and that reports of the evaluation be forwarded to the federal government. Failure to comply with this requirement could result in a loss of program funding. Since considerable monies were involved, this requirement was to be taken seriously. The fact that many, if not most, local educational agencies had little idea of how to go about evaluating their programs did not receive adequate consideration. Certainly, the educational community was ill-prepared to undertake such a massive amount of evaluation work. There was a great deal of scurrying around in the early years of the ESEA, and many of the evaluation efforts, or what passed as evaluation, were poor. Nonetheless, the intent of Congress was clear. If the monies being invested in education were to have any chance of significantly improving the enterprise, then it was important to keep track of how they were being spent and what results were being obtained.

It was unfortunate that what came to be known as the "evaluation requirement" was introduced in the manner that it was. Still, it seems unlikely that the need to evaluate educational programs would have been taken so seriously or so quickly acted on without such a spur. One unfortunate aspect of the evaluation requirement arose from the fact that evaluation was viewed by many as an activity engaged in to satisfy an external funding agency, that is, the federal government, rather than as an integral part of the educational enterprise. It was also unfortunate that only externally funded programs were, in fact, evaluated. Resources were often not available for evaluating conventional programs.

The view that developed in the mid- to late-1960s regarding the evaluation requirement was, to say the least, lamentable. It was also in marked contrast to the view that evaluation was an integral part of the educational process that had been developing since the late 1920s and early 1930s, principally under the leadership of Ralph Tyler. Briefly, Tyler's rationale postulated three major elements in the educational process: objectives, learning experiences, and appraisal procedures.[2] Since objectives will be treated in detail in chapter three, it is only necessary to mention here that *objectives* refers to one's intentions for an educational endeavor. They represent desired, or valued, performances or behaviors that individuals in a program are intended to develop. An educational program's purposes may range from having learners (whatever their age or other characterisitcs) acquire a narrowly specified set of skills to reorganization of an entire life style. The nature of the objectives is not important at this point. What is important is that an educational program be undertaken with some intentions in mind and that these intentions refer to desired changes in the learners served by the program.

The term *learning experiences* refers to those activities and experiences that learners undergo in order to acquire the desired behaviors. For example, if a program in nutrition education is concerned with learners acquiring information about the importance of including various food groups in a diet, the learning experiences designed to help students acquire this information might include reading, lectures, audiovisual presentations, and the like. "Learning experiences" is a broad term that includes both individual and group activities carried on in and out of class at the instigation of educators for the sake of attaining the program's objectives. Thus, if a teacher requires that learners visit a museum to view a particular exhibit, this would be classified as a learning experience, provided it is intended to help attain a particular objective. Correspondingly, homework assignments, individual projects, and term papers—completed outside of school—would also be classified as learning experiences. According to Tyler, learner appraisal in the educational process is critical because it is concerned with ascertaining the extent to which the objectives of the program have been met. For a representation of the educational process as formulated by Tyler see Figure 1.1.

The representation in Figure 1.1 is a dynamic one as signified by the two directional arrows linking each element with each of the others. Beginning

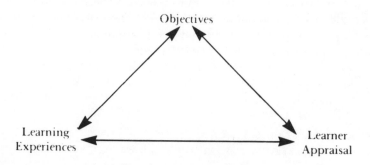

FIGURE 1.1: Representation of Educational Process

Source: Adapted from R. Tyler, ed., *Educational Evaluation: New Roles, New Means.*
Yearbook of the National Society for the Study of Education. Chicago: University of Chicago
Press, 1969.

with objectives, the arrow pointing to learning experiences indicates that objectives serve as a guide for the selection or creation of learning experiences. For example, if a geometry course is supposed to develop deductive thinking abilities that can be used in real life situations, then learning experiences that require work with other than geometry content, such as newspaper editorials, advertisements, and the like, will have to be included in the program. Other examples could easily be cited. The key point is that objectives will be an important determiner of the learning experiences that constitute the operational program. The arrow pointing from objectives to learner appraisal indicates that the primary (some would maintain the exclusive) focus of appraisal is on gathering evidence about the extent to which the objectives of a program have been attained. Just as the objectives provide specifications for the establishment of learning experiences, they also furnish specifications for learner appraisal. To return to the previous example, a program that seeks to have students develop and use deductive thinking in life situations might require, in its appraisal of learning, evidence regarding student ability to apply deductive principles to the analysis of a variety of material outside the realm of geometry.

The two arrows stemming from objectives in Figure 1.1 are easily explained. The meaning of the other arrows is less apparent but no less important. The arrow pointing from learning experiences to learner appraisal is indicative of the fact that learning experiences can provide exemplars for the development of appraisal tasks. The activities that students engage in during the learning phase of a program should furnish ideas for appraisal situations. In fact, there must be fundamental consistency between learning experiences and appraisal tasks for learners. If there is not, something is amiss in the program. This is not to say that learning experiences and appraisal tasks must be identical. Appraisal tasks should contain an element of novelty for the learner. This novelty may appear in the content of the evaluation task, the form of it, or both. If there is no element of novelty, one does not have an educational program but, rather, a training program where learning experiences are designed to develop relatively narrow behaviors in the learner, and appraisal procedures are expected to ascertain only whether the narrow set of behaviors have been acquired. Education, on the other hand, involves the acquisition of fairly broad *classes* of behaviors. Thus, the arrow pointing from learning experiences to learner appraisal indicates that learning experiences furnish ideas and suggestions for learner appraisal, but there should not be an overspecification of appraisal procedures.

The two arrows pointing from learner appraisal to (1) objectives, and (2) learning experiences are especially important. In the case of the former, the arrow signifies that appraisal procedures should furnish information about the extent to which the objectives are being attained. This is an important function of learner appraisal. In addition, appraisal information can furnish valuable information that may result in the modification of some objectives and the elimination of others. Particular objectives may have been included as a result of noble but unrealistic intentions on the part of educators, but an appraisal may yield information that indicates the goals were not attained. This should prompt the educators to reconsider the objectives. Should the objectives be modified or perhaps eliminated? Are the objectives realistic for the group of learners served by the program? Are the resources and time necessary for achieving the objectives available? Such questions will, of course, have to be answered within the context of a particular situation. In raising these questions here, the intention is to illustrate how the results of appraisal activities can provide information pertinent to the review of objectives.

The arrow pointing from learner appraisal to learning experiences is suggestive of two important notions. First, just as appraisal activities can furnish information about which objectives are being successfully attained and which are not, learner appraisal can also provide information regarding learning experiences that appear to be working well and ones that are not. In any educational enterprise there will be a variety of learning experiences. It is unrealistic to expect that all will be equally effective. Appraisal procedures can furnish information about which learning experiences are succeeding, which ones may be in need of modification, and which ones should, perhaps, be eliminated. This is the notion of formative evaluation described by M. Scriven (1967) and discussed in some detail by Cronbach (1963). A second important idea suggested by the arrow pointing from appraisal to learning experiences is that tasks, exercises, and problems developed by evaluation specialists may be suggestive of new learning experiences. The incorporation of novel and imaginative appraisal materials into the learning program has, on occasion, contributed significantly to the improvement of learning. Of course, the appropriation of such materials for the improvement of the quality of the learning experiences renders the materials unusable for appraisal purposes. However, this is usually considered a small price to pay for improving the quality of the learning experiences.

The last arrow, which points from learning experiences to objectives, denotes that learning activities can result in encounters involving teachers, learners, and learning materials that suggest new objectives. Alert and sensitive teachers can identify potentially important new objectives. A teacher, for example, may be conducting a discussion with a group of learners and, as sometimes happens, the discussion will take a turn in an unexpected direction. The teacher may allow the discussion to follow this new course with considerable benefit to all. Such a development may lead the teacher to ask that specific provisions be made to ensure such benefits by incorporating one or more new objectives into the program. If one does not make formal provision for such activities, then they may not occur in the future, the basic limitation of incidental learning being that if it is not formally provided for, it may not take place. For this reason the arrow pointing from learning experiences to objectives has been included.

The above characterization of the educational process is attributed to Tyler (1950); its roots can be seen in his earlier work (1934). It is important to note that Tyler saw evaluation as central to the educational process and not as an appendage, useful merely to satisfy the demands of an outside funding agency. All serious writers about evaluation share Tyler's basic view about the critical role evaluation has to play in education's improvement, although there is considerable variance as to how this role should be fulfilled. Unfortunately, the view about the centrality of evaluation in the educational process is neither universally shared by educational practitioners nor, when it is held, necessarily applied. For example, a number of writers in the field of curriculum development exhort practitioners to engage in the systematic evaluation of educational programs but furnish little guidance about how to carry out this function. Even practitioners will often give lip service to the importance of evaluation but will do little or nothing about it.

While Tyler's view of education and the role of evaluation in the educational process has been of enormous value to persons in curriculum development as well as to those in educational evaluation, it provides only a foundation for current evaluation thought and practice. Technical developments in the methods of evaluation, measurement, research, decision theory, information sciences, and other related areas, as well as new demands for educational planning, have resulted in additions and modifications to Tyler's basic views.

There has been a notable shift in thinking about the role of evaluation in the educational process since Tyler's original formulation. Tyler viewed evaluation primarily as the assessment of learner performance in terms of program objectives. For Tyler, evaluation was virtually synonymous with what was previously defined as learner appraisal. There was good reason for this. At the time that Tyler formulated his rationale, evaluation work was not only quite spotty but largely haphazard. Tyler sought to make evaluation a more systematic and rational process. Accordingly, he urged that clear objectives be formulated and that they serve as the basis for the development of evaluation instruments. The results obtained from the use of such instruments would permit people to determine how well program objectives were being attained and thus enable them to judge program success. Given the level of educational thought and practice at the time that Tyler formulated his rationale, it was clearly a great leap forward.

A number of contemporary writers have argued for an expanded role for evaluation. Their reasoning is that strict fidelity to a program's objectives can place an evaluation worker in a very difficult position. What if a program is pursuing worthless or unrealistic objectives? Must the evaluation worker restrict his activities to assessing the extent of attainment of those objectives or is the worker to be allowed to question or even challenge the objectives themselves? Opinion and practice are divided on this issue. The emerging consensus is that evaluation workers should be free to question and challenge dubious objectives when there is a real basis for doing so. This avoids the issue, however, since one needs to know what constitutes a "real basis" for questioning or even challenging a program's objectives, especially if the evaluation worker had no part in the development of the program.

There appear to be two bases for doing so. The first is more obvious than the second. If an evaluation worker has had considerable experience in evaluating the types of programs that he or she has been called on to study, then the evaluation worker might be able to question or challenge a program's objectives in light of this experience. For example, an evaluation worker who is also a specialist in elementary school mathematics might be in a strong position to question the appropriateness and even the worth of a particular set of objectives for an elementary school mathematics program. The second basis for questioning or challenging a program's objectives is the need that a program was designed to meet. Programs are established to meet some need as Tyler clearly showed in his classic monograph (Tyler, 1950). It is one thing to determine whether a program is achieving its objectives; it is another to say whether the objectives, even if they were achieved, would meet the need that gave rise to the program. Thus, the need furnishes a basis for reviewing a program's objectives. More important, it frees an evaluation worker from having to slavishly accept a program's stated objectives.

This does not mean that one can freely criticize program objectives. One should question or challenge program objectives only after careful study of the relationship between a program's objectives and the need the program was designed to meet, or on the basis of sufficient expertise about the nature of the program and the learners to be served.

The acceptance of objectives as part of an educational enterprise to be evaluated rather than as an external set of specifications that are beyond question is part of the contemporary view of educational evaluation. An attempt has been made to represent this view of the role of evaluation in Figure 1.2. Eval-

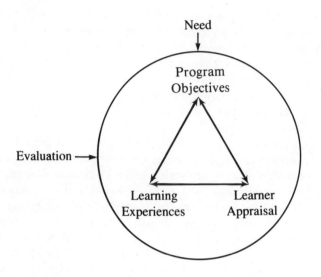

FIGURE 1.2: Representation of the Role of Evaluation in the Educational Process

uation has as its province objectives, learning experiences, learner appraisal, and the relationship between the three. Note, however, that the need that the program is based on is not included. The reason for this is that evaluation workers, because of their training, experience, and often limited view of a total institution, are usually not in a position to say whether particular needs are valid, or which of several needs should be addressed. Such matters are usually left to a group of professional workers called policy analysts working closely with decision makers.

SUMMARY

This chapter has sought to introduce the reader to the concept of evaluation and to describe it in some detail. An important feature of a definition is not only to say what something is but also what it is not. Accordingly, evaluation was contrasted with two related activities, measurement (including learner appraisal) and research, and some basic differences were noted. Also presented was a summary of a view of the educational process that placed evaluation squarely in that process. Attention was given to the role of evaluation by relating evaluation elements in the educational process: objectives and learning experiences. Finally, the chapter concluded with a discussion of what was and was not included in an evaluation enterprise.

The Nature of Educational Evaluation / 17

Notes

1. Throughout this book the term "evaluation worker" is used to designate an individual who plans, works, or assists in the conduct of an evaluation study. While not as succinct as the term "evaluator," it seems more apt. A comprehensive evaluation of an educational enterprise requires the skills and expertise of a number of people. The term "evaluator," on the other hand, implies that a single individual can plan and carry out a comprehensive evaluation study. This is not likely to be the case. For example, an individual who has competence in the area of instrument development is not likely to be also proficient in the area of cost analysis.

2. Tyler originally used the term *evaluation* to denote procedures used to appraise learner progress towards the attainment of objectives. He saw such procedures as being vital for furnishing information about the extent to which objectives were being attained and about the appropriateness and efficacy of learning experiences (Tyler, 1934). In this book the term *evaluation* is used in a broader way. It includes not only Tyler's views but also procedures used in judging the overall merit of an educational enterprise. Judgments of overall merit involve consideration of the worth of the objectives being pursued, their costs, and some measure of their acceptance by learners, teachers, and community.

References

Beeby, C. E. 1977. "The Meaning of Evaluation." In *Current Issues in Evaluation: No. 4, Evaluation*. Wellington, New Zealand: Department of Education.

Campbell, D. T. and Stanley, J. 1966. *Experimental and Quasi-Experimental Designs for Research on Teaching*. Chicago: Rand McNally.

Cook, T. and Campbell, D. T. 1979. *Quasi-Experimentation: Design and Analysis Issues for Field Settings*. Chicago: Rand McNally.

Cronbach, L. J. 1963. "Course Improvement Through Evaluation." *Teachers College Record*. 64: 672–83.

Cronbach, L. J. and Snow, R. 1977. *Aptitudes and Instructional Methods*. New York: Irvington Publishers.

Cronbach, L. J. and Suppes, P. (eds.). 1969. *Research for Tomorrow's Schools: Disciplined Inquiry for Education*. New York: MacMillan.

Cronbach, L. J., et al. 1980. *Toward Reform of Program Evaluation*. San Francisco: Jossey-Bass.

Kaplan, A. 1964. *The Conduct of Inquiry*. San Francisco: Chandler.

Kerlinger, F. 1986. *Foundations of Behavioral Research*, 3rd ed. New York: Holt, Rinehart and Winston.

Popham, W. J. 1988. *Educational Evaluation*. Second edition. Englewood Cliffs, N.J.: Prentice-Hall.

Scriven, M. J. 1967. "The Methodology of Evaluation." in Stake, R. E. (ed.) *Curriculum Evaluation*. AERA Monograph Series on Evaluation, No. 1. Chicago: Rand McNally.

Tyler, R. 1934. *Constructing Achievement Tests*. Columbus, Ohio: Ohio State University.

—— 1950. *Basic Principles of Curriculum and Instruction.* Chicago: University of Chicago. Press.

Additional Readings

Borich, G. 1974. *Evaluating Educational Programs and Products.* Englewood Cliffs, N.J.: Educational Technology Publications.
House, E. R. 1980. *Evaluating with Validity.* Beverly Hills: Sage.
House, E. R. (ed.) 1986. *New Directions in Educational Evaluation.* Philadelphia: Farmer Press.
Joint Committee on Standards for Educational Evaluation. 1981. *Standards for Evaluation of Educational Programs, Projects and Materials.* New York: McGraw-Hill.
Madaus, G. F., Scriven, M., and Stufflebeam, D. L. 1983. *Evaluation Models: Viewpoints on Educational and Human Services Evaluation.* Hingham, Mass.: Kluwer Academic Publishers.
Smith, E. and Tyler, R. 1943. *Appraising and Recording Student Progress.* New York: Harper.
Walberg, H. (ed.) 1974. *Evaluating Educational Performance.* Berkeley: McCutchan Publications.
Worthen, B. R. and Sanders, J. R. 1987. *Educational Evaluation: Alternative Approaches and Practical Guidelines.* White Plains, N.Y.: Longman Inc.

—— *2* ——

A FRAMEWORK FOR EVALUATION

INTRODUCTION

The purpose of this chapter is to present a clear, coherent, and comprehensive view of educational evaluation. In addition, it is intended to be sensible and practical. Since evaluation work so often involves teachers, administrators, lay boards, consumers, and community members in the planning, execution, or reporting of results, it is important that the general form of an evaluation study be understandable, appear reasonable, and easy to accomplish in a real-life situation with all of the attendant problems of a natural setting.

The formulation of a view of evaluation that meets the above requirements is no easy task. It is not that there are no guides to help one. Over the past fifty years, a number of individuals have proposed how educational endeavors should be evaluated. Stake (1975, p. 53) summarized nine general approaches to evaluation that, counted conservatively, encompassed no less than twenty specific models of evaluation. More recently, Popham (1988, pp. 24–45) described fourteen specific evaluation models or approaches in five broad categories. It is not within the purview of this book to attempt to describe and compare all or even some of the models; that would probably be more confusing than enlightening. Fortunately, descriptions and comparisons of a number of these models already exist and the interested reader is referred to those sources (Worthen and Sanders 1987; Popham 1988; Stake 1975).

While discussion of various evaluation models is beyond the scope of this book, some of the ways in which they differ can be noted to assist in formulating a view of evaluation that attempts to transcend, take account of, and, in some way, accommodate these differences. One way that evaluation models differ is in terms of what are considered to be the major purposes of educational evaluation. One group of writers, perhaps best exemplified by Cronbach

(1963), sees improvement of instructional programs as the chief goal of evaluation. Educational programs are developed, tried out, modified, tried out again, and eventually accepted for adoption on a broad scale. Whether one holds a linear view of the process of research, development, and dissemination, characteristic of much of the curriculum development work of the early and mid-1960s, or some alternate view of the process of improvement of education, is not critical here. Evaluation in any case is seen as supplying the information that will lead to improvement of the instructional endeavor. Evaluative information provides feedback to curriculum workers, teachers, and administrators so that intelligent decisions regarding program improvement can be made. Such a feedback and quality control role for evaluation, if carefully planned and executed, is supposed to doom curriculum development enterprises to succeed!

In contrast with this view is the position that evaluation efforts should be directed toward formal, experimental comparative studies. In such instances evaluation efforts are directed at producing educational analogues of environmental impact reports. Just as an environmental-impact report estimates the likely effects of a particular planned project, educational evaluation in such cases should be able to inform educators and others of the likely effects of adopting a particular educational program. The methods used to arrive at such estimates center around planned, comparative studies. In well-conducted research studies, it should be possible to conclude that one program outperforms another (or fails to) in terms of various criteria, usually some measures of student performance. Advocates of such a role for educational evaluation are often concerned with overall judgments about educational programs based on a comparison with one or more alternative programs.

The difference in views of the major purposes to be served by evaluation presented above has been drawn as sharply as possible. In reality, there is general acknowledgment of the validity of alternative purposes to be served by educational evaluation by writers holding different views. Unfortunately, the acknowledgment is not always translated into a modification of one's approach so as to accommodate alternative viewpoints. This is not to say that a particular purpose for educational evaluation is necessarily wrong. In many instances it may be correct and highly appropriate. The point is that most models of evaluation are generally limited in terms of the purposes envisaged for educational evaluation, each tending to emphasize a limited set of purposes.

A second basis for distinguishing among various approaches to evaluation is the training and background of the proponents of those approaches. Although evaluation work has been going on for a long time, it has only attained prominence in recent years. Consequently, many workers in this "new" field received their training in more conventional disciplines. Each area of training, whether it be curriculum development, educational psychology, measurement and statistics, or whatever, has its own theoretical concerns, methodological emphases, and outlook. The models proposed by different evaluation workers often reflect their own scholarly orientation although there is often some attempt to accommodate their views to the realities and demands of real-world evaluation situations. Sometimes such effort succeeds reasonably well; sometimes it does not. For example, some writers received extensive training in behavioral research methods. Such writers are often strong advocates of formal experimental studies for evaluating educational endeavors. The procedures of experimental research, while ideally suited for laboratory studies in which the experimenter can exercise almost total control over all relevant conditions (including breeding several generations of laboratory animals in order to have just the right strain of animal), can hardly be applied to actual educational settings where the evaluation worker typically exercises an extremely limited degree of control. Yet, some writers seriously suggest that such tightly controlled studies not only are desirable but are indeed the only permissible ones. Fortunately, there are very few such advocates. It is clear that, by training or background, people bring particular views, concerns, or emphases to the field of evaluation from other disciplines. Sometimes this can be beneficial when it raises new issues and problems. To the novice, however, such divergence can be a source of confusion because it suggests an absence of a basic structure to the field.

A third and somewhat related distinguishing characteristic among the various approaches to educational evaluation stems from the nature of the subject or discipline that is the focus of evaluation efforts. Specialists in subject-matter areas in which evaluative work is contemplated or already underway can be counted on to have something to say about what should be evaluated and how this should be done. Differences among specialists from various fields often reflect basic differences in orientation about the nature of the subject and what can be gained from studying it. In art education, for example, Eisner (1977) presents a view of his subject (and a list of claimed benefits for studying it) that is vastly different from that held by such writers as E. G. Begle (1963) and M. Beberman (1958) in mathematics education. The differences cannot be lightly dismissed. They are genuine and reflect basically different orientations arising out of the nature of each subject. Any comprehensive view of evaluation must be based on a recognition of such differences.

A fourth distinguishing characteristic in approaches to evaluation stems from the emphasis that each accords to different parts of the evaluation process. Such differences in emphasis can come from a variety of sources; their origin is not of concern. The emphasis accorded to a particular aspect of the evaluation process can serve as the basis for an entire approach to evaluation. For example, workers with a background in or disposition toward administration may view decision making as the key element in the evaluation process and develop a scheme for educational evaluation in which decision making is the cornerstone. Others with a concern for precision and careful measurement will advocate an approach in which precise specification of learner behavior and the development of instruments to ascertain this becomes the dominant concern. Likewise, individuals concerned with social cohesion may devote considerable effort to studying how programs function, and how individuals relate to one another within the program and to others outside the program. There are any number of points of emphasis that can be adopted in an evaluation enterprise. Such points can become not only the focal point for evaluation work but, in extreme cases, an almost exclusive concern. Imbalance like this is, of course, to be avoided.

A FRAMEWORK FOR EVALUATION

In formulating a framework, a conscious effort has been made to accommodate a variety of viewpoints about educational evaluation. Obviously the framework cannot be all-inclusive; some approaches are mutually exclusive and contradictory. When the purposes of evaluation differ, different parts of the framework will receive different emphases. The framework presented here should not be regarded as a model. While various writers have proposed different models of evaluation, what is presented here does not claim to be a model. It is hoped that it will be helpful to the reader in thinking about educational evaluation and will be useful in planning and conducting evaluation studies.

Comprehensive evaluation of educational treatments, whether they be units of instruction, courses, programs, or entire institutions, requires the collection of five major classes of information. Each class of information is necessary although not sufficient for evaluation of an educational enterprise. In setting forth these five major classes, it is recognized that some may be of little or no interest in a particular evaluation enterprise. What is to be avoided is the possibility of omitting any class of information important for determining the worth of a program. Thus, the framework allows for possible errors of commission, for example, collecting information that will have little bearing on the determination of the worth of a program while avoiding errors of omission that may lead to a failure to gather information that may be important. There are two reasons for this position. First, if a particular class of information turns out to be unimportant, it can simply be disregarded. Second, if it is known in advance that a particular class of information will have little bearing on the outcome of the evaluation, it simply need not be gathered. This does not reflect on the framework per se but only on the inappropriateness of a part of it in a particular situation. On the other hand, failure to gather information about particular relevant aspects of an education venture indicates a faulty evaluation effort and should be avoided.

Initial Status of Learners

The first class of information relates to the initial status of learners. It is important to know two things about the learners at the time they enter the program: who they are, and how proficient they are with regard to what they are supposed to learn. The first subclass of information, who the learners are, is descriptive in nature and is usually easily obtained. Routinely, one wants to know the age, sex, previous educational background, and other status and experiential variables that might be useful in describing or characterizing the learners. Strictly speaking, such information is not evaluative. It should be useful in interpreting the results of an evaluation study and, more important, serve as a baseline description of the learner population. If subsequent cohorts of learners are found to differ from the one that received the program when it was evaluated, then it may be necessary to modify the program to accommodate the new groups. The second subclass of information, how proficient the learners are with regard to what they are supposed to learn, is more central to the evaluation. Learning is generally defined as a change in behavior or proficiency. To demonstrate learning, it is necessary to gather evidence of performance at, at least, two points in time: (1) at the beginning of a set of learning experiences and (2) at some later time. Gathering evidence about the initial proficiencies of learners furnishes the necessary baseline information for estimating, however crudely, the extent to which learning occurs during the period from start to finish. (Determining whether the learning occurred as a direct result of the program or was due to other factors is an issue that will be dealt with in chapters nine and eleven.) A related reason for determining the initial proficiency level of learners stems from the fact that some educational enterprises may seriously underestimate initial learner status with regard to what is to be learned. Consequently, considerable resources may be wasted in teaching learners who are already proficient. Mere end-of-program evidence gathering could lead one to an erroneous conclusion of program effectiveness when what had actually happened was that already developed proficiencies had been maintained.

It is important that a determination of the initial level of learners' proficiencies be undertaken before an educational enterprise gets seriously underway. Only then can one be sure that the learners are assessed independently of the effects of the program. Studying learners after they have had some period of instruction makes it impossible to determine what they were like before instruction began. While the point seems self-evident, it has been violated so often in recent years that several methodologists have published articles about this in professional journals to sensitize workers in the field.

The one instance in which gathering data about the initial proficiencies of learners can be omitted is when what is to be learned is so specialized in nature that one can reasonably presume that the initial status of learners is virtually nil. Examples where such a presumption could be made reasonably would include entry-level educational programs in computer programming, welding, and cytotechnology. Outside of such specialized fields, however, it is worth the relatively small investment of time and expense to ascertain the initial status of learner proficiency.

To determine the initial status of learners can be a large order. If complete information about every variable of interest were obtained for every learner, several hours at the very least, more likely several days, of information-gathering would be necessary. This would, in effect, curtail the amount of time available for instruction.

Since any evaluation scheme must be practical, it is worth digressing to comment on how relevant information can be gathered with a minimum of intrusion on instructional time. (Details regarding these procedures will be given in chapters five, nine, and ten.) First, much of the background information that is useful in describing a group of learners can be located in existing records, thus eliminating the need for gathering the information directly from learners during instructional time. Second, it is not necessary to require all learners to respond to a full set of instruments. A sample, chosen so as to be representative of all learners enrolled in a program, curriculum, or institution, can be studied to furnish information that characterizes the total group. Third, it is not necessary to examine a group of learners with regard to all the objectives of a program. A sample of program objectives will usually suffice. What one is looking for is some estimate of the initial level of learner proficiency. Fourth, a sampling of individuals and a sampling of questions, items, and tasks that probe the proficiencies, abilities, and even affective outcomes an educational enterprise seeks to develop can be undertaken. This dual sampling, which will be discussed at length in chapter ten, is referred to as *multiple matrix sampling* and lends itself particularly well for use in evaluation studies. One of its chief advantages is efficiency. Economies of 75-80 percent in the time required for information gathering are commonplace with multiple matrix sampling with no great loss in the precision and quality of the information obtained. In practical terms, this means that it should be possible to obtain the necessary information about the initial status of learners in no more than twenty to thirty minutes.

Learner Performance after a Period of Instruction

The second major class of information required in evaluation studies relates to learner proficiency and status after a period of instruction. The notion here is that educational ventures are intended to bring about changes in learners. Hence, it is critical to determine whether the learners have changed in the desired ways. Changes could include increased knowledge, ability to solve various classes of problems, ability to deal with various kinds of issues in a field, proficiencies in certain kinds of skills, changes in attitudes, interests and preferences, etc. The changes sought will depend on the nature of the program, the age- and ability-levels of the learners and a host of other factors. Whatever changes a program, curriculum, or institution seeks to effect in learners must be studied to determine whether they have occurred and to what extent. The only way this can be done is through a study of learner performance. Whether the particular changes in learner behavior can be attributed to the effects of the educational experience is, however, another matter (to be dealt with in detail in chapter nine). Before such a determination can be made, however, it must be ascertained whether learning has occurred and, if so, to what extent.

The notion that information about what has been learned should be obtained after a period of instruction has often been interpreted to mean that learners must be examined at the end of a program or course. This is not quite correct. When information should be gathered is a function of the purposes of those who will be the major consumers of the evaluation. The developer of a program, for example, might be keenly interested in finding out how effective particular units of instruction are in bringing about particular changes in learners, for example, increased knowledge, ability to solve certain kinds of problems, and also in the effectiveness of specific lessons. Such information can help the developer to detect flaws in the program and make appropriate modifications. The same program developer might be relatively uninterested in learner performance at the end of the program. Moreover, summative information may be at such a general level as to be virtually useless in helping him or her detect where the program is working, and where it is not. Someone else, on the other hand, who is considering the adoption of a program, may have little interest about how learners are performing at various points in the program; his or her interest lies chiefly in the final status of the learners. That is, have they learned what was expected by the conclusion of the program? A positive answer could lead to a decision to adopt the program, a negative one, to possible rejection. Different persons approach an evaluation enterprise with different questions, and such differences should be reflected in decisions concerning what information should be gathered and when it should be gathered.

The above distinction closely parallels the one between formative and summative evaluation noted earlier. It is not, however, the only distinction that can be made. What is important is that a schedule of information gathering with regard to learner performance should be consistent with the purposes for undertaking the evaluation and that the phrase "after a period of instruction" not be restricted to end-of-course information gathering.

There are two kinds of learner-performance information to be gathered after a period of instruction. One is interested in the particular abilities, skills, affective outcomes, and the like that are intended to result from a set of organized educational experiences. (The technical term for such outcomes is "objectives" and will be discussed in some detail in the next chapter.) Collecting information regarding the attainment of the objectives of an educational venture is vital. The aim in gathering such information is to ascertain as fully as possible to what extent objectives are being met. Evaluation work should furnish information with regard to each and every educational objective for an educational enterprise.

The second kind of information about learner performance that should be gathered is less well known and not universally accepted. It involves learner proficiency with regard to outcomes not formally included in the stated objectives of the program. Because of the somewhat special nature of such outcomes, they are not included here. They will be presented below in the fifth class of information (Supplemental Information). Incidental outcomes are mentioned here solely because they complement the learner-performance information gathered with regard to stated program objectives.

Execution of Treatment

The third class of information collected in an evaluation study centers on the educational treatment being dispensed, whether it is a course, program, curriculum or an entire institutional setting. At the very least, one needs to know whether the treatment was carried out. If so, to what extent? Did the treatment get started on time? Were the personnel and materials necessary for the program available from the outset or, as has been the case in a number of externally-funded programs, did materials and supplies not arrive until shortly before the conclusion of the program? Questions regarding the implementation of the intended program may seem trivial but, in fact, are critical. Often it is simply assumed that program was carried out on schedule and in the way it was intended. This assumption is open to question but, more important, to study. Any responsible evaluation enterprise must determine whether and how an educational program was carried out.

Information about the execution of a program should not only meet the minimal requirement of determining whether a program has been carried out as intended; it should also furnish some descriptive information about the program in operation. Such information can often be used to identify deficiencies in the program as well as possible explanations for success. The collection of information about the program in operation will rely heavily on the use of observational procedures, and in some cases, on the use of narrative descriptive material. Who actually gathers such information is a matter that can be decided locally. Evaluation workers, supervisors, or other administrative personnel can share in the performance of this critical function. Maintenance of logs or diaries by teachers in the program can also contribute to meeting informational needs in this area. Even participant-observer instruments, along the lines developed by Pace and Stern (1958), where individuals are asked to report on particular practices and features of an environment, could be useful.

Failure to determine the extent to which a designed program was implemented opens evaluation studies to serious criticism. One of the classic educational studies in the United States, the Eight Year Study of the Progressive Educational Association, suffered from this fatal flaw. The thirty schools in the experimental group did not, in fact, modify their programs sufficiently from those of traditional schools so as to constitute an experimental treatment. More recently, some observers have noted one possible explanation as to why evaluations of early Headstart Programs failed to show any effects:

their failure to get started on time, secure the necessary qualified personnel, obtain adequate materials and supplies, and operate with any clear set of plans. It is hoped that educational programs, developed to meet particular needs, will not be subject to the criticism Shaw leveled in a different context when he observed that the main problem with Christianity was that it had never been tried.

The study of program implementation is not undertaken just to determine how faithfully a program was carried out. Rather, the program that is evaluated is the implemented program. The implemented program can differ markedly from the designed or intended program. Further, there may be very good reasons for such differences. One of the evaluation worker's responsibilities is to describe and compare the intended program, the implemented or actual program, and the achieved program. The achieved program refers to learner performance in terms of program objectives. In order to fulfill this task, the evaluation worker will need to know not only the intended program or learning experiences and the achieved program or learner performance in terms of program objectives, but also the implemented or actual program in order to make the necessary comparisons. This is why this class of information, execution of treatment, is included as one of the five major classes of information to be gathered in an evaluation study. Failure to gather such information can be a fatal flaw since it prevents one from knowing what exactly was being evaluated.

Costs

The fourth major class of information is costs. Unfortunately, costs have not received adequate attention in evaluation work. The reason for this is not clear. Perhaps early educational evaluation efforts were directed toward ascertaining the efficacy of competing instructional treatments that had equal price tags. In such cases, cost considerations would not be a major concern. Today, however, the range of available treatments—in the form of units of instruction, courses, programs, curricula, and instructional systems—have widely varying costs. These need to be reckoned so that administrators and educational planners, as well as evaluation workers, can make intelligent judgments about educational treatments. Not only must direct costs be reckoned, for example, the cost of adoption, but indirect costs as well. Costs of in-service training for teachers who will use a new program, for example, must be determined if a realistic estimate of the cost of the new program is to be obtained. An evaluation specialist whose training and experience may be in measurement, research methodology, or curriculum development may not be able to carry out such cost estimations. If he or she cannot, then someone who can must be found. An evaluation making no reference to costs is rarely of practical value, however interesting it may be academically. The educational administrator probably has a fair idea of what can be accomplished if money were no object.

The real problem for the administrator is to make wise decisions when cost is a factor.

Information about costs should be considered as early as possible in the evaluation of educational programs. (One recognizes, of course, that cost information may need to be modified as time passes.) Careful cost estimation can lead to better planning and more intelligent decision making when laudable but costly programs are considered for trial or adoption. Traditionally, evaluation workers have neglected the entire issue, leaving administrators to worry about such mundane matters. This has been unfortunate. An evaluation worker's professional function involves gathering all relevant information about an educational enterprise. Costs are certainly relevant and, in some cases, may be critical in judging the worth of an educational venture.

Supplemental Information

The fifth class involves supplemental information about the effects of a program, curriculum, or institution and is composed of three subclasses. The first includes the reactions, opinions, and views of learners, teachers, and others associated with the enterprise being evaluated. The latter could be administrators, parents, other community members, and even prospective employers. The purpose of gathering such information is to find out how an educational treatment is viewed by various groups. Such information is no substitute for more direct information about what is actually being learned, but it can play a critical role in evaluating the overall worth of a program in a larger institutional context. There have been occasions when programs, instituted by well-intentioned educators, have succeeded in achieving their objectives, and at a reasonable cost. However, controversy about such programs, inside or outside the institution, have led to their termination. One can cite as examples the installation of sex education programs in schools in highly conservative communities or the adoption of textbooks that were considered to contain offensive material by a sizable segment of a community.

Supplemental information, in the form of views and reactions of groups connected with an educational venture, can be highly instructive in a number of ways. It can (1) provide information about how a program is being perceived by various groups, (2) help formulate information campaigns, if there is a serious discontinuity between what is actually taking place in a program and what is perceived to be taking place, and (3) alert evaluation workers and administrators to the need for additional information about why a particular program is being viewed in a certain way by one or more groups. Such information may also prevent evaluation workers from developing what Scriven (1972) has described as a kind of tunnel vision that sometimes develops from overly restricting evaluation efforts to determine how well program objectives have been achieved. For example, attaining a limited set of objectives in a sex education program for elementary school students, at the cost of a sizable amount of local support and conflict between school and community, might simply be too high a price to pay.

Information about the views and reactions of various groups connected with an educational enterprise can be gathered fairly easily through the use of questionnaires and interview techniques. The value of gathering such information should not be underestimated. Neither should it be overestimated. A number of evaluation efforts have relied solely on the collection of the views and reactions of individuals and groups having some connection to a program. Educational evaluation should not be confused with opinion polling. It is important to find out how well an educational venture is succeeding in terms of what it set out to accomplish. This requires the collection of information about learner performance outlined in the first two classes of information. In addition, supplemental information about how a program is being received by various groups is important to an overall evaluation of its worth.

The instances cited above, where supplemental information in the form of views and reactions of various groups showed them to be rather extreme, do occur. The frequency of such occurrences, however, is low. Generally, reactions to educational programs tend to be on the mild side with a tendency on the part of the public to view new programs in a somewhat favorable light, especially if they have been fairly well thought through and reasonably well-presented. If reactions to educational programs are fairly mild, ranging, for example, from acquiescence to some positive support, little further attention need be accorded such information. However, one is not apt to know in advance what the views and reactions of various groups are likely to be. Accordingly, it is necessary to find them out consciously.

The second subclass of supplemental information involves learner performances not specified in the program's objectives. Developers of educational programs, courses, and curricula are improving in their ability to specify what should be learned as a result of exposure to instruction, and the importance of assessing learner performance with regard to specified objectives is now generally accepted. However, it is also reasonable to inquire how well broader goals of education are being served by a particular program. That is, how well is the need which the program was developed to meet being satisfied. "An ideal evaluation" Cronbach points out (1963, pp. 121–122):

would include measures of all the types of proficiency that might reasonably be desired in the area in questions, not just the selected outcomes to which this curriculum directs substantial attention. If you wish only to know how well a curriculum is achieving its objectives, you fit the test to the curriculum; but if you wish to know how well the curriculum is serving the national interest, you measure all outcomes that might be worth striving for. One of the new mathematics courses may disavow any attempt to teach numerical trigonometry, and indeed, might discard nearly all computational work. It is still perfectly reasonable to ask how well graduates of the course can compute and can solve right triangles. Even if the course developers went so far as to contend that computational skill is no proper objective of secondary instruction, they will encounter educators and laymen who do not share this view. If it can be shown that students who come through the new course are fairly proficient in computation despite the lack of direct teaching, the doubters will be re-assured. If not, the evidence makes clear how much is being sacrificed. Similarly, when the biologists offer alternative courses emphasizing microbiology and ecology, it is fair to ask how well the graduate of one course can understand issues treated in the other. Ideal evaluation in mathematics will collect evidence on all the abilities toward which a mathematics course might reasonably aim; likewise in biology, English or any other subject.

Cronbach's view is not universally accepted. Some writers assert that any attempt to test for unintended outcomes by the program developers is imposing inappropriate and unfair criteria on the program. There is always a danger of being unfair. Present also is the highly practical problem of deciding what kinds of learner-performance information, not specified in the objectives, should be obtained. It would seem that some information along these lines should be gathered. The examples cited by Cronbach furnish some useful guides about the kind of additional information program developers should obtain. It is important that supplemental information about learner performance, when obtained, be analyzed and reported separately from information bearing directly on the intended outcomes of a program. Any evaluation effort must not only be done fairly, but appear to be done fairly. The inclusion of information about learner competencies, not intended as part of an instructional program, must be handled delicately. Separate treatment and reporting of such information is a minimal prerequisite of fairness.

While Cronbach maintains that an ideal evaluation effort would gather evidence about learner performance on all outcomes an educational enterprise might reasonably expect, in practice the amount of supplemental performance information will, of necessity, be limited. Unless a program is heavily funded and has the requisite staff to develop evidence-gathering measures for the whole range of supplemental performance information desired, it is unrealistic to expect that very much can be done. Some efforts, albeit modest ones, can be made. It would be best to use the bulk of available resources to obtain learner-performance information with regard to intended outcomes and to supplement this with some additional measures. One should not dilute an evaluation effort by trying to measure everything and end up doing a mediocre or even poor job. This is a matter of planning and strategy. One can always expect that the resources available for evaluation will be limited. This is not a tragedy. Failure to use available resources effectively, however, can lead to undesired results. It is recommended that the major use of available resources be devoted to obtaining the most relevant information about learner performance. This entails examining how much has been learned with regard to the intended outcomes; some provision can (and should) be made with regard to other learner-performance outcomes that might result from the kind of program being evaluated.

The third subclass of supplemental information has to do with the side effects of educational programs, courses, and curricula. Admittedly, this is not an easy matter. Just as pharmaceutical researchers have long known that drugs can have effects on patients other than the ones intended, educators are realizing that their undertakings can have side effects, too. Sometimes such unintended effects can be beneficial, for example, when a program designed to improve reading skills of learners not only improves reading proficiency but increases self-esteem. Negative side effects may also occur: in a rigorous academic high-school physics course students may learn a great deal of physics but their interest in learning more physics in college may be markedly reduced or extinguished.

While one can cite the side effects of educational programs at length, prescriptions about what to look for and how to detect them are hard to give. Evaluation workers must first recognize that side effects can occur in any educational program. They must then strive to be as alert and sensitive as possible about what is happening to learners as they move through a set of educational experiences. This means attending not only to learner performance in relation to stated objectives, but to any general class of behaviors, including interests and attitudes, that may be developing. This is not an easy task, but if the evaluation workers can maintain a level of receptivity about effects not directly specified by the objectives of a program, there is a fair chance that such behaviors will be discerned when they appear.

Another way of detecting the side effects of educational programs is through the use of follow-up procedures. Following up learners into the next level of education or into their first year of employment can furnish clues. In the example cited above about the rigorous high-school physics course, the critical information about the negative effect of the program on interest in learning more physics came from a follow-up study. Students who had taken the innovative physics course were taking additional physics courses in college at less than one-half the rate of comparable students who had taken a conventional high-school physics course. However, it is not likely that formal follow-up studies will yield such clear-cut results. Moreover, formal follow-up studies often require more resources than are available at most institutions. Even when such resources are plentiful, it is not usually clear how they should be put to use. The detection of unintended effects is an elusive business. Rather than attempt to conduct formal follow-up studies, it is usually better to employ rather loosely structured procedures. Open-ended questionnaires and relatively unstructured interviews with teachers at the next level in the educational ladder, with employers of graduates as well as with graduates themselves, can furnish clues about side effects of programs that could then be studied more systematically. It is also possible that the first subclass of supplemental information, views and reactions of various groups connected with a program, can provide clues about program side effects. Whatever strategy is employed to detect side effects, it should probably be somewhat loosely structured and informal.

The framework for evaluation presented above sets forth the major classes of information required for a comprehensive evaluation of an educational enterprise. Detailed procedures for the collection of each class of information are presented in subsequent chapters along with discussions about the analysis and interpretation of evaluative information and the synthesis of results into judgments of worth. Before such complex undertakings can be initiated, however, it is critical that the necessary information is obtained. The framework presented in this chapter is an agenda for information gathering.

Three major features that underlie the framework should be made explicit. First, at the core of the framework is the notion that learner performance is a major basis for evaluation of educational courses, programs, and curricula. That is, educational ventures are set up to bring about certain changes in learner performance. How well they succeed in doing so is considered essential for evaluating their worth. This is the reason for inclusion of the first two classes of information. A second major feature of the framework is that learner performance is a necessary although not sufficient condition for the evaluation of educational treatments. How effectively the program was carried out, how much the program costs, what people think of the program, and what unintended effects the program has are considered vital to a comprehensive evaluation. This is somewhat of an expansion over a number of previous attempts to deal with the evaluation function. Lest this expansion be considered too burdensome for effective evaluation because of the ever present fact of limited resources, it should be noted that conventional evaluation efforts usually waste a good deal of time and money. A number of specific and detailed suggestions will be made later about how a comprehensive evaluation effort can be planned and executed without any increase in resources allocated to evaluation.

The third major feature underlying the framework is the idea that evaluation is central to the educational process. This view was presented in chapter one when evaluation was related to objectives, learning experiences, learner appraisal, and educational need. It is a notion that has been endorsed by educators for a long time. Unfortunately, it has been practiced far less than it has been preached. By requiring the involvement of evaluation workers in the execution of the intended program, in the reckoning of costs, and the collection of a range of supplemental information, the evaluation function should become more closely allied with the educational process. No longer can the evaluation worker be one who is only present at the start of a program, when the objectives are presented, and at the conclusion of a program, when data are gathered; rather he or she will have a continuing role to play throughout the course of an educational venture. This centrality of the evaluation role is perhaps the most noteworthy feature of the framework.

This expanded and more central role of evaluation in the educational process should lead not only to higher quality evaluation work but to more useful evaluation information. It would seem likely, for example, that the distinction between formative and summative evaluation that has held sway for a number of years might be considerably diminished, if evaluation were an ongoing operation rather than an episodic one. While the prospect of a continuing role for evaluation that is central to the educational process has a number of attractive features, it is not without risks. One of the oft-observed phenomena is the general mistrust that program developers and teachers have of evaluation workers. Such suspicion is, of course, understandable. Evaluation workers are often seen as threats to the continued existence of programs because of their judgmental function. Certainly, as long as evaluation workers have little contact with the programs they are supposed to be evaluating, there may be good reason for such suspicion and distrust. Closer contact between evaluation workers, program personnel, and the programs being evaluated is needed if the evaluation specialist's professional function is to be fulfilled. Such increased contact can also serve to ameliorate the traditional suspicion and distrust directed at evaluation workers by increasing the amount and kinds of information that they are not only exposed to but need in order to fulfill their professional functions properly.

Some evaluation workers tend to be wary about increased contacts with program developers, teachers, and the ongoing program itself. Such caution is based on a belief that their objectivity as evaluation workers may somehow be compromised by closer contact with program personnel. This concern is probably more imagined than real, but evaluation workers must be prepared to deal with it. Some ideas about how to deal with it will be presented in chapters eleven through thirteen. The point to note here is that while limited contact with a program, course, or curriculum may preserve the detachment of the evaluation worker, it will deprive him or her of a considerable body of information that is needed to perform the evaluation function. Much of the information specified in the framework requires that the evaluation worker be in close and continuing contact with personnel connected with the enterprise that is being evaluated. There is no way to avoid it.

SUMMARY

In this chapter, a framework for educational evaluation was presented. The framework is composed of five major classes of information judged necessary for a comprehensive evaluation of an educational enterprise. They are (1) initial status of learners, (2) learner performance after a period of instruction, (3) execution of the treatment, (4) costs, and (5) supplemental information. The latter class has three subclasses: opinions and reactions of various groups connected with the enterprise, supplemental learnings, and side effects.

Each class of information is necessary for a total evaluation effort. The amount of resources devoted to the collection of each class of information may vary considerably, however, depending on the purposes for which the evaluation is undertaken. If the major purpose of an evaluation is to determine whether to adopt a particular program or not, one pattern of resource allocation may be adopted; if the chief purpose is improvement of an existing program, another strategy may be followed. In each case, however, attention needs to be given to each of the major classes of information. It is possible that a decision may be made not to gather information in one or more classes in a particular evaluation study. Such a decision should be made only after careful deliberation about the informational needs in a particular situation.

References

Beberman, M. 1958. *An Emerging Program of Secondary School Mathematics*. Cambridge, Mass.: Harvard University Press.

Begle, E. G. 1963. "The Reform of Mathematics Education in the United States." In *Mathematical Education in the Americas*, edited by H. Fehr. New York: Bureau of Publications, Teachers College, Columbia University.

Cronbach, L. J. 1963. "Course Improvement through Evaluation." *Teachers College Record* 64: 672–83.

Eisner, E. 1977. "On the Uses of Educational Connoisseurship and Criticism for Evaluating Classroom Life." *Teachers College Record* 3: 345–58.

Pace, C. R. and Stern, G. 1958. "An Approach to the Measurement of Psychological Characteristics of College Environments." *Journal of Educational Psychology* 49: 269–77.

Popham, W. J. 1988. *Educational Evaluation*, 2nd ed. Englewood Cliffs, N.J.: Prentice-Hall.

Scriven, M. 1972. "Prose and Cons About Goal-Free Evaluation." *Evaluation Comment* 3.

Stake, R. E. 1975. "Program Evaluation, Particularly Responsive Evaluation." *Occasional Paper Series* 5. Kalamazoo: The Evaluation Center, Western Michigan University.

Worthen, B. R. and Sanders, J. R. 1987. *Educational Evaluation: Alternative Approaches and Practical Guidelines*. Worthington, Ohio: Charles A. Jones.

3

EDUCATIONAL OBJECTIVES

Much has been written on the subject of educational objectives in the past twenty years. Some of it has been highly personalistic, fetishistic, idiosyncratic; some, pure nonsense. Disagreements remain today over what educational objectives are and controversy over how they should be expressed. The purpose of this chapter is to define and describe educational objectives, noting areas of disagreement among specialists, tracing where educational objectives come from, and, finally, addressing the issue of how educational objectives should be expressed. Throughout the chapter an attempt will be made to present a balanced and sensible view of educational objectives, noting areas where problems remain and identifying points of contention.

One may begin by stating what educational objectives are and describing the critical aspects of such statements. An educational objective is a statement of a desired change in the behavior of a learner. There are several elements in this definition. First, an objective is a statement about a learner. This immediately distinguishes objectives from three other things with which they are often confused. First, objectives are *not* statements of subject matter to be covered, for example, fractions, plane geometry, or American history up till World War II, since they do not say anything about the learner. Second, objectives are *not* statements of teacher behavior. Thus, for example, statements such as, "to provide a range of reading materials for students," or "to lead a discussion of O. Henry's *Gift of the Magi* " refer to what a *teacher* will do, not the learner. Third, objectives are *not* statements about learning experiences. Teachers who have students "work in small groups" or "go to the library for project work" are directing learning activities that should lead to attaining objectives. The learning activities, however, are not the objectives. Whatever other deficiencies may be noted about the statements above, their failure to be about learners (rather than teachers) renders them unacceptable as statements of educational objectives.

A second element in the definition of an educational objective is that it is a statement about a desired change in the learner. The term "desired" indicates that the particular behavior the learner is expected to develop is prized; it is valued. Educators are interested not in just any changes in learners that come as a result of a planned set of learning experiences: they look for particular changes. The word "desired" indicates that certain changes in learners are considered important and others are not. It is simply not possible to study every change that might occur in learners as a result of a set of educational experiences. Educational objectives represent the outcomes of a process of valuation and, consequently, certain learner behaviors will be given priority over others. In other words, educational objectives are values.

The third element in the definition is "change." Learning denotes a change in the behavior of an individual. In fact, this is the common definition of learning. If a group of learners already exhibits a set of desired behaviors before they undergo a set of educational experiences, then it is foolish to accord these behaviors the status of objectives. For example, if students in a nutrition education program can correctly distinguish protein-rich foods from foods that are not, then it is unnecessary to make this an objective of the program. It would not only be a waste of time but might delude educators into thinking they were accomplishing something when they were merely certifying a proficiency the learners already possessed. Educational programs, curricula, and institutions are intended to help learners acquire new sets of behaviors, not affirm things they already know and can do.

The last element in the definition is "behavior." This is an often troublesome term since it has been subject to such an array of interpretations that one is obliged to specify how it is to be used in any situation. In this book, behavior will be used to denote what an individual says or does. Learner behavior can range from a response given to a specific question such as "What is the name of the capital of Idaho?" to the organization and expression of a set of ideas in written or oral form. It would include not only the ability to reproduce acquired information but to apply principles in novel situations, carry out various kinds of analyses, and exhibit particular response tendencies in various situations, such as approaches to dealing with certain classes of phenomena and generating novel products. In short, anything that the learner might say or do is an example of a behavior.

The definition is purposely broad. It does, however, exclude certain internal states of individuals. For example, the term "understands" would not, in itself, be considered behavioral, since it does not require any saying or doing on the part of the learner. For this reason some writers would exclude the use of such terms as "understands, knows, comprehends," etc., from the language of educational objectives since they are not behavioral in nature. Besides not meeting the definitional requirement of behavior, terms that are descriptive of learners' internal states present formidable problems in evidence gathering. How, such writers ask, is one to ascertain whether a learner understands something? What is meant by the term "understands"?

No doubt these are troublesome questions and evaluation work would be less complex and difficult if nonbehavioral terms were routinely excluded from the language of educational objectives. There are, however, three reasons for including them. First, terms such as "understands" and "knows," have long been a part of the vocabulary of educators, and to exclude them unilaterally seems unwise. While evaluation workers may be dubious about the ability of teachers to assess learner understanding, teachers often are confident of their ability to do so. It would seem more productive to investigate such contentions than to exclude them on an a priori basis. Second, teachers often have in mind certain kinds of behavior, however imperfectly formulated, when they use terms referring to internal states. It would appear to be more productive for teacher and evaluation worker to clarify what is meant by such terms than to simply reject them. Very likely teachers do have in mind a particular set of behaviors when they use terms such as "understands." Since one of the initial tasks in evaluating an educational enterprise is to obtain a clear set of statements of educational objectives, evaluation workers would be advised to employ all avenues of approach to this task. Accepting teacher nomenclature, however imprecise and nonbehavioral it may be, as a point of departure could prove productive. A decision initially to accept the terms used by program developers and teachers and explore their meaning in a particular situation is, thus, not only an acknowledgment of their equal professional role but the first step toward a clarification of those intentions. This is one service that evaluation workers can provide to teachers that can be of immediate and sometimes considerable benefit.

A third reason for accepting nonbehavioral terms is that they often serve as concise and useful summarizations for a set of behaviors a teacher wishes to develop. A problem frequently encountered in expressing educational objectives is that such statements become lengthy and wordy. If a fairly full expression of objectives becomes too cumbersome, teachers will likely pay it little attention. Whatever can be done to express educational objectives as succinctly as possible is usually well worth the effort, since it increases the likelihood that teachers will attend to them. Thus, the use of terms such as "understands," "knows," etc., may serve as useful summarizations for elaborated sets of behaviors. This can be satisfying for both teacher and evaluation worker. Consider the list of behaviors (shown in Table 3.1) that could clarify "understanding." In given situations teachers might endorse several, most, or all of them as constituting proficiencies they have in mind when using the term "understanding." An evaluation worker, although perhaps disinclined to use the term, is still in a position to proceed with developing ways of determining whether students have attained specific proficiencies.

SOURCES OF EDUCATIONAL OBJECTIVES

The definition presented earlier and described in some detail above can only be considered an opening volley in any discussion of educational objectives.

TABLE 3.1: Outline of Proficiencies Indicating Understanding

1. States concepts, ideas in own words.
2. Recognizes whether there are sufficient data to solve a problem.
3. Recognizes relevancy of data for a particular problem.
4. Identifies errors in procedure and structure.
5. Given situation, identifies applicable principle.
6. Given a principle, identifies situation using it.
7. Makes reasonable inferences from data.
8. Given set of data, predicts outcomes.
9. Predicts consequences if errors or changes in procedures occur.
10. Detects similarities and differences, and relationships.
11. Given outcome, reconstructs data to support it.
12. Generalizes or classifies.
13. Identifies underlying principles or causes of several events.
14. Organizes ideas, objects, events, etc., into new patterns.
15. Gives novel examples.

Source: Compiled by the author.

Before proceeding to the ways that educational objectives can be formulated and expressed, let us briefly consider how educational objectives come into being. An examination of the bases for the development of educational objectives will provide a base for dealing with them (Tyler, 1950).

The three major sources for educational objectives are (1) the needs of the learner, (2) the needs of the society, and (3) the material to be learned. Careful investigation into the nature of the learners can help identify the learner needs that an educational program might meet. For example, in an area where persons find it difficult to organize themselves to study, an educational program may attempt to ameliorate this problem through systematic instruction and guidance. Investigators in a number of fields of human development seek to identify various kinds of individual needs. The general aim of such work is to describe the status of a group of learners with respect to a characteristic, or set of characteristics, and compare this with what the best-of-present knowledge and theory would indicate is a desirable state of affairs. Any gap would then indicate a need that exists for a given group of learners. An attempt to formalize this process and so make it usable by educators and community members, at a local level, has resulted in the development of various needs-assessment procedures and instruments. Possible areas in which needs might be identified for learners at the junior high-school level, for example, could include (1) health; (2) immediate social relationships, including life in the family and with friends and acquaintances; (3) sociocivic relationships, including civic life, the school, and the community; (4) consumer aspects of life; (5) occupational life; and (6) recreation. These categories are only suggestive of broad areas within which needs could be identified. Needs of the learner, once identified, could furnish one basis for the formulation of educational objectives.

The second source for educational objectives relates to the needs of the society. It has been well described by Tyler (1950, p. 11).

The effort to derive objectives from studies of contemporary life largely grew out of the difficulty of accomplishing all that was laid upon the schools with the greatly increased knowledge which developed after the advent of science and the Industrial Revolution. Prior to this time the body of material that was considered academically respectable was sufficiently small so that there was little problem in selecting the elements of most importance from cultural heritage. With the tremendous increase in knowledge accelerating with each generation after the advent of science, the schools found it no longer possible to include in their program all that was accepted by scholars. Increasingly the question was raised as to the contemporary significance of particular items of knowledge or particular skills and abilities.

An educational institution simply cannot teach everything; choices must be made. One basis for selection lies in the needs of contemporary society. Need here refers to a competency that the individual must have in order to function effectively, productively, and satisfactorily as a citizen in society. Identifying such needs is somewhat hazardous because society is constantly changing. Too close a focus on a society's transitory needs could lead to developing educational programs that provide individuals with outdated skills and proficiencies. For example, establishing a program to train people to perform tasks that will soon be automated is not only economically wasteful but constitutes a grave disservice to the learners who go through such a program. The identification of societal needs must be based on a careful analysis of the kinds of competencies likely to be in high demand for some time to come. Such competencies may include being able to gather and analyze information so as to make intelligent choices as consumers, being able to get along with others in a work situation, and so forth. Identifying societal needs is not restricted to vocational requirements; it can include a broad range of skills and abilities required for effective functioning in contemporary society.

The third source for educational objectives comes from the nature of the material to be learned. Subject-matter specialists have much to contribute. While structure, methods of investigation, principles, and information in a discipline will serve in part as determiners of what is to be taught in a particular subject, subject-matter experts should be consulted at length about which aspects of a subject to include in an educational program. A note of caution should be added. The educator's concern with teaching a subject to a group of learners is not the same as the specialist's. In fact, the concerns of the two can diverge sharply. An educator is primarily interested in identifying and organizing those aspects of a subject judged relevant for learners at a particular age and ability level, having specific sets of needs and interests. Subject-matter specialists, however, tend to be concerned with the training of specialists in their areas. They may see little difference between the general educational needs of learners and the educational needs of future specialists. Those charged with the development of educational programs need to make sure that the expertise of subject-matter specialists is used wisely in educational planning. A lax stance by program developers regarding this can result in educational programs that fail to meet either the needs of the learners or the needs of the larger society.

Curriculum development in the United States, from the launching of the first Soviet sputnik in 1957 until the mid-1960s, can be interpreted historically as a period in which subject-matter specialists largely dominated the process of curriculum development. From various fields, they produced educational programs that were highly effective in training budding physicists, chemists, etc. The programs, unfortunately, were not as effective in meeting the educational needs of the broad group of learners served by the schools. Certainly, educational planners need to make use of all the expertise they can get in fashioning sound educational programs. However, the decision-making function can neither be delegated away nor wrested from them by any single group, whether these be specialists in subject-matter areas, manpower experts, psychologists, human development specialists, or whatever. The planners of educational programs must maintain control over their endeavors.

The needs of the learner, the needs of society, and the nature of study materials, while the three major sources for educational aims, do not constitute educational objectives in their own right. Before a learner need, societal need, or any part of a subject can achieve the status of educational objective, it must undergo a valuation process; that is, it must be judged important and desirable by some group of educators. Thus, perceived deficiencies in the writing abilities of young people do not in themselves define a set of educational objectives with regard to writing; they are only suggestive. Only when a group of educators consciously decides that writing proficiency is an important matter for an institution to develop will writing proficiency achieve the status of an objective. Such conscious decision making is what results in objectives.

In formulating educational objectives, the process by which a need or an aspect of subject is assigned value may be deliberate or casual; it must take place, however. It is frequently extremely complex: there can be conflicts between the needs of the learner, the needs of society, and the nature of the subject to be learned. The conflict between proponents of general education and those who advocate the kind of specialized education that equips learners with marketable skills reflects a continuing debate regarding the basic mission of an educational institution. In one case, the basic educational mission is viewed in terms of meeting a set of identified learner needs; in the other, it is seen in terms of meeting a set of societal requirements. When formulating a set of objectives for an educational program, choices have to be made; such choices are usually among competing alternatives from each of the three sources of educational objectives.

A major basis for deciding what will become an objective is a philosophy of education. It may not be clearly and explicitly formulated (and often is not), but in one way or another choices get made, and needs or aspects of a subject are transformed into objectives. A philosophy of education serves, as it were, to screen or filter a variety of often competing needs and subject-aspects, letting through as objectives only what is considered educationally worthwhile.

A second screen for filtering information about learner needs, societal needs, and the nature of the subject material to be learned is a psychology of learning. Educators may recognize a set of needs, wish to meet them through an instructional program, but decide not to do so because the likelihood of succeeding is too small. The reason for such a decision may be that the age or ability of a group of learners is simply too low to give much chance of success. For example, the decision not to adopt a highly rigorous physics program could be based (quite realistically) on the fact that high-school students could not handle the material. Some of the questions that may be asked with regard to contemplated objectives according to Furst (1958, p. 45) are:

To what extent is growth toward the objective a function of general maturation or general intelligence as contrasted with instruction?

Can the objective be reasonably attained at a given level of maturity?

At what levels of maturity are particular objectives best attained?

How much growth can be expected of different kinds of learners with respect to a set of objectives?

Does the attainment of one objective facilitate attainment of other objectives?

What is the retention value of different kinds of outcomes? Are some more lasting than others?

There are no complete or definitive answers to these questions. Yet they must be addressed and answered, to some degree, if educational planning is to be realistic. Research exists that can be of use in obtaining partial answers. The collective experience of teachers with particular kinds of learners is another important guide in formulating tentative answers to the questions; thus, contemplated objectives can be subject to at least some reality testing.

In sum, educational objectives originate as a result of a deliberative process, which begins with a consideration of learner needs, the needs of society, and the nature of the subject matter to be learned. These three sources of educational aims are intended to answer the question, "What needs to be done?" A philosophy of education and the psychology of learning serve to answer the questions of what should be done and what can be done. Ideally, the process by which educational objectives are formulated is a conscious and rational one. This does not mean that it is antiseptic. Differences in value orientations, political realities, and economic constraints all influence the process of formulation and selection of objectives. In actuality, things are not usually particularly tidy. Nevertheless some set of educational objectives, no matter how crudely stated, emerges from the planning process.

EXPRESSING EDUCATIONAL OBJECTIVES

While there is general agreement about where educational objectives come from, considerable disagreement exists about how educational objectives should be expressed. Ignoring those writers who despair about ever expressing educational intentions in written form, a wide range of views remains about how objectives should be expressed. At one extreme are writers who prescribe precise, detailed statements about each proficiency learners should develop as the result of exposure to an educational treatment. Such statements, these writers argue, should contain four essential elements (Mager, 1962). They should (1) be about the learner, (2) refer to an observable behavior, (3) specify the conditions under which the behavior is to occur, and (4) state the standard for judging what is an acceptable level of behavior. In the view of such writers, the objectives of a program would be expressed by a string of such statements, each containing the four essential elements listed above. At the other extreme stand those writers who think a short, discursive statement that tries to convey the intent of an educational course, program, or curriculum institution will suffice, and that considerable autonomy should be left to the teachers charged with carrying out the treatment. There are, of course, a number of intermediate positions.

Evaluation specialists have faced considerable problems in working with educators to express educational objectives. Some of the problems are political in nature, while others are conceptual or practical. The political problems stem from a resistance by some educators to clearly and explicitly state objectives since, by doing so, it becomes possible to determine to what extent the objectives are being attained. This is seen as a threat by some educators since, if a program is found to not be achieving its objectives, resources for the program may be withdrawn. In the view of such educators, unfavorable results can be highly threatening to their program's existence and to their own professional role. One way to avoid this is not to state program objectives explicitly so that no clear target is presented.

While feelings can run high and resistance to expressing objectives can be quite strong, there is little evidence to support the notion that the results of an evaluation study serve as the sole or even the major basis on which a decision is made to retain, radically alter, or terminate a program. Some educators fear, however, that unfavorable results will lead to the abolition of a program. This fear is more imaginary than real. Even if it were real, the need that the program was developed to meet would remain and something would still have to be done. Nevertheless, some educators are reluctant to expose their intentions and can devise rather clever and, to the evaluation worker, often maddening ways of resisting expressing their educational intentions in clear and explicit terms. In such cases, it is the job of the evaluation worker to reassure the educator that systematic evaluation is intended to help improve a program and not to exterminate it.

While the political problems that the evaluation worker must sometimes confront in order to identify and express a set of program objectives are considerable, they are minor when compared to the conceptual ones. These center around the issue of the level of generality or specificity at which objectives should be expressed. Some evaluation specialists have urged that objectives be stated in the most concrete and specific terms possible. The reason for this is fairly obvious. The more specificity there is in a set of objectives, the easier it will be to determine whether learners have attained them. Such an approach is not without its problems. First, in striving to achieve maximum specificity, the number of objectives can multiply at an alarming rate. For example, in one case where a dozen or so general and reasonably clear objectives had sufficed to express the intentions for a tenth-grade English course, attempts to spell out learner proficiencies in specific terms resulted in 1,084 specific objectives. Clearly, such an extended list is utterly unrealistic. No teacher can attend to such a list, provide learning experiences designed to achieve each of the objectives, and monitor student progress toward their attainment. An evaluation worker would be equally hard-pressed to gather evidence with respect to all the objectives.

While the quest for specificity in objectives can lead to an outlandish increase in the number of objectives, there are other problems as well. A quest for specificity in the expression of statements of educational objectives can lead one into the trap of concentrating on objectives that can easily be expressed in specific terms and abandoning objectives that do not lend themselves to such expression. Since the acquisition of knowledge and skills can be easily expressed as objectives, they are sometimes given prominence in statements of objectives while more complex but elusive objectives are neglected or, unfortunately, abandoned. This is indeed unfortunate since it is the evaluation worker's responsibility to show fidelity to the program developer's intentions, not to decide what objectives should be kept or discarded on the basis of ease of expression. Evaluation workers must, at the minimum, make sure that all the desired learner performances are included in a statement of objectives even if they are somewhat inadequately expressed.

Another aspect of the conceptual issue centers on the unity and integrity of complex objectives. Consider swimming as an example. One might have as an objective for a swimming program that learners will swim one hundred yards freestyle without stopping. The freestyle stroke requires a number of behaviors that must be integrated into an overall performance—flutter kick, arm motion, rhythmic breathing, etc. Mere enumerations of each of the component performances would not suffice. What is needed is a statement of an objective that will encompass not only each component of the freestyle stroke but the overall performance. The same holds true in the intellectual area as well. Many elementary school teachers are concerned with students learning to write reports on various topics. Usually, students must gather information from a variety of sources, distinguish between relevant and less relevant material, organize information into a sensible order, and write a coherent report. While the process can be broken down into a series of behaviors, it is the finished report that is paramount. Fractionalization of the process into the component behaviors can undermine the integrity of the main goal. Evaluation workers need to be sensitive to an objective's intent so that it can be expressed in a way that is relevant to the intentions of the people who developed the program and not just in a way that lends itself to ease of evaluation.

Finally, one frequently voiced dissatisfaction with statements of educational objectives, both general and specific, is that they fail to say anything about the basic structure, orientation, or framework of an educational enterprise. For example, two mathematics courses for the same grade level might have very similar statements of objectives, but one may adopt an approach that emphasizes conceptual development, while the other stresses application of principles to practical problems. In the opinion of many educators, statements about objectives, no matter how carefully constructed, are simply not capable of conveying anything about the orientation or flavor of a course, program, or curriculum. The absence of such information is not only distressing to educators, it is often a loss for evaluation specialists as well. Evaluation workers need all the information they can get in order to perform their professional function. The failure to obtain basic information about the educator's intents can pose serious problems for an evaluation enterprise.

This discussion is intended to expose one of the major conceptual issues in expressing educational objectives. While clarity is always a goal in expressing educational objectives, specificity may not be. Accordingly, evaluation workers, while desirous of seeking clear and specific terms for expressing educational objectives, must be alert and sensitive to program intentions. These intentions must be expressed as completely and as clearly as possible. Unfortunately, there is no single level of abstraction that can be relied on to achieve this goal.

It seems that educational intentions need to be expressed on three levels. First, a short, discursive exposition (less than five pages) is required to communicate the basic intentions of an educational enterprise: its orientation, framework, and broad goals. Second, a set of clear, general statements of objectives should describe the major areas in which changes in learner performance are being sought. For a single course that runs for a semester or a year, a list of, perhaps, six to fifteen general statements should be adequate to characterize its intentions; a program or curriculum running for several years would have somewhat more. The purpose of such a set of statements is to describe in general terms what is included in the enterprise and, by implication, what is excluded; this should serve as a convenient summarization of goals to direct teacher and learner efforts. Third, a set of clear and specific objectives is needed to give further meaning to each general objective where this is possible or necessary. Where it is not, illustrative proficiencies for each general objective should be supplied. The term "specific objectives" used here is similar to N. Gronlund's term "specific learning outcomes" (1985, p. 30) and is somewhat related to R. F. Mager's and W. J. Popham's term "instructional objectives," although there are some basic differences (Mager, 1962; Popham, 1988). It is important that all three types of statements be obtained in order to express as fully as possible the intentions of an educational enterprise. Each type serves a particular purpose that cannot be met by either of the other two.

Lest the reader think that preparing three different kinds of statements creates an unreasonable burden, it should be pointed out that our intention is just the opposite. Educators and even evaluation specialists will encounter considerable difficulty in trying to express adequately a set of educational intentions with a set of statements at a single level of abstraction. In trying to decide how general or specific a statement of an educational objective should be, the educator and the evaluation worker run a risk, on one hand, of being too general and omitting important, detailed material; on the other, of producing unwieldy strings of specific and detailed statements that will resemble a laundry list. By stating objectives at several levels, such difficulties can be avoided. The opportunity for a full expression of a set of educational intentions can then be realized.

These statements, of course, must be arranged in a clear and logical relationship. Unfortunately, no formula for constructing the three interlocking sets now exists. One need not, for example, begin with an expository statement, then proceed to the general and specific objectives, although that is one procedure and certainly logical. One can just as well start with a set of general objectives and proceed in either direction. The only requirement is that a clear relationship among the three sets of statements be maintained.

There are different requirements for formulating each kind of statement. The least restrictive of these applies to the general expository statement: an educator is free to express the basic intent of an educational venture in a discursive form. This may include the basic orientation, organizational framework, content coverage, and general expectations with regard to learner performance. Descriptive material of some of the learning experiences might even be included to convey some of the flavor of the enterprise. While one would place few restrictions on the development of such an expository statement, its purpose as a descriptive rather than promotional document must remain central at all times. It is a necessary but not sufficient expression of educational intentions.

GENERAL OBJECTIVES

Developing a set of general objectives is a more demanding business than preparing an expository statement. A general objective is a unitary statement, describing a learner state after exposure to an educational treatment. While some writers argue that such statements should refer to observable behaviors in learners, I do not regard it as essential. General objectives can refer to internal states in the learner, as indicated by use of terms such as "knows," "understands," and "comprehends," provided these terms are clarified either in an accompanying set of specific objectives, or in a set of illustrative examples, that clearly conveys the nature of the proficiency that is intended. In formulating a set of general objectives, several guiding principles are useful.

1. Objectives should be stated in terms of the learner and not in terms of subject matter to be learned, teacher activities, or learning experiences. This point becomes increasingly important as one moves from an expository statement to a listing of outcomes. An objective expressed as "participates in group discussions" would be considered unacceptable, since it refers to a learning experience rather than to what a student should show as a result of such an experience. Why does a teacher want learners to participate in group discussions? Perhaps a teacher wants learners to participate in group discussions so they can effectively present their points of view, adjust their positions on the basis of evidence or soundly presented argument, and, with other learners, reach sound and reasonable conclusions. If these are the benefits the teacher seeks from participation, then they should be stated as the objectives. Mere participation in an activity is not an acceptable objective.

2. Statements of objectives should begin with a verb, denoting the desired learner behavior or state. This format tends to assure that the focus of the objective will be on the learner and what he or she does. It should not be a recital of subject-matter to be learned. To illustrate, the statement "A set is a well-defined collection of objects or elements" is a statement about subject matter to be learned. "Knows the meaning of basic terms in mathematics" is a statement of an objective.

3. Objectives should be stated in terms that have uniform meanings. Unfortunately, language used in expressing educational intentions is often vague. Terms such as "good citizenship," "conceptual ability," "critical thinking," and "appreciates" can mean very different things to different people. Furthermore, deciding what would constitute admissible evidence of appreciation, critical thinking, and good citizenship is itself a formidable problem. Such problems can be avoided by not using ambiguous terms. When used, it is the responsibility of the educator, with assistance from the evaluation specialist, to define them with precision, clarity, and specificity, in a set of specific objectives.

4. Objectives should be unitary statements. For example, the objective "knows basic principles of balancing chemical equations and can apply them in the solution of problems" refers to two processes. The first refers to a knowledge state in the learner, the second to an ability to use the principles in the solution of novel problems. If both of these are important, then each should be accorded the status of an objective.

5. Objectives should be stated at an appropriate level of generality. They should be expressed at a level general enough to be further defined in a set of specific objectives. Thus "knows the meaning of basic mathematical terms"

would be an acceptable statement of a general objective since it could be defined further in a series of specific objectives. Listing the specific terms to be learned—such as set, subset, intersection of sets, union of sets, etc.—in a set of general objectives would be inappropriate; it would be too cumbersome to work with. It would also convey an impression that the course or program was atomistic in nature, and this might be untrue. On the other hand, an objective such as "knows mathematics" is stated far too broadly to serve any useful purpose.

6. Objectives should be related to the learning experiences provided. This point was made earlier in characterizing the educational process (see chapter one). Put simply, it is unrealistic to expect learners to achieve objectives when little or no opportunity is provided to attain them. In a biology course, where the learning experiences consisted of having to read printed material, attend lectures, and carry out explicitly-formulated experiments in a laboratory, it would not only be unrealistic but highly unfair to expect students to write short, learned essays on biological topics at the end of the course. No opportunity to develop the ability was provided. Either the objective or the learning experience needs to be modified.

7. Objectives should be realistic in terms of the time available for instruction, the characteristics of the learners, and the present state of knowledge. An illustration of an unrealistic objective would be "understands the causes of alcoholism," since no one knows the causes of alcoholism. Similarly, an objective for a group of seventh-graders that reads "understand the use of non-literal statements in literature" would probably be unrealistic because of the maturity level of the learners, and the limited time available for instruction in a general course in English.

This last principle is of special importance. Educational programs are developed to achieve particular goals. If the goals or objectives are unrealistic for a group of learners, then the evaluation will undoubtedly show that the goals have not been achieved. This result is not likely to satisfy the program's developers, administrators, or teachers. But it could have been predicted with near certainty before the program ever began. The simplest way to avoid such an unfortunate situation is to try to ensure that program objectives are realistic for the learners being served and the time and resources that are available. It is far better to have a program consisting of realistic and achievable objectives than one that has unrealistic and unattainable ones.

SPECIFIC OBJECTIVES

General objectives are the competencies that learners are supposed to acquire after exposure to a set of learning experiences. Since these objectives are stated in general terms, further elaboration is often necessary. This is done by listing specific objectives. Usually, each general objective needs to be followed by more specific and detailed statements that define the particular learner performances that would constitute the achievement of a general objective. One of the best guides for formulating specific objectives is furnished by Gronlund (1985). There is one slight difference between the terminology used by Gronlund and the terminology used in this book. We have used the term "specific objectives" to refer to the detailed behavioral statements of learner behaviors. Gronlund has chosen to use the term "specific learning outcomes." The difference is simply one of nomenclature; the meanings are the same. If a learner approached a teacher and asked, "What do I have to say or do to convince you that I have achieved a particular general objective?" the answers to such a question, in clear and specific form, would constitute a set of specific objectives for a general objective.

Most general objectives require elaboration in a set of specific objectives in order to convey fully a set of educational intentions. The behaviors described in Table 3.1 (to indicate understanding) provide one example of a set of specific objectives. It is not necessary that all possible behaviors be listed. What is needed is a set of clear and specific behaviors that could be considered representative of a general objective, and that one is willing to accept as evidence of the general objective's attainment. Thus it might be possible to analyze a general objective into five or six specific behaviors that, taken together, would constitute a reasonably full explication of a general objective. It is usually pointless to try to generate lengthy and exhaustive lists of specific objectives for each general objective. In the first place, it is unlikely that the proficiency represented in each specific objective will receive separate attention in instruction. Second, it is equally unlikely that an attempt will be made to test for every proficiency. Third, long lists of specific objectives are extremely cumbersome for teachers to work with. Hence, they are apt to be ignored. Finally, an attempt to define exhaustively a general objective may give the erroneous impression that a general objective is nothing but the sum of discrete proficiencies, rather than a generalized proficiency. Too detailed an analysis of a general objective may undermine the unity and, consequently, the integrity of the objectives.

One example of such overanalysis is in the area of reading comprehension where attempts have been made to break this competency into a number of different abilities. Some of the specific skills that have been noted are ability to follow directions, identify direct details, draw inferences from written material, find antecedents of words and phrases, identify motives of characters, and identify the writer's purpose. The above analysis may be helpful in suggesting instructional emphases and specific test questions. Still, it does convey the impression that reading comprehension is made up of many separate skills, which is not true. Reading comprehension is a fairly generalized ability that manifests itself rather uniformly through a variety of specific abilities as shown by Thorndike (1973) and others. Attempts to overanalyze reading comprehension, or any other general objective that is unitary in nature, into a large number of specific skills can undermine the integrity of the general objective.

SUMMARY

One of the contributions that an evaluation worker can make to the educational process is to help program developers and teachers clarify their educational intentions. It is neither necessary nor realistic for evaluation specialists to expect that a well-formulated set of objectives already exists for the course, program, or curriculum they are called upon to evaluate. One of the first orders of business for the evaluation worker is to determine how the objectives of an enterprise are expressed, if at all, and then work with program developers and teachers to clarify them if necessary. The development of the expository statement of the enterprise's intentions might be undertaken first. Such an undertaking should provide necessary background information about the enterprise, its orientation and direction. The formulation of a set of general objectives would then follow. Here the evaluation worker can assist the program developer and teachers by helping them formulate objectives as clearly as possible. Guidelines for formulating general objectives given in this chapter should be of assistance in the task. Last, the evaluation worker can help program developers and teachers define the general objectives in terms of the more specific learning outcomes that constitute the specific objectives. What are the things learners must say or do to convince program developers and teachers they have achieved each general objective? This is the key to defining specific objectives. The evaluation worker can help fashion such answers into clear, specific, behaviorally-oriented statements of learner performance. The assistance an evaluation worker can provide in each of these tasks should not only enable program developers and teachers to clarify their educational intentions, it should also furnish them with the basic specifications for evaluating an educational enterprise in terms of the changes it produces in the learners it serves.

References

Furst, E. 1958. *Constructing Evaluation Instruments*. New York: Longmans Green.
Gronlund, N. 1985. *Measurement and Evaluation in Teaching*, 5th ed. New York: Macmillan.
Mager, R. F. 1962. *Preparing Educational Objectives*. Belmont, Cal.: Fearon Publications.
Popham, W. J. 1988. *Educational Evaluation*, 2nd ed. Englewood Cliffs, N.J.: Prentice-Hall.
Thorndike, R. 1973. "Reading as Reasoning." *Reading Research Quarterly* 9, no. 2: 135–47.
Tyler, R. 1950. *Basic Principles of Curriculum and Instruction*. Chicago: University of Chicago Press.

Additional Readings

Bloom, B. (ed.). 1956. *Taxonomy of Educational Objectives: Handbook I, The Cognitive Domain*. New York: Longmans Green.

Bloom, B., Hastings, T. and Madaus, G. (eds.). 1981. *Evaluation to Improve Learnings.* New York: McGraw-Hill.

de Landsheere, V. 1977. "On Defining Educational Objectives." *Evaluation in Education: International Progress*, vol. 1, no. 2.

Harrow, A. 1972. *A Taxonomy of the Psychomotor Domain.* New York: David McKay.

Henry, N. (ed.). 1946. *The Measurement of Understanding.* Yearbook of the National Society for the Study of Education. Part 1. Chicago: University of Chicago Press.

Kibler, R., et al. 1977. "Behavioral Objectives." In *Curriculum Handbook: The Disciplines, Current Movements and Instructional Methodology*, edited by L. Rubin. Boston: Allyn and Bacon.

Krathwohl, D., et al. (eds.). 1964. *A Taxonomy of Educational Objectives: Handbook II, The Affective Domain.* New York: David McKay.

Smith, E. and Tyler, R. 1943. *Appraising and Recording Student Progress.* New York: Harper.

Struenig, E. and Guttentag, M. 1975. *Handbook of Evaluation Research*, vols. 1 and 2. Beverly Hills: Sage.

Walberg, H. (ed.). 1974. *Evaluating Educational Performance.* Berkeley: McCutchan Publications, 1974.

——— *4* ———

RELATING EVALUATION PROCEDURES
TO OBJECTIVES

The identification of general and specific objectives for courses, programs, or curricula is critical to the evaluation enterprise. Without a clear set of objectives it is impossible to ascertain whether an educational enterprise is accomplishing what it has set out to do. In the framework for evaluation presented in chapter two, the first two classes of information require data about learner performance at the start of an educational treatment and at a later period, often at the program's conclusion. The objectives provide specifications for much of the information to be collected. Any educational enterprise seeking to bring about changes in learners is duty bound to collect information about the extent to which such changes have occurred.

Measurement of learner performance, in relation to a set of objectives, is not limited to the measurement of factual information acquired during a period of instruction. Neither is it limited to paper-and-pencil tests measuring the effects of formal instruction. Evaluation is a continuous and comprehensive process, using a variety of evidence-gathering procedures. It is inextricably linked to the objectives and learning experiences of an educational venture.

In the previous chapter attention was focused on the process of formulating and expressing a set of educational objectives. In this chapter attention will be paid to the problem of identifying those evaluation procedures that provide the best and most direct evidence concerning the attainment of general and specific objectives.

Relating evaluation procedures to general and specific objectives requires logical analysis and judgment. There are, however, several principles to guide such an activity. Figure 4.1 sets forth the relationship between general objectives, specific objectives, and evaluation procedures.

```
 ↓General Objectives ª
   Specific Objectives ᵇ
 ↓Evaluation Procedures ᶜ
```

FIGURE 4.1: Relationship of Evaluation Procedures to Objectives

[a]Goals which direct educational courses, programs, and curricula.
[b]Learner behaviors accepted as evidence of attainment of objectives.
[c]Procedures for obtaining evidence of learner behavior described in the specific objectives.
Source: Adapted from N. Gronlund, *Measurement and Evaluation in Teaching,* 4th ed.
New York: Macmillan, 1981, p. 31.

The important point to be made about the information presented in Figure 4.1 is that a clear and logical relationship must be established among the three elements—general objectives, specific objectives, and evaluation procedures. The direction of the arrows shows that general objectives serve as the specifications for the development of the specific objectives; specific objectives are the determiners for the selection of evaluation procedures. This close logical relationship must be maintained if the evaluation enterprise is to have validity.

In selecting evaluation procedures, three general principles hold. First, an evaluation procedure should be appropriate; that is, the evaluation procedure chosen must produce the requisite information about learner behavior. Second, of several equally appropriate evaluation procedures, the one that is most efficient and practical should be employed. The reason for this is to insure that the evaluation enterprise is realistic and manageable. Third, wherever possible, but especially with objectives that are considered to be critical, multiple measures should be used (reference on triangulation). The purpose of this practice is to fortify the validity of evaluation results by obtaining relevant data (1) in several different ways or (2) on several occasions. Any particular evidence-gathering procedure is bound to have its own irrelevancies: a specific format, procedures for administration, specific item content, etc. The use of more than one procedure or occasion for evidence gathering should supply a variety of information bearing on the same objective or set of objectives.

Of the three principles presented above, the one concerning appropriateness is critical. (*Appropriateness* means that the evaluation procedure requires the learner to perform the behavior specified in the objective.) If an evaluation procedure is not appropriate for a particular objective, the resulting information is irrelevant at best and misleading at worst. For example, if a specific course objective requires learners to produce a plan for testing a hypothesis in a certain subject area, then the evaluation procedure must insure that students produce such a plan. Nothing less and nothing more will do. Questions asking students which of several plans would be most adequate for testing a hypothesis are invalid; the objective requires that students construct a plan, not select one from a number of alternatives. Clearly, the ability to select a plan correctly is no guarantee that the learner will be able to construct one.

It frequently happens that inappropriate evaluation procedures are selected for evidence gathering. For example, there is a tendency to overrely on objective written tests in many evaluation studies. Such tests include a number of item types among which are true-false and matching questions, one- or two-word fill-in items, and multiple-choice questions. Objective written tests are, generally, highly efficient in sampling learner performance on a wide range of subject matter. They can also be used to test a variety of objectives. They become appropriate, however, when the specific objective of a course, program, or curriculum specifies that the student identify, recognize, or select a correct response. They are inappropriate whenever an objective requires that the learner recall an item of information or develop his own response. It is, clearly, the evaluation worker's responsibility to make sure that every evaluation procedure used is appropriate for each objective.

The principle of choosing the most efficient evaluation procedure is important for practical reasons: an evaluation enterprise should be as unobtrusive, practical, and economical as possible. To achieve this goal, one should use evaluation procedures that (1) are inexpensive, (2) require a minimum amount of time (from both learner and teacher) for obtaining the necessary evidence, and (3) yield the most reliable estimates of learner behavior.

To illustrate this principle, consider an objective that requires learners to identify prime numbers. There are three general ways to test learners on this objective. First, they can be given an objective written test, consisting of a list of numbers, and asked to make an x next to the numbers that are prime. Second, learners can be asked to list all prime numbers between two given numbers. Last, they can be questioned orally by a teacher or assistant as to which numbers in a given set are prime and which are not. All three ways of gathering the requisite learner-performance information are appropriate to the objective. Of the three, however, the objective written test is most efficient: it requires the least amount of time on the part of both learners and teacher. Administered in a matter of minutes, it can be scored quickly by the teacher, an aide, or even a machine. What's more, it can be administered to an entire class at the same time. For this objective an evaluation worker would be wise to use an objective written test.

Table 4.1 relates a variety of educational objectives to their appropriate evaluation procedures. Listed on the left side of the table are sixteen different objectives. The list is not exhaustive, merely suggestive of a range of possible objectives. In all likelihood a given course, program, or curriculum would not include every one of them. The lower-numbered objectives are largely cognitive, while the higher-numbered ones are principally affective. Objectives eight and nine sometimes have a substantial psychomotor component. This distinction, considered important by some educators, is of no concern here. The view

TABLE 4.1: Procedures for Evaluating Sixteen Objectives

Evaluation Procedures

Objective	Objective Written Test	Objective Self-reports of Feelings	Objective Self-reports of Past Actions	Essay Written Test	Oral Questioning	Planned Observation by Checklist or Rating	Paper, Theme, or Report	Product, Scored or Rated	Performance, Observed and Rated	Incidental Observation by Teacher or Evaluation Worker	Situational Test
1. Recalls, recognizes, identifies specific facts, concepts	X	—	—	X	X	—	—	—	—	—	—
2. Identifies, describes, names orders	X	—	—	X	X	—	—	—	—	—	X
3. Makes set of plans, devises procedures or experiments	—	—	—	X	—	—	X	—	—	—	X
4. Communicates through writing	X	—	—	X	—	—	X	—	—	—	—
5. Communicates orally	—	—	—	—	X	X	—	—	X	X	—
6. Comprehends oral communication	X	—	—	X	X	—	—	—	—	—	—
7. Judges, compares, interprets	X	—	—	X	X	—	X	—	—	—	X
8. Carries out task or process	—	—	—	—	—	—	—	—	X	—	X

	1	2	3	4	5	6	7	8	9	10	11
9. Produces product to meet certain criteria	—	—	—	—	X	—	—	—	—	—	—
10. Displays specified attitudes, values	—	X	X	—	X	—	—	—	—	X	—
11. Displays specified interests	—	X	X	—	X	—	—	—	—	X	—
12. Displays specified character traits (honesty, loyalty, etc.)	—	—	—	—	X	—	—	—	X	X	X
13. Displays leadership	—	—	—	—	X	—	—	—	X	X	X
14. Displays specified work habits (initiative, promptness, responsibility, etc.)	—	—	—	X	—	—	—	—	X	—	—
15. Displays social adjustments to peers, superiors, group	—	—	—	—	—	—	—	X	X	X	—
16. Displays personal adjustment (self-esteem, reactions to thwarting, handling of anxiety, etc.)	—	X	—	—	—	—	—	X	X	X	X

Source: Compiled by the author.

throughout this book is that educational objectives are values; each one is important in its own right. Whether objectives should be classified as belonging to a cognitive, affective, or psychomotor domain is relatively unimportant.

The column headings in Table 4.1 present sixteen common types of evaluation procedures. The first, the objective written test, includes a variety of item-types. Typically, a learner selects a response from several choices or supplies one- or two-word answers to specific questions. Similarly, self-reports of feelings or past actions can be obtained in multiple ways: for example, by having learners indicate their agreement or disagreement with particular statements of feeling, or by having them rank statements in order of "most-to-least descriptive" of their feelings. Each general evaluation procedure thus represents a class of techniques to be used in gathering certain kinds of evidence.

Evaluation procedures may be arranged in a rough order of efficiency. The first procedure, an objective written test, is the most efficient; objective self-reports of feelings and past actions are second; and so on down to situational tests which are the least efficient. The checks in the boxes in the body of Table 4.1 indicate that a particular evaluation procedure is appropriate for a given objective. The chart shows that the seventh objective, which specifies that learners correctly interpret material presented to them, could be tested by an objective written test, an essay examination, oral questioning, or a situational test. All of the checked evaluation procedures would be appropriate for gathering evidence with regard to the attainment of the objective. The objective written test, however, is the most efficient procedure for obtaining the relevant information. Nevertheless, while an objective written test is most efficient, an essay test might in some cases be more suitable; for example, in a situation where the persons charged with evaluation did not have the requisite expertise to develop objective items necessary for objective testing. In practice, one uses the available resources to do a job. Many people do find it easier to develop essay rather than objective-type questions to measure complex intellectual performances. Consequently, while one would consider efficiency first by choosing evaluation procedures as far to the left as possible in Table 4. 1, there are sometimes good reasons for not doing so. The important point is to choose an appropriate evaluation procedure for a given objective.

As noted above, one may choose to use a less efficient procedure for highly practical reasons. One may also wish to consider, where resources permit, using more than one procedure to determine to what extent an objective has been achieved. The use of multiple measures of outcomes is generally recommended as a means of overcoming the idiosyncrasies associated with a particular evaluation instrument or procedure. In the case of an objective requiring learners to identify prime numbers, three different procedures could be used to determine learner proficiency. The use of multiple measures of educational outcomes is strongly recommended as a means of insuring that learner performance, after a period of instruction, is due to the effects of instruction, not to the irrelevancies of specific evaluation procedures. The extent to which multiple measures of learner performance can be employed will often depend on the exigencies of local circumstances, for example, the amount of evaluation material that can be produced, the time available for administering and scoring tests, etc. In chapter ten, ways of collecting information efficiently are described to enable evaluation workers to gather more information than they might have thought possible. In any event, local conditions will be the overriding determiners of how much information can be gathered.

The evaluation procedures listed in Table 4.1 are ones generally employed to gather data about learner behavior. A brief description of each will be given to acquaint the reader with the general characteristics and main feature of each. Detailed presentations of each procedure can be found in general textbooks on measurement (Anderson, 1981; Gronlund, 1985; and Thorndike and Hagen, 1977).

OBJECTIVE WRITTEN TEST

Objective written tests consist of a number of different item-types. The learner operates within a highly structured situation and selects his answer from a limited set of choices, supplied by the test constructor. He typically responds to a large number of items and receives a score, usually right or wrong, according to a predetermined set of correct answers. Item-types used in objective tests include true/false, matching, multiple choice and, sometimes, short one- or two-word fill-in questions. The term objective refers to this last characteristic, namely, that competent judges can agree on the correctness of a learner's answer. Objective tests have been used extensively to test for possession of factual information; they can also be used to assess ability to draw inferences, make interpretations from presented material, apply principles to novel situations, make comparisons and elementary kinds of analyses. Two examples of objective test questions that go beyond the testing of factual information are reprinted from Comber and Keeves (1973):

(Example 1)

Tom wanted to learn which of three types of soil—clay, sand, or loam—would be best for growing beans. He found three flowerpots, put a different type of soil in each pot, and planted the same number of beans in each, as shown in the drawing. He placed them side by side on the window sill and gave each pot the same amount of water.

Why was Tom's experiment NOT a good one for his purpose?
A. The plants in one pot got more sunlight than the plants in the other pots
B. The amount of soil in each pot was not the same.
C. One pot should have been placed in the dark
D. Tom should have used different amounts of water
E. The plants would get too hot on the windowsill

(Example 2)

John put some seeds on moist cotton in a dish. Jane put some seeds of the same kind into a glass full of water by the side of his. After two days John's seeds sprouted but nothing seemed to happen to Jane's. Which of the following is the most probable explanation?
A. Jane's seeds had been kept dry for too long
B. Jane did not allow her seeds enough air
C. Jane did not put the glass in a warm enough place
D. Jane should have used a different kind of seed
E. Jane did not use any cotton

OBJECTIVE SELF-REPORTS OF FEELINGS

Objective self-report measures of feeling, typically, consist of a number of non-factual statements that learners are asked to respond to by indicating their extent of agreement or endorsement. Some illustrative items, intended to measure learner attitudes toward science, are given by Comber and Keeves (1973):

> Science is steadily destroying the world.
>
> Science helps to make the world a better place to live in.
>
> Science is making us slaves to machines.

For each item the learner is furnished a set of response options such as "I strongly agree," "I agree," "I am uncertain," "I disagree," and "I strongly disagree," and is asked to check the one that best corresponds to his feelings. By summing the learner's responses to a number of items measuring the same characteristic, it is possible to describe an individual's affective disposition with respect to a particular area.

Three major assumptions underlie the use of objective self-report measures of feeling. These are: (1) the learner is able to read and understand the statements; (2) the learner is aware of his feelings toward the characteristic being measured; and (3) the learner is willing to indicate his feelings toward the characteristic being measured.

If one or more of these assumptions is not met, the use of objective self-report measures of feelings would be a questionable undertaking. For example, in a science course that seeks to influence attitudes in a particular way, learners may be reluctant to express their real feelings toward science. Evaluation workers need to be sensitive about the prospects of obtaining honest information through the use of such measures. One obvious way of increasing the likelihood of obtaining honest answers is to have learners respond anonymously. Since the goal of an evaluation is to make statements about treatments rather than individual learners, it is unnecessary for individuals to be identified by name.

OBJECTIVE SELF-REPORTS OF PAST ACTIONS

These are often employed to gather supplemental information that will help interpret results of learner performance in a particular course, program, or curriculum. For example, a social studies course may seek to develop learner interest in governmental affairs. It may achieve this goal with some learners but not with others. The use of a self-report measure of learner's previous contacts and activities in governmental affairs might reveal that those who had a history of involvement in civic activities demonstrated increased interest, while those who had not, did not. The use of an objective self-report of past actions can be of considerable help in explaining why some learners change in desirable ways while others do not. It can constitute an invaluable aid for future course-planning as well.

Questionnaires are the main vehicle for gathering information about the past actions of learners. Well-constructed questionnaires can result in the collection of a considerable amount of information in a short time. One of the major problems in the use of questionnaires, however, is that they appear easy to devise. Unfortunately, this is not the case. The development of good questionnaires requires considerable expertise; anyone planning to use them would be well advised, at the very least, to study carefully the principles and procedures of questionnaire development (see Kornhauser and Sheatsley, 1959; Oppenheim, 1966; Wolf, 1985). The same assumptions that underlie the development of objective self-reports of feelings apply to instruments measuring past actions. However, it is probably less likely that individuals will withhold reporting about past actions (unless they are deemed socially undesirable).

ESSAY WRITTEN TEST

An essay written test usually consists of a few questions. Learners are required to organize their own answers and use their own words and style of writing (usually including their own handwriting) to produce answers with varying degrees of correctness and completeness. The essay written test is particularly useful when what is required is that learners produce their own answers rather than merely recognize a correct one. Where objectives require that students be able to describe, give examples, make comparisons, develop a plan, etc., the essay written test is best suited for testing such proficiencies.

While it is generally recognized that the scoring of essay written tests can pose problems, it is less widely acknowledged that the development of such tests also presents considerable difficulties. One must have clearly in mind the mental processes one wants the learner to use in answering an essay question before starting to write it. The use of novel material, or novel methods of presentation in stating an essay question, may be necessary to test proficiencies beyond mere recall of knowledge. The task for the learner must be clearly presented and unambiguously defined. In scoring essay questions it is generally recommended that qualities on which answers are to be judged be defined in advance of scoring and, where multiple criteria are employed, that provisions be made for a separate evaluation of each quality. Preparing model answers, reading all responses to one question before going on to another, and scoring questions as anonymously as possible are all recommended practices for achieving maximum accuracy in scoring.

ORAL QUESTIONING

Oral questioning is in some ways similar to the use of essays. Learners are presented with problems that require them to organize their answers and express them in their own words. Answers, of course, can have varying degrees of completeness and correctness; however, oral questioning permits an examiner to ask follow-up questions and obtain elaboration on the part of respondents. As such it is a highly flexible method of assessing learner proficiency. On the negative side, it is often difficult to judge the quality of a learner's answers. Unless the questioning is tape-recorded, no permanent record exists that can be studied in detail while making a thoroughgoing appraisal. Judging learners' responses as they occur places a considerable burden on an examiner. The flexibility of oral questioning also poses problems; actual questions asked of one learner can differ markedly from those asked of another, resulting in a basic noncomparability. Finally, as a method, oral questioning is comparatively inefficient, since only one learner can be examined at a time.

PAPER, THEME, OR REPORT

The use of an assigned paper, theme, or report as an evaluation procedure is often undervalued. It has a number of the same features that essay written tests have. Learners organize their own answers and express themselves in their own style of writing. In addition, learners ordinarily have the opportunity to review and edit their work so that the resultant product usually represents their best efforts.

In many cases the learner is given some latitude in selecting the particular topic he or she will write on, thus introducing a certain degree of noncomparability into the situation. However, this can be remedied somewhat by specifying the limits within which choices for topics can be made, or by having an approval procedure before learners are allowed to begin to work in earnest. Another difficulty in the use of papers, themes, or reports prepared outside of a classroom setting is that it is seldom possible to know how much the product represents the learner's own efforts, and how much the efforts of others. For this reason, it is usually considered wise to supplement papers, themes, and reports with evidence gathered under supervised conditions.

PRODUCTS, SCORED OR RATED

Educational enterprises, having among their objectives the production of objects, will necessarily require product evaluations. Products that are scored or rated resemble essay questions in that the learner produces an object in his own style. The product can have varying degrees of correctness or completeness. For example, in a course in carpentry a learner may be required to build a sawhorse according to a set of specifications. The product can then be judged on the basis of several criteria: stability, sturdiness, closeness of fit of joints, etc. Separate scores or ratings can be given for each criterion. In appraising learner products it is usually not possible to make judgments about the process used in production. In the construction of a sawhorse, for example, we cannot rate the learner's proficiency in using a T-square, saw, or hammer merely by observing the finished product; only tentative inferences can be made. These, of course, would need confirmation in another situation where the process can be directly observed.

PERFORMANCES, OBSERVED AND RATED

Some objectives demand that learners carry out a particular kind of performance. Making a speech before a group, playing a musical instrument, or leading a discussion are examples of behaviors that can only be evaluated by direct observation and rating of the performance. Judging learner performance in this way requires time and effort to closely observe the performance and, either while it is going on or immediately after its conclusion, rate it according to previously determined criteria and standards. The usual device employed is a scale, with one or more characteristics, on which the performance is to be rated. In addition, for each characteristic there is a set of graded categories representing different levels of quality. Observing and rating performances is often laborious and time-consuming. It also demands that the individual doing the rating is sufficiently familiar with the rating scale to use it as intended. Usually, this requires training in the use of rating scales so that various kinds of errors can be avoided. Used properly, rating scales can be important sources of information about learner behavior; in some cases, they may be the only source available.

INCIDENTAL OBSERVATION

Unlike planned observations and ratings of learner performance, incidental observation, often coupled with rating, is employed to assess typical learner behaviors. Planned observation and rating could be used, for example, to appraise learners' speaking or oral reading performances. In these cases, learners are called on to perform. Social skills, use of time and equipment, initiative, persistence, adaptability, and other similar behaviors are best appraised when the individual is unaware that he or she is being observed and when observation occurs over an extended period of time. Incidental observation by a teacher or evaluation worker, coupled with some procedure for recording such as a checklist or a rating scale, can yield useful information about a number of important objectives in the areas of skills, work habits, social behavior, interest, and adjustment.

The main requirement for the use of incidental observation is that the observer should be conscious of the characteristics and behaviors singled out for observation and sensitive to their occurrence. Observation normally occurs during the course of regular activities in the educational situation, placing a real demand for versatility on the part of the observer. If observations are to have any validity, they should be made during the normal course of educational activities when the individual being observed is least aware of being observed. Observation should also continue over some period of time, since the behavior that is sought may not occur naturally in many situations. Heavy requirements are placed on observers; they must detect the behaviors considered important and keep a record of their occurrences. Incidental observation frequently requires more time and effort than usual testing procedures, and it is more subjective than one would wish. However, if the behaviors being assessed are considered educationally important, there is no alternative but to gather evidence about them, however fallible the methods employed may be.

SITUATIONAL TEST

The situational test is a mixture of a standard testing approach and a real-life situation. It is created as naturally as possible to evoke particular kinds of learner behaviors that are considered educationally important. At the simplest level, the teacher may call upon a learner to read unfamiliar material in order to note the kinds of errors made. At a more complex level, a group may be formed to discuss a particular topic, and learners are observed for the incidence of particular discussion-group behaviors such as clarification, facilitation, reaction to different points of view, etc. The difficulty in developing situational tests is making them appear spontaneous and making sure the learners are unaware that they are in an evaluation situation. This sometimes requires elaborate efforts. A situational test is useful for assessing character traits, such as honesty and loyalty, and various social skills and leadership qualities. Along with a system for recording performance data, it can be used to gather evidence about types of behavior that might otherwise go unassessed.

The special feature of the situational test is that it is intended to elicit certain kinds of learner behavior. One can wait for a learner to display these behaviors in an educational setting and not see them occur, because nothing occurs to evoke them. The situational test attempts to overcome this by structuring the situation in such a way that conditions call for a demonstration of the required behavior. For example, if one wanted to know whether a learner knew the meaning of the word "eleemosynary," one could follow the learner around for a year and never hear him utter the word. Still, it would be unwarranted to infer that he did not know it. The occasion for its use simply never arose. The situational test is intended to remedy this by arranging conditions in the situation so that the only way the learner can perform successfully is by using the word "eleemosynary."

SUMMARY

The above sketches of major evaluation procedures are intended to acquaint the reader with a variety of ways of gathering information about learner behavior with regard to educational objectives. They are, however, no substitute for the extensive treatment provided in standard texts. A number of these can be found in the references and list of additional readings. The key to relating objectives to evaluation procedures is appropriateness. An evaluation procedure should be selected on the basis of its chances of yielding the kind of evidence that will permit an evaluator to make an unequivocal statement about the extent to which a particular objective has been achieved. Table 4.2 was developed to assist in accomplishing this goal.

The tendency to equate evaluation with formal testing has been an unfortunate development. The evaluation worker has an arsenal of techniques and procedures available to obtain evidence of learner achievement of program objectives. While each evaluation procedure has its strengths and its limitations, judicious use of appropriate procedures should furnish the evaluation worker with the information to assess the extent of attainment of program objectives. To emphasize the variety of evaluation procedures and show how objectives can be related to them, Table 4.2 has been developed. This table presents four general objectives for a high-school chemistry course (the actual course would probably have more). Each general objective has been broken down into a group of specific objectives. One, and sometimes two or three, evaluation procedures are presented for each specific objective. For each specific objective the evaluation procedures selected are those that will provide the most direct and adequate evidence of learner behavior. Such a table should be developed in connection with the planning of any evaluation enterprise.

TABLE 4.2: Procedures for Evaluating Objectives for High School Science Course

General and Specific Objectives	Evaluation Procedure
1. Knows common terms	
Defines common terms	Short answer essay test
Distinguishes between corret and incorrect use of terms	Objective written test
Identifies meaning of terms when used in context	Objective written test
2. Understands principles and generalizations	
Recognizes major principles and generalizations	Objective written test
States principles and generalizations in own words	Short answer essay test
Given a principle or generalization, identifies situation using it	Objective written test
Given a situation, identifies principle or generalization that applies	Objective written test
3. Applies principles to novel material	
Identifies elements in situation needed to establish problem type	Short answer essay test
Selection of abstraction (principle, method or idea) suitable to problem type	Objective written test,
Use of abstraction to solve problem	Short answer essay test
	Short answer essay test
4. Plans and carries out a study to test a hypothesis	
Develops a plan for hypothesis testing which can yield unequivocal results	Paper
Carries out study in a technically correct way	Planned and incidental observation
	Product (Laboratory notebook)
Prepares a report of results of the study	Paper and Product (Laboratory notebook)

Source: Adapted from N. Gronlund, *Measurement and Evaluation in Teaching*, 5th ed. New York: Macmillan, 1985.

References

Comber, L. and Keeves, J. 1973. *Science Education in Nineteen Countries*. New York: Halstead Press (John Wiley).

Gronlund, N. 1985. *Measurement and Evaluation in Teaching*, 5th ed. New York: Macmillan.

Komhauser, A. and Sheatsley, P. 1959. "Questionnaire Constuction and Interview Procedures." In C. Sellitz, et al., *Research Methods in Social Relations*, revised ed., edited by C. Sellitz, et al. New York: Holt, Rinehart and Winston.

Oppenheim, A. 1966. *Questionnaire Design and Attitude Measurement*. New York: Basic Books.

Thorndike, R. and Hagen, E. 1977. *Measurement and Evaluation in Psychology and Education*, 4th ed. New York: Wiley.

Wolf, R. 1985. "Questionnaires." In *International Encyclopedia of Education*. T. Husen and T. Postlethwaite (eds.). Oxford, England: Pergamon.

Additional Readings

Bloom, B. (ed.). 1956. *Taxonomy of Educational Objectives: Handbook I: The Cognitive Domain*. New York: Longmans Green.

Bloom, B., Hastings, T. and Madaus, G. (eds.). 1981. *Evaluation to Improve Learning*. New York: McGraw-Hill.

Harrow, A. 1972. *A Taxonomy of the Psychomotor Domain*. New York: David McKay.

Henry, N. (ed.). 1946. *The Measurement of Understanding*. Yearbook of the National Society for the Study of Education, Part 1. Chicago: University of Chicago Press.

Krathwohl, D., et al. (eds.). 1964. *A Taxonomy of Educational Objectives: Handbook II: The Affective Domain*. New York: David McKay.

Smith, E. and Tyler, R. 1943. *Appraising and Recording Student Progress*. New York: Harper

Struenig, E. and Guttentag, M. 1975. *Handbook of Evaluation Research*, vols. 1 and 2. Beverly Hills: Sage Publications.

Walberg, H. (ed.). 1974. *Evaluating Educational Performance*. Berkeley, Cal.: McCutchan Publications.

5

GATHERING EVIDENCE ABOUT LEARNER PERFORMANCE

The importance of information about learner performance in evaluating an educational course, program, or curriculum cannot be overestimated. Properly gathered, analyzed, and interpreted, such evidence enables an educator to determine how well an educational enterprise is succeeding in achieving what it set out to accomplish. What it "set out to accomplish" invariably involves changing the behavior of learners in directions considered educationally desirable: an increase in knowledge, skills, and problem-solving abilities; a change in attitudes; or other more complex performances.

Previous chapters presented and discussed (1) the processes by which objectives are formulated and expressed, and (2) how appropriate evaluation procedures are chosen for gathering evidence about learner achievement of these objectives. This chapter attempts to describe a number of the more relevant aspects of the actual process of gathering information about learner behavior. (Detailed descriptions of procedures for evidence-gathering, however, will not be dealt with since they are readily available in standard texts on measurement and testing.) Of concern here is the role it plays in the evaluation of educational courses, programs, and curricula. Evidence-gathering, it cannot be noted too often, refers not only to conventional testing, but to a wide range of procedures available for the collection of relevant information about learner behavior in relation to educational objectives.

The formulation of a set of general objectives and its elaboration in the form of specific objectives, although critical, is only one step in the evaluation process. For each specific objective, one or more suitable evaluation procedures must be selected. Evaluation exercises, items, tasks, questions, observation forms, and so on are then developed to elicit relevant learner performance information. Conventional procedures for instrument development are followed, fidelity to the objectives being the overriding consideration. Occasionally, concessions have to be made for practical reasons—such as limitations on time, lack of expertise with a particular technique, or because of difficulties of use in an actual situation. For instance, a specific objective might ideally require the use of extensive observation of learner performance, but practical considerations might lead one to settle for a self-report instrument. Of course, once one decides to substitute a less direct means of gathering information for a more direct one, some check should be made to obtain assurance that the two procedures yield essentially similar results.

The actual development of evaluation instruments is often undertaken jointly by those charged with the evaluation of educational courses, programs, and curricula and those charged with developing and conducting them. Evaluation workers should bring to the task a body of professional and technical expertise in the development of evaluation instruments; those who develop and conduct the programs should bring a body of substantive knowledge about the material they will teach and the nature of the learners they will serve. Their joint efforts (in some limited endeavors it might be only two individuals) should produce a set of evaluation instruments that are relevant for the program and reasonable for learners.

Ideas for evaluation exercises can come from program, personnel, or evaluation specialists; whatever the source, they need to be reviewed by those involved in the evaluation. Such a review would result in a decision as to whether (1) an evaluation exercise or procedure is faithful to the objective being measured and (2) suitable to the learners. These are crucial considerations. If security is a factor, evaluation workers and program personnel can develop prototype exercises and procedures to serve as models for the development of parallel material by evaluation specialists. While less than ideal, such arrangements are sometimes necessary. It will protect the professionals most closely associated with the program's operation by insuring that beneficial program effects cannot be ascribed to overfamiliarity with the actual test questions, items, and exercises.

Once developed, the material should be grouped on the basis of similarity of procedure, not objective being measured. Thus, objective written questions would be grouped in one pile, regardless of objective being tested, essay questions in another pile, and so on. In doing this, workers should make sure that the objective being tested is not overlooked, since at some later date all information will have to be reassembled objective by objective.

WHEN SHOULD EVIDENCE BE GATHERED

Information about learner performance must be obtained on at least two occasions—before instruction gets seriously underway, and after a specified period of instruction. The phrase "before instruction gets seriously underway" indicates that an estimate of learner performance before a treatment begins is important. Specifically, educators not only need to know that learners are not already proficient in what they are expected to achieve, some estimate of how unaccomplished they are is also required. To this end measures of achievement, for example, objective written tests, essay tests, etc., could be administered during the first few sessions that learners are together. The administration of such measures at the beginning of a set of learning experiences is a somewhat delicate undertaking: teachers and learners will not have developed a working relationship yet, and learners presumably will be answering questions and items covering unfamiliar material. One commonly used procedure is to include in the test directions a statement acknowledging the learners' general lack of familiarity with the material, but requesting them to try to do their best. It can also be announced that the resulting information will be of assistance in planning specific learning experiences for the group. Often, assurance that these test performances will not influence students' grades is given; however, this may prevent individuals from putting forth their best effort in answering various questions and items. This is a real problem, and there is no easy solution. Some assurance should be offered that performance will not influence the learners' marks. Frankly given, it may even contribute to the development of a sense of trust between teachers and learners. It should not be assigned undue prominence. Instead, educators should emphasize that information, representing the best efforts of the learners, will be of considerable importance in planning an appropriate set of learning experiences for the group.

Information relating to intellectual outcomes can be gathered during the beginning sessions of a course, program, or curriculum. For several reasons information about nonintellectual outcomes should probably not be gathered until somewhat later, perhaps three to four weeks after a program has started. First, learners may be reluctant to respond frankly to measures dealing with attitudes, feelings, and interests. Rather than run the risk of obtaining incorrect information or no information at all, it seems wise to hold off a little until some relationship has been established. Second, some measures, notably those dealing with social relationships, cannot be administered until a group of learners has been together for a period of time. For example, sociometric measures cannot be administered until a group has been together long enough for social relationships to develop. If a program has objectives dealing with social aspects associated with learning, this will usually be the case.

The chief danger in delaying initial information gathering about learner performance is that the information may be influenced by the effects of the program. Called "confounding," this unwanted influence can result in problems in the interpretation of results from evaluation studies. Confounding usually results in an underestimate of program effects. Consequently, delays in pretesting must be avoided. As a rule, initial information should be gathered as early as possible. However, in regard to nonintellectual outcomes, it may be necessary to delay administering some measures for a few weeks until the learners have adjusted to the situation and feel comfortable enough to give frank answers to items of a personal nature.

How much information should be gathered about the initial performance of learners is an open question. While some would advocate as much as possible, a good case could be made for obtaining as little as possible; keeping the amount of testing time down to a minimum at the beginning of a period of instruction has distinct advantages. First, the less time that is taken for testing, the more that is left for learning. Second, the chief purpose of measuring learner performance at the beginning of a course, program, or curriculum is to obtain a rough estimate of learners' proficiencies regarding program material. Third, one would expect that minimizing testing time at the beginning of a treatment period would increase the likelihood of learners making an honest effort to answer questions and items and to respond frankly to attitudinal items and the like. That is to say, increasing the test burden is likely to decrease the willingness of learners to furnish useful information. In a few special cases, most initial information gathering can be dispensed with entirely: programs to train welders, electricians, joiners, computer programmers, health technicians, and the like involve such specialized knowledge and skills that it is safe to assume that entering learners have little, if any, initial proficiency. The same holds true for beginning courses in foreign languages or specialized math and science programs. In programs that are developmental in nature, however, learners typically enter with some previously acquired proficiencies. Reading, mathematics, and a number of other school subjects are examples of programs where entering learners have already attained some proficiency. In such cases, it is important to make some assessment of initial proficiency. To sum up, assessment of the initial proficiency of learners with respect to the objectives of the course, program, or curriculum is important. The sole exception is programs that are highly specialized in nature, where prior competence can be presumed low or nonexistent.

In addition to performance data, information descriptive of the learners to be served must be gathered. Data on sex, socioeconomic status, or previous educational history of the learners can either be gathered directly from the learners themselves or from institutional records. Depending on the nature of the educational enterprise, additional items of information descriptive of learners should be collected. Such information serves three purposes. First, educational workers should be able to characterize their learners correctly. Interpretations of the results of evaluation studies must take into account the nature of the learners. Second, educational courses, programs, and curricula are designed to serve a particular group of learners (usually referred to as the intended, or target population). The question is if the intended beneficiaries of an educational venture are the ones actually being served. Only by systematically gathering information about the learners themselves and comparing this with the defined target population can a determination of a match be made. From time to time it does happen that the actual learners being served by a program are not the ones for whom the program was intended. Voluntary educational programs such as "Sesame Street" and "The Electric Company" have experienced such outcomes; it can even happen in institutional settings. Thus an important feature of any evaluation study is determining whether the intended group of beneficiaries is being reached. A third reason for gathering information describing the learners being served by an educational enterprise is to detect shifts in the nature of the group over a period of time. While it is usually hoped that a program, course, or curriculum, found to be reasonably successful in one institution at one period in time, will continue to be effective with succeeding groups of learners, any changes in learner populations signals a need for reexamination. Systematic collection of descriptive information about learners being served can be useful in detecting whether changes in the nature of the group occur. Appropriate modifications in the program can then be considered.

Collecting information about learners and how proficient they are relative to what is to be learned is a relatively straightforward matter compared to the gathering of subsequent information. Even the phrase "after a period of instruction" is vague, although for good reasons. When subsequent information is collected is largely a function of the uses to be made of the results. If the purpose of evaluating a course, program, or curriculum is to improve it at certain points, then it may be necessary to gather information repeatedly. Each time would be deemed critical in the life of the enterprise, representing a major decision point or milestone. In a science course, for example, it might occur at the end of each major unit of work or even at a critical point within a unit, for example, when the basic principles of a given class of phenomena have been presented and discussed, and learners are about to move into an application phase or embark on a series of laboratory experiments. The function of evaluation in such a situation is to track learners through a series of activities in order to determine group progress, identify problems in learning, and so on. As previously noted, such activity is termed "formative" evaluation and is undertaken with the explicit intent of program improvement. In contrast, collecting information at the end of a program is done to determine the effectiveness of the program in terms of its objectives. Here, information is gathered as close to the end of the program as possible so that learners can be tested with regard to the attainment of all the program's objectives. Such end-of-program data gathering can also be undertaken for formative evaluation purposes. For example, end of program results may indicate that certain skills and concepts were not learned satisfactorily. Further study would be needed, however, to identify the reasons for such failures.

It sometimes happens that decisions regarding the future of courses, programs, and curricula cannot await the completion of a program. Budgets for most educational institutions need to be drawn up months in advance, requiring programmatic decisions well in advance of full and final information. While it is highly desirable that decisions be made on the basis of complete information, it may not always be possible. In such circumstances, even in the case of summative evaluation, it is well to gather evaluative information before the close of a program. It may be necessary to collect information halfway through a program. This is clearly not an ideal state of affairs, but it is sometimes unavoidable. Better something than nothing; in the words of Sir Robert Watson-Watt, the inventor of radar: "Give them the third best to go on. The best never comes, and the second best comes too late."

In summary, decisions about when evidence should be gathered are open-ended questions. The collection of information about the nature of the learners and their initial level of proficiency is a relatively clear issue. The uses to be made of the results of the evaluation govern the collection of subsequent information. The program developer must work these out as he goes along. All in all, the uses to be made of the results of an evaluation study should be clarified as early as possible and a schedule for collecting information about learner performance that is consistent with these intended uses should be developed. It is because there is no universal set of uses of evaluation information that the ambiguous phrase "after a period of instruction" must be used to characterize when subsequent information about learner performance should be gathered.

HOW SHOULD EVIDENCE BE GATHERED

Some mention has already been made about the conditions under which learner-performance information should be gathered. For example, for objectives that involve evaluating the learner's typical behavior in a group setting, unobtrusive procedures, such as planned or incidental observations, should be employed; for objectives demanding the best efforts of the learner, a task must be specified and the learner encouraged to do his best.

There are a number of other considerations in the collection of information about learner performance. Of critical importance is time. One should always try to keep the time for information gathering to a minimum. There are a number of obvious reasons for this, the major one being that the less time used for evidence-gathering, the more time there is for teaching and learning. In most cases, fortunately, this is not a major problem, it is simply not necessary to examine each learner with respect to every general or specific objective. One can, for example, divide a group of learners, at random, into four equal subgroups and gather one-fourth of the required information from each quarter. This represents a saving in time of 75 percent—not an inconsiderable economy. Details as to how such procedures can be developed and implemented will be described in chapter ten. The point is that it is not necessary to gather information on every learner with regard to every objective when evaluating an educational enterprise. These economies, beside allowing more time for teaching and learning, should increase cooperation by reducing the testing burden for each individual learner. In many evaluation situations it should be possible to gather the bulk of the required learner performance information in about thirty to forty minutes. Observational procedures or out-of-class learner projects would, of course, require additional time, but they would, at least, not interfere with normal teaching and learning operations

The use of procedures that require each learner to respond to only a fraction of the total amount of evaluation material has several important consequences. One, the scope of an evaluation study need not be unduly limited because of time restrictions. In fact, it should be possible to gather full information with regard to all objectives without making excessive demands either on teachers and learners or the time allotted for instruction. Two, through judicious allocation procedures, the same set of instruments for gathering information about learner performance may be used before instruction gets underway and after a period of instruction. If the total amount of testing material has been divided at random into fourths, a learner can be asked to respond to one set of exercises before instruction begins and a different set after a period of instruction. In this way, a single set of material could be used several times. Furthermore, no individual would be required to respond to the same material more than once. In fact, if it is decided that information about learner performance is required at four points during the course of an educational enterprise, then a single set of material, appropriately divided into fourths, and carefully assigned to learners, could suffice for an entire class. The saving in time, effort, and expense from not having to develop parallel sets of items should be obvious.

The idea of not administering the same set of questions, exercises, etc., to every learner may appear to be somewhat unusual. However, when one remembers that the purpose of evaluating an educational treatment is to say something about the worth of the treatment, and not to describe the performance of each and every learner, the procedure makes sense. Just as we routinely accept the results of surveys that poll a small sample of persons, we should be prepared to accept studies in which 20 to 25 percent of the learners respond to any given item or exercise. (A more detailed discussion on procedures for allocating evaluation exercises among learners and analyzing the results will be found in chapters ten and eleven.)

ISSUES IN THE GATHERING OF INFORMATION ABOUT LEARNER PERFORMANCE

Testing each learner on only a fraction of questions, items, and exercises immediately raises the issue of noncomparability. It will not be possible to compare one learner's performance with another if they have not been tested on the same set of material. This is quite correct. However, evaluation and learner appraisal are two distinct enterprises. The former is much broader in scope; it considers not only treatment effects on learners but matters of cost; reactions of learners, teachers, administrators, and others; even the worth of the objectives being pursued. Learner appraisal, on the other hand, involves assessing the progress of learners in terms of a set of stated objectives. This is normally the teachers' responsibility. (In some cases external testing and certifying by accrediting boards, as in professional schools and certain vocational programs, constitutes normal practice. This, however, is the exception, not the rule.) The appraisal function is generally best handled by those who work closely with learners and are therefore in a position to observe and record their progress; these would obviously be the teachers. However, the evaluation enterprise should not be confused with the appraisal of learner performance.

If the evaluation of courses, programs, and curricula is handled separately from the appraisal function, then those charged with appraising learning performance must organize and conduct such activities themselves. Evaluation personnel may furnish assistance, if requested and if time and resources permit but, in general, teachers have to bear the major responsibility for appraising learner performances. In carrying out this responsibility, teachers should keep in mind that the gathering of learner-performance information for evaluation purposes will usually not contribute to the appraisal function. This is obviously true if not all learners are given the same set of questions, exercises, scales, etc. The distinction between evaluation and learner appraisal should be clarified from the beginning, otherwise false or unrealistic expectations will develop and the professional integrity of each kind of educational worker (teacher, evaluation specialist) may be jeopardized. Systematic evaluation of educational programs by teachers does not alter the basic responsibility of teachers for learner appraisal. In many cases, evaluation will not facilitate it, either.

Another issue of importance that has been raised in connection with evaluation in recent years is the place of norm-referenced and criterion-referenced measurement of learner performance. Considerable confusion still surrounds the basic conception of what criterion-referenced measurement is. This is partly due to the novelty of criterion-referenced measurement (although it has been shown that the basic notion has existed for decades) and partly to the confusion that naturally surrounds a newly presented concept (Airasian and Madaus, 1972). The presentation of rather idiosyncratic views of what criterion-referenced measurement is or should be has not helped the situation, either.

Criterion-referenced measurement has two major characteristics. First, the domain measured is limited to a very clear but narrowly defined topic or skill. The one hundred basic addition facts and the use of commas in series are examples of such clear and narrowly defined domains. Second, there is a predetermined standard that separates acceptable from unacceptable performance. In addition, a number of other characteristics exist that serve to distinguish criterion-referenced measurements from norm-referenced ones. However, these are generally either minor ones or stem from the two major characteristics noted above or involve technical issues of no concern here. By having a predetermined dividing line between acceptable and unsatisfactory performance (some writers use the terms mastery and nonmastery), it has been possible to obtain results from criterion-referenced testing showing that a particular percentage of learners has achieved an acceptable level of performance on a particular topic or skill. The prospect of obtaining such results has probably been one of the major appeals of criterion-referenced measurement. Learners are not judged on the basis of how they stand in relation to the rest of the members of a group but, rather, in terms of whether they have met a predetermined level of acceptable performance. No fixed percent of a group must be consigned to a low level of performance; every learner can be a winner!

The use of criterion-referenced measurement in the evaluation of courses, programs, and curricula is not especially recommended. On the contrary, evaluation studies need to determine learner performance at several levels of proficiencies rather than a single one. In evaluating a special reading instruction program for seventh graders, for example, it would be helpful to know how learners perform on simple material, on material of average difficulty, and on difficult material. Since performance information, gathered in connection with evaluation studies, is generally not used to appraise individual learners, there is little danger that learners will be harmed by responding to material at varying levels of difficulty and complexity. Indeed, considerable benefit may accrue from ascertaining the range of attained proficiency. The situation here is similar to a high jumping contest where the bar is set at 3' 8". Finding that all contestants can jump that high is far less instructive, in terms of information gained about jumping proficiency, than having contestants continue to jump at successively greater heights until they reach their maximums. It is this latter kind of information that is particularly important in evaluation studies. Evaluation workers seek to measure actual levels of achievement, rather than some single arbitrary level.

Another problem with the use of criterion-referenced measurement in evaluation studies arises because many of the objectives of instruction do not meet the specifications of a clear and narrowly defined domain. Important educational objectives are highly complex, even specific objectives are, and require the use of several concepts, skills, and abilities. A relatively clear objective, for example, the preparation of a report on some aspect of Greek civilization, requires the use of a broad range of competencies. In contrast, criterion-referenced measurement necessitates narrowly defined domains if the results are to be clearly interpretable. Faced with a variance between the nature of educational objectives and a method of testing, educators should put objectives first. Testing procedures must be appropriate for the objectives, not vice versa.

This does not mean that criterion-referenced measurement has no place in instruction, it doubtless does. But its place is restricted to those areas where there are clear and narrowly defined domains. Indeed, such measures seem best suited for making instructional decisions about individual learners.

A third issue in the gathering of evidence about learner performance in evaluation studies centers on the use of nonlocally produced questions, exercises, tests, scales, and so on. This would include the use of published instruments as well as standardized tests. Opinion in this area varies greatly. On the one hand, some will argue that only locally produced measures, tailored to the objectives of a particular program, can be used with confidence. The use of externally developed measures can be exceptionally unfair if they measure proficiencies not emphasized in a particular program. To judge a program on the basis of such irrelevant measures, some argue, is not only a disservice to the program but poor evaluation practice. Situations have been known where only 10 to 15 percent of the questions in a standardized test measured proficiencies relevant to course objectives. The maxim "test what you teach" is particularly germane in evaluation.

In contrast to this position is the view that nonlocally produced measures are not only useful and desirable but essential. Several reasons have been cited for this position. First, it is unlikely that there will be enough resources available locally to produce all the instruments needed to gather information about learner performance. Judicious selection and use of nonlocally produced measures is considered not only desirable but essential. Second, it is unlikely that the objectives of a particular program are so specialized or idiosyncratic as to make nonlocally produced instruments wholly inappropriate. Third, for a number of educationally important objectives, for example, reading comprehension and math computation, published standardized tests are substantively and technically better than measures locally produced. Finally it is argued that when the goal of evaluation is to find out what changes a course, program, or curriculum produces in learners, measures should not be limited to the specific objectives of instruction. "An ideal evaluation," Cronbach (1963) writes, "would include measures of all the types of proficiency that might reasonably be desired in the area in question, not just the selected outcomes to which this curriculum directs substantial attention." This, of course, opens the door to any and all measures that are related to the program under study.

While the two positions would appear irreconcilable, the problem can be handled in a fair and evenhanded way. The selection or development of measures for gathering information about learner performance should be based on the objectives themselves. If the objectives are the determining consideration, then whether measures are locally developed or not is simply irrelevant. Most efficient would be to use already developed measures, including published ones if such are available, and supplement these with locally developed ones. Measures not directly related to the specific objectives of the program can be used to gather information about other kinds of learner proficiency in the general area of study as long as the results are analyzed and reported separately. In terms of the framework for evaluation presented in chapter two, such results would more appropriately be regarded as belonging to the class of supplemental information. If the evaluation enterprise is appropriately and judiciously organized and conducted within the framework set forth in chapter two, distinctions between locally and nonlocally developed measures, measures related to program objectives, and measures not related to objectives lose much of their importance.

A TECHNICAL NOTE

For several reasons the discussion in this chapter has avoided any detailed consideration of the issues of validity and reliability. In the first place, these subjects are dealt with at length in standard references on measurement and evaluation (Messick, 1989; Gronlund, 1985; Wolf, 1982). Second, it was felt that the evidence-gathering considerations, issues, and problems discussed in this chapter were the important ones for evaluation studies. Third, the issue of validity—the paramount one in testing—has been emphasized throughout. This has been done, however, in context: wherever the importance of choosing or devising measures of educational objectives that faithfully and fully reflect the objectives has been emphasized, the notion of content validity has been stressed also.

The issue of reliability, in contrast, has not been considered for two reasons. First, the precision with which a characteristic is measured is a secondary consideration to validity. Second, conventional notions of reliability do not apply to the evaluation of courses programs, and curricula in the same way as to the measurement of individuals. Reliability theory and procedures for estimating the reliability of measures developed out of a concern for estimating the precision of scores of individuals. When a reading test is administered to a single learner, it is important to know how accurately the learner's reading proficiency is being measured. This involves knowledge of the standard error of measurement. In evaluation studies, however, concern focuses on estimating performance for a group of learners—from a particular subgroup exposed to a treatment to all individuals exposed to the treatment. Thus, in evaluation studies, concern centers on the reliability of group estimates of performance.

Typically, the reliability of group performance estimates is higher than the reliability of individual estimates (Feldt and Brennan, 1989), principally because individual differences among members of a group are treated as errors of measurement in estimating group performance, and formulas for estimating the reliability of group measures are readily available (Feldt and Brennan, 1989). The practical import of the heightened reliability of estimates of group performance is twofold. First, one can use instruments with reasonable confidence in evaluation studies that would be marginally acceptable, or even unacceptable, for purposes of individual measurement. Thus an attitude scale with a reliability coefficient of .60 for individual measurement can be reliably used to estimate the attitude of a class of twenty to thirty learners. By shifting the focus from individuals to groups, a greater range of measures becomes available. The second consequence of the greater reliability of group estimates is that it permits one to use subscores and even single items to characterize group performance in fairly reliable fashion. This is especially important in evaluation studies where performance information in relation to program objectives is sought. In contrast, total scores that summarize several aspects of performance may mask more than they reveal. The average score of an arithmetic test, administered to a group of learners, tells one nothing about how the learners performed with regard to particular topics. Using subscores and even single items can provide program personnel with important information about successful and unsuccessful aspects of the program, and, furthermore, such information for a group will be fairly dependable. Thus the concern for reliability of measures of learner performance is nowhere near as critical in evaluation studies as in individual measurement.

SUMMARY

This chapter has set forth a number of important considerations in the collection of evidence about learner performance in evaluation studies. Issues regarding the nature of the evidence to be obtained, the points at which it should be gathered, and the ways in which it can be gathered, have been taken up one by one. In addition, several important theoretical, procedural, and practical considerations have been introduced and discussed. Throughout, emphasis has been placed on the importance of using appropriate evaluation procedures and collecting relevant information. This is the critical point in all evaluation work. Details of instrument development were not given since they are readily available in conventional texts on testing.

References

Alrasian, P. and Madaus, G. 1972. "Criterion-referenced Testing in the Classroom." *Measurement and Education 3*. Reprinted in R. Tyler and R. Wolf (eds.) *Crucial Issues in Testing*, pp. 73–88. 1974. Berkeley: McCutchan Publishing Corporation.

Cronbach, L. J. 1963. "Course Improvement through Evaluation." *Teachers College Record* 64: 672–83.

Feldt, L. S. and Brennan, R. L. 1989. "Reliability." In R. L. Linn (ed.) *Educational Measurement*, 3rd edition. New York: Macmillan.

Gronlund, N. 1985. *Measurement and Evaluation in Teaching*, 5th edition. New York: Macmillan.

Messick, S. 1989. "Validity." In R. L. Linn (ed.), *Educational Measurement*, 3rd edition. New York: Macmillan.

Millman, J. and Greene, J. 1989. "The Specification and Development of Tests of Achievement and Ability." In R. L. Linn (ed.), *Educational Measurement*, 3rd edition. New York: Macmillan.

Wolf, R. 1982. "Validity." In *Encyclopedia of Educational Research*, 2nd edition. Edited by H. Mitzel. New York: Macmillan.

Additional Readings

Anderson, L. W. 1981. *Assessing Affective Characteristics in the Schools.* Boston: Allyn and Bacon.

Berk, R. A. (ed.). 1980. *Criterion-Referenced Measurement: The State of the Art.* Baltimore: The Johns Hopkins University Press.

Bloom, B. (ed.). 1956. *Taxonomy of Educational Objectives: Handbook I, The Cognitive Domain.* New York: Longmans Green.

Bloom, B., Hastings, T. and Madaus, G. (eds.). 1981. *Evaluation to Improve Learning.* New York: McGraw-Hill.

Harrow, A. 1972. *A Taxonomy of the Psychomotor Domain.* New York: David McKay.

Krathwohl, D., et al. (eds.). 1964. *A Taxonomy of Educational Objectives: Handbook II, The Affective Domain.* New York: David McKay.

Lake, D., Miles, M. and Earle, R. (eds.). 1973. *Measuring Human Behavior.* New York: Teachers College Press.

Nitko, A. J. 1989. "Designing Tests That Are Integrated with Instruction." In R. L. Linn (ed.), *Educational Measurement,* 3rd edition. New York: Macmillan.

Popham, W. J. 1988. *Educational Evaluation,* 2nd edition. Englewood Cliffs, NJ: Prentice-Hall.

Shaw, M. and Wright, J. 1967. *Scales for the Measurement of Attitudes.* New York: McGraw-Hill.

6

MONITORING THE IMPLEMENTATION OF THE PROGRAM

While information about the effects of courses, programs, and curricula on learners is widely accepted as an essential part of an evaluation enterprise, the collection of information about how programs are actually carried out has not received adequate attention. This is unfortunate since it is critical to any systematic evaluation study. The collection, analysis, and interpretation of such information is vital to the success of any evaluation enterprise. The number of educational undertakings that have been judged unsuccessful because the intended program was never really carried out can only be surmised. In recent years, a sizable number of ESEA programs for the disadvantaged as well as Headstart programs were considered to have failed when, on closer examination, they were found not to have been carried out at all or, at most, minimally. Whether the programs would have succeeded had they been carried out is a matter of speculation. The fact remains that in many instances programs that were judged to be unsuccessful were simply not carried out.

Information about the way an intended course, program, or curriculum has been implemented is needed for two major reasons. First, it is vital to the interpretation of information about learner performance. If an intended program was not properly executed, or in certain cases not executed at all, information about learner performance in relation to the objectives of the program is open to serious misinterpretation. For example, in one school district, a fifth-grade mathematics curriculum called for teachers to teach a unit on prime numbers. An end-of-grade, locally-devised mathematics test revealed that learner performance on this topic was abysmally low. This was in marked contrast to the other topics in the curriculum, where learner performance was generally high. Only the most casual investigation was needed to uncover the reason for the low performance of students: the unit had not been covered in instruction.

Further inquiry showed that the teachers were not sufficiently knowledgeable about prime numbers to feel comfortable teaching them and, consequently, omitted the topic from their classroom instruction. The remedy for this situation was simple. A single workshop on prime numbers was conducted for the fifth-grade teachers in the district. Not surprisingly, learner performance on problems involving prime numbers on the end-of-grade mathematics test improved markedly the next year. The learners, in fact, performed as well on that topic as they did on the others. Clearly, it is vital to know what has occurred in the teaching-learning situation in order to be able to properly interpret learner-performance information with regard to the instructional objectives.

A second reason for gathering information about the way that an educational treatment has been carried out is even more basic. Evaluation involves more than the assessment of learner performance in terms of objectives. One of the additional elements in evaluation is an examination of the relationship between objectives, learning experiences, and appraisal procedures. Judgments need to be made about the relationships among these three elements of the educational process. For instance, are the learning experiences consistent with the stated objectives? What is the relationship between the learning experiences and the evaluation procedures? Answers to these questions require direct information about the learning experiences.

Unfortunately, this aspect of an evaluation study is often overlooked. While many people accept the tripartite characterization of the educational process formulated by Tyler and outlined in chapter one, a corresponding effort has not been made to gather information about the extent to which an intended program was implemented or the way that it was done. One major exception to this in the field of evaluation was the work *Thirty Schools Tell Their Story*, which was part of the Eight-Year-Study of the Progressive Education Study (Van Til, 1943). Ironically, this volume chronicles the fact that when the thirty schools constituting the experimental group were freed from traditional college and university entrance requirements, they did not modify their programs sufficiently to constitute an innovative treatment. In light of this, the failure to find any significant performance differences between the graduates of the experimental and control school is hardly surprising.

Information about the actual set of learning experiences is needed as part of the evaluation enterprise so that an analysis of the relationship between objectives, learning experiences, and appraisal procedures can be made. Discontinuities between objectives and learning experiences may easily arise. For example, in a college course in the biological sciences the objectives called for students to be able to write about conceptual issues in biology, to analyze problems, design experiments to test hypotheses, etc. The learning experiences, in contrast, consisted exclusively of lectures and set experiments in the laboratory. Failure to achieve the objectives could be traced in large measure to the fact that the learners were not provided any opportunities to develop the proficiencies that were stated in the objectives. Similarly, elementary school mathematics programs often espouse an intention to have students develop problem-solving abilities, but the learning experiences may contain an inordinate amount of computational work and simple drill, leaving little or no time to devote to solving the more complex kinds of problems stressed in the objectives.

There are numerous instances of educational courses, programs, and curricula that failed to achieve their objectives. Unfortunately, evaluation work often does little more than document such failures. Good evaluation work should not only establish the extent to which objectives have been attained, it should also attempt to explain why they were or were not attained. This is extremely difficult to do. Education does not have a well enough established body of theory to allow one to say unequivocally why a program succeeded or not. The evaluation specialist, however, with the assistance of other educational specialists in curriculum, administration, and the teaching of particular subjects, should be able to offer some reasons for why educational ventures turned out as they did. Such explanations may have to be presumptive and based on logical analysis. They will probably also need to be strongly qualified, regarded as suggestive rather than definitive. The important point is that some attempt needs to be made to explain the results or lack of results if evaluation studies are to be more than a box score of the successes and failures of educational treatments.

METHODS OF GATHERING INFORMATION ABOUT THE EXECUTION OF EDUCATIONAL PROGRAMS

There are three principal ways of gathering information about how an educational treatment has been carried out. The purpose of this section is to describe each way and show how it can be used to obtain the necessary information about program execution.

The first way to obtain information about the extent of program implementation involves the use of observational procedures. Information about aspects of learner performance is not being sought; observational procedures are focused on learning activities and instructional materials. Ideally, a trained observer would be present at all times to observe and record what occurs in the learning situation: the organization and conduct of activities, the groupings of learners, the kinds of learning materials used and the ways, the time devoted to various activities, and so on. Such information, systematically recorded, could furnish one basis for sound evaluative judgments. Obviously, few if any programs can afford to have full-time, highly-trained observers present for the duration of the treatment period. It is possible to make periodic visits, however. Weekly, biweekly, or even monthly visits can be made to programs, and observation periods of one-half hour to several hours in duration are clearly within the realm of possibility. Exactly how much observational work will be undertaken would be determined to a large extent by available resources.

Given a limited amount of resources, the most productive deployment would probably be to have a substantial number of periods of observations, each of limited duration, rather than a small number of observations of extended duration. If resources were available for ten hours of observation for a course lasting an academic year, it would be preferable to hold forty observations of fifteen minutes each than to have ten one-hour observation periods spread throughout the year. Each short observation period yields fresh information; all other things being equal, the more observations the better.

Another highly practical reason for having a large number of observation periods involves the perceptions of learners and teachers. Infrequent visits will tend to be perceived as official inspections whereas shorter, more frequent visits can be accepted and handled more casually. As long as it is clear at the outset that the purpose of such observations is not to judge the teacher's effectiveness but to gather information about the program and that a number of short visits are essential for this purpose, apprehensions can be minimized. Teachers must be assured that information obtained from observations will not be turned over to administrators, that no judgments about teacher performance will be made, and that the anonymity of individual teachers will be preserved. Further, it is recommended that teachers be given assurance, in writing if necessary, that no information obtained from observations will be included in an evaluation report until teachers have had a chance to review the information and to suggest alterations that they feel need to be made. Such assurances are considered necessary if the teacher's full cooperation is to be obtained.

Once a schedule for observation has been established and cooperation elicited from teachers, attention must be given to the form in which observational information is to be recorded. Few observers are qualified to record observational information in a discursive form. Too much occurs in any learning situation for even the most sensitive observer to capture and record everything. Accordingly, some guidance must be furnished to the observer. An observer may be presented with a brief guide, indicating in general terms what to look for in the learning situation. In other cases, an observer may be presented with a series of general dimensions to direct the observation. These dimensions might be (1) activities engaged in by learners, (2) grouping procedures employed, (3) instructional materials used, (4) amount of time devoted to various activities, and so on. More specific guidance may be provided: scales for rating specific aspects of the learning situation, for example, or a checklist covering a substantial number of features of the learning situation. Rating scales are used to rate the strength or quality of particular aspects of the learning situation; checklists are employed to determine the presence or absence of particular items of interest.

Which features of the learning situation are attended to and which are ignored will hinge to a large extent on the nature of the objectives and the intended learning experiences. Consequently, specific prescriptions about what to observe cannot be given. At a minimum, one needs some information about the physical setting where learning takes place, the kinds of activities and materials used, the amount of time devoted to various activities, and how the learning situation is organized and conducted. Beyond these minima, the specific objectives of the program and the planned learning experiences related to their attainment would determine what is of interest and should be observed and recorded.

Whatever form of recording is employed, even a detailed checklist of items would need to be supplemented by observer comments. It is highly unlikely that any recording system could be devised that is so comprehensive that comments, that amplify and qualify the formal record would be unnecessary. On the contrary, it is recommended that whatever form for recording observations is used provide ample room for comments by observers. Comments should be encouraged as much as possible.

While there have been a number of attempts in recent years to develop observational instruments for classroom use and an anthology of such instruments has even been produced (Simon and Boyer, 1970), it seems unlikely that any existing instrument will be entirely adequate for use in a particular evaluation enterprise. Existing instruments, however, can furnish suggestions and in some cases be adapted for use in a specific situation.

One fairly recent development is the introduction of techniques of ethnography into evaluation. Persons with training and background in the field of anthropology have been working to apply ethnographic field procedures to evaluation work. To date, there have been a number of articles in journals such as *Educational Researcher* and *Evaluation Practice*. The amount of actual use of such techniques in evaluation studies, however, is not known. At this time, the move to use ethnographic procedures in evaluation work should be welcomed since, by and large, little is generally done to obtain information about what is happening in teaching-learning situations. How much of a contribution ethnographic procedures can make to the field of evaluation can only be determined in the future.

A second way of gathering information about the way that a course, program, or curriculum is being implemented is through the use of teacher reports. These might be in the form of teacher lesson plan books, supplemented by elaborating comments or log/diaries that teachers submit on a regular basis. The latter are intended to serve as records of what happened in the learning situation and to preserve teachers' comments on those events.

Using what is essentially a kind of self-report from the teacher is not without its drawbacks. As in self-report information about personal characteristics, such instruments are limited by the nature of the reporters: their ability to observe and comment objectively, and by their willingness to do so. This is not to suggest that professionals would willfully engage in deception; rather, it might occur unconsciously or reporting may be selective. It is generally presumed that people wish to think well of themselves and what they do; this could easily influence their ability to report fully and accurately about what occurred in the learning situation. Furthermore, maintenance of a log/diary or an elaborated set of lesson plans with supplemented comments is laborious and time-consuming. It may be unreasonable to expect teachers to bear such a reportorial burden. To rely heavily on such teacher reports is highly questionable. Their use should probably be quite restricted; they should never be expected to provide the sole, or even main, basis for describing what occurred in the learning situation.

The third way to gather information about the extent of implementation of educational programs is through learner reports. These reports, usually termed participant observations, call on the group members, in this case the learners, to report on a number of aspects of the situation in which they find themselves. While the pioneer work in the methods of participant observation occurred in the field of anthropology, in the work of Margaret Mead and others, such methods have been adapted, systematized, and applied to the field of education. The work of C. R. Pace and G. Stern on the measurement of psychological characteristics of college environments (1958) was one of the first attempts to apply psychometric principles to the measurement of environments. Pace's subsequent development of the College and University Environment Scales (CUES) modified and extended this original work (1969). Recently, descriptive scales have been used in connection with the studies conducted by the International Association for the Evaluation of Educational Achievement (IEA). The scales consist of a number of short items that require the learner to indicate whether certain activities or events occur in the classroom. Some illustrative items, from a scale descriptive of science teaching and learning, are given by Comber and Keeves (1974):

> We use a textbook for science.
>
> Our science teacher tests us only on what is in the textbook.
>
> The main aim of our science lessons is to understand our textbooks.
>
> Our science lessons include laboratory experiments in which we all take part.
>
> We make observations and do experiments during our science classes.

The three response categories for these items were "always or almost always," "sometimes," and "hardly ever or never." The purpose of such items is to have the learner serve as a reporter. If a number of learners respond to a set of such items and there is substantial agreement among the learners' responses in a single setting (as a rule of thumb two-thirds agreement is regarded as acceptable), then it should be possible to use such information to characterize aspects of the learning situation.

While descriptive scales are a relatively new development, they offer the promise of furnishing important information about the nature of learning experiences. Since this information has often been lacking or, at best, inadequately gathered in most previous evaluation work, a clear need exists for the further development of descriptive scales. One can easily envisage the development of several dozen items that attempt to characterize important aspects of an educational program. Such items can be included in a questionnaire administered to learners at periodic intervals as part of a systematic information-gathering operation. Further, to achieve economy in information gathering, a collection of such items can be randomly split into several subsets, in much the same way that a pool of items measuring learner proficiency can be. Thus, no individual learner would need to respond to more than a fraction of the descriptive items yet the resultant information could be used to characterize the learning situation.

There is an ethical question relevant to the use of participant-observer reports. Such reports call on learners to observe and report on their learning environments. To a large extent this entails responding to statements intended to describe instructional procedures, learning activities, use of materials, etc. It sometimes becomes difficult to separate items descriptive of such aspects of classroom life from evaluations of the teacher; thus, learners may end up serving as reporters on teacher behavior. With the growing acceptance of course evaluations in recent years, the use of participant-observer instruments may not seem objectionable. But unless it is clear at the outset that learners will be asked to respond to descriptive items from time to time, there is a possibility these instruments could be viewed as an unwarranted invasion of the learning situation. To counter the possibility of such an objection, it is suggested that all descriptive items used be carefully scrutinized and any that are possibly offensive be eliminated. In addition, teachers should be informed as early as possible that learners will be asked to respond to items intended to describe the learning situation. It is the responsibility of evaluation personnel to make sure that information so obtained is used to describe the learning situation and not to judge individual teachers. Such precautions are necessary if ethical problems are to be avoided and a climate of trust, so necessary for evaluation work, is to be maintained.

MULTIPLE SOURCES OF INFORMATION

The need for information about the execution of an educational treatment cannot be stressed enough. Not only is information needed regarding the availability of learning materials and supplies, the time devoted to instruction, and the adequacy of resources; the fidelity with which a designed treatment was carried out must be known also. The assumption that an intended treatment was executed as planned is one of the most naive ones that can be made in education. Recent educational history is studded with examples of programs that were not carried out as intended.

Given the importance of information regarding the execution of educational treatments, as much information as possible should be obtained. Yet evaluation endeavors must generally operate with meager resources. The practicing evaluation specialist realizes that resources devoted to the collection of information concerning program execution usually means fewer resources for gathering learner-performance information. Consequently, decisions have to be made regarding the amount of resources to be allocated to gathering each kind of information.

Rather clear costs are associated with each type of information concerned with program implementation. Observational information obviously will involve the heaviest costs. At the same time, it can be expected to yield the highest quality information. Self-report information from teachers is probably the least costly to gather. Considerable effort, however, must be devoted to analyzing, organizing, and summarizing such information. Moreover, as previously noted, self-report information can be rather incomplete and somewhat inaccurate. Participant-observer information, in the form of descriptive items, requires some time and effort to develop but generally little time to administer, tabulate, summarize, and interpret. Certainly, a mixture of all three kinds of data would be highly desirable in an evaluation study: each would provide a partial picture of the nature of the treatment dispensed. Together, they should furnish a reasonably complete description of an educational treatment as implemented.

When different methods of gathering information about program execution are used, inconsistencies will occur. Two principal kinds are to be expected. The first is within a data source, the second between data sources. Differences of the first kind, for example, different activities and procedures observed at different times, are likely to reflect genuine differences in the program from one time to another. Similarly, differences in teacher reports of activities will usually reflect actual changes in the program's activities. On the other hand, differences between data sources at a given time will likely be indicative of errors in the measuring process. For example, when reports by an external observer show little provision for individual difference in rate of learning, while a teacher's log or diary states that provision has been made, the evaluation worker will have to seek a resolution between the conflicting accounts.

At this point, having all three kinds of information about program implementation should prove valuable. Usually two of the data sources will be in agreement, and discrepancies can be reconciled fairly easily. However, if the external observer's report, the information with the highest presumed level of validity, is out of line with the others, it may be necessary to gather additional observational information. In most cases, however, the use of multiple sources of information about program implementations can be expected to fortify the validity of the results obtained. Discrepancies can be expected to be small and erratic in comparison to the agreement; where they do occur, it should be possible to resolve them with reasonable dispatch (Mark and Shotland, 1987).

While the analysis and interpretation of information about program execution will be taken up in chapters eleven through thirteen, it is important to note that discrepancies between a planned and an implemented program are not necessarily a bad thing. There may be perfectly good reasons for such discrepancies. If the planned program was unrealistic for a particular group of learners, then it is the responsibility of teachers to adjust the program to the level of the learners. Similarly, a planned program may have assumed that particular resources such as laboratory equipment, space, and materials would be available. If those resources are not available, adjustments may have to be made. There are a number of other reasons why discrepancies between an intended and actual program may arise. The task for the evaluation worker is to identify such discrepancies by collecting information on the program that was implemented and to compare it to the intended program. Only then will the evaluation worker be able to determine if there are any sizable discrepancies between the two and begin to find the reasons for those discrepancies.

SUMMARY

This chapter has stressed the importance of gathering information concerning the implementation of courses, programs, and curricula. There may be considerable discrepancies between a designated treatment and the way it is actually carried out. Gathering information relating to program implementation is considered as valuable to an evaluation enterprise as gathering information about learner behavior. Information about program implementation serves two purposes. First, it permits an evaluation worker to properly interpret learner-performance information. Second, it can be directly used in assessing the relationships among objectives, learning experiences, and appraisal procedures.

Three principal ways of gathering information about implementation were discussed: (1) observations by evaluation personnel; (2) teacher reports in the form of plan books and, sometimes, logs and diaries; and (3) student reports on activities and features of the learning situation. Each type of data has its advantages and disadvantages. All three, when systematically gathered, analyzed, and properly interpreted, should provide sufficient information to describe adequately the program that was actually carried out.

References

Comber, L. and Keeves, I. 1973. *Science Education in Nineteen Countries* . New York: Halstead Press (John Wiley).

Mark, M. M. and Shotland, R. L. (eds.). 1987. *Multiple Methods in Program Evaluation* . San Francisco: Jossey Bass.

Pace, C. R. 1969. *College and University Environment Scales* . Princeton: Educational Testing Service.

Pace, C. R. and Stem, G. 1958. "An Approach to the Measurement of Psychological Characteristics of College Environments." *Journal of Educational Psychology* 49: 269–77.

Simon, A. and Boyer, E. 1970. *Mirrors for Behavior: An Anthology of Classroom Instruments*, vols. 1–15. Philadelphia: Research for Better Schools.

Van Til, W. (ed.). 1943. *Thirty Schools Tell Their Story* . New York: Harper.

Additional Readings

Boehm, A. and Weinberg, R. 1977. *The Classroom Observer: A Guide for Developing Observation Skills.* New York: Teachers College Press.

Hall, G. and Louchs, S. 1977. "A Developmental Model for Determining Whether the Treatment is Actually Implemented." *American Educational Research Journal,* 14, no. 3: 263–76.

──── 7 ────

PROGRAM COSTS

The area of cost has been much neglected in educational evaluation for reasons that are not very clear. Recently, however, economists and finance specialists have turned their attention to education and educational evaluation. The field of educational evaluation should benefit considerably from this attention if current work is any guide (Haller, 1974; Levin, 1983).

Reckoning educational costs is an exceedingly complex and difficult undertaking. While most tend to view cost estimation as providing relatively hard information, specialists in the field constantly emphasize its slippery character. Few, if any, educators, for example, are prepared to say how much it costs to teach the average learner to read at a given level of proficiency. At a more detailed level, it is not possible to state what it actually costs to teach a learner multiplication of fractions. Cost information is simply not recorded in a way that permits answers to such seemingly straightforward questions. And even if it were, cost experts assert, the determination of costs would require a substantial number of difficult decisions as to what should be counted as costs, and in what way they should be counted. When costs are determined also makes a difference. If a local school board decided to provide dental care to its employees in the middle of a school year, the cost estimate for all instructional services would immediately change even if everything else remained constant.

WHAT IS A COST?

Traditionally, costs have played a minor part in educational evaluation. To decision makers—administrators and governing boards—evaluations that make no reference to costs are rarely of much practical value, however interesting they may be pedagogically, since educational decision makers have a fairly good idea of what they could do if money were no object. Their job lies in choosing among alternatives most of which are, in their own way, good. Thus value choices are involved as well as cost considerations. However, since few if any programs can be justified at any cost, cost considerations must be given some weight in decision making. How much weight they will carry in any situation will vary enormously. The responsibility of the evaluation specialist is to try to see that cost considerations are explicitly included in an evaluation.

It would be desirable if a clear definition of what a cost was, and how it could be determined, existed. Unfortunately, there is no universally accepted definition and no set of procedures to guide evaluation personnel. The standard definition of a cost is that it is a lost benefit: this definition ties costs to decisions. That is to say, deciding to do one thing implies that something else cannot be done. Under this definition a set of instructional materials has no inherent value. Rather it is the decision—to purchase those materials and (consequently) not buy something else—that constitutes the real cost of the materials. Cost determination, under such a definition, involves identifying and comparing alternative courses of action; thus the cost of a decision is tied to the various alternatives. Since every decision involves alternatives, the value of the most highly prized alternative *not chosen* becomes the cost of a decision.

One consequence of this definition is that it places costs in the future. Since a cost depends on an alternative not chosen, it cannot be determined with complete accuracy; it must be estimated. As in most estimation situations, the usual procedure is to use present expenditures as a basis for estimating costs. This generally serviceable guide for cost estimation, however, cannot be depended on without reservation. Consequently, additional guides for cost estimation, including what should and should not be reckoned as costs, are required.

The notion of a cost as an opportunity foregone is generally accepted by economists and finance experts. It is not always relevant in a particular educational setting, however. For example, a local school district might be able to obtain money from a state department of education to run a special program for gifted learners (in fact legislation may have been passed especially for this purpose). On the other hand, the most pressing local need may be for something entirely different. The school superintendent, with local board approval, will prepare a request and secure the funds to run a program for gifted learners. From the point of view of the local school district this program costs nothing; it is wholly funded by the state. Of course, the program has a cost attached to it, paid here by the state. Generally, however, this does not concern the local school district. The point is that it is sometimes possible to obtain money for one purpose, but not for another. Such specially funded programs may cost nothing from the standpoint of the local school district.

From the standpoint of the economist, the alternatives being considered in a cost situation may be virtually limitless. There is no end to the ways that money can be spent. In a school situation, money can be spent to improve instruction in basic subjects, for purposes of remediation, to pay off debts on buildings, to mount new programs, improve the coaching of athletic teams, field teams in new sports, purchase musical instruments, etc. An exhaustive examination and cost estimation of every alternative is quite beyond the resources of a single evaluation enterprise. Accordingly, cost estimation in an evaluation situation is usually limited to considering one or two plausible alternative ways of meeting a particular educational need. For example, where deficiencies exist in the reading achievement of learners at a particular grade level, alternative ways of remedying such deficiencies must be identified and several contemplated for trial. Cost estimation in such a case would be restricted to specific alternative ways of meeting this need, ignoring other possible uses of funds outside the area of reading, or the grade level in question.

HOW ARE COSTS DETERMINED?

There are several ways of measuring costs. Not all of them involve dollars. One might merely list the resources required for a particular program. Thus, if a new reading program was being contemplated, one could develop an inventory of resources, including personnel, that would be required. Such a list would give the number of teachers with specified qualifications, the space requirements, the books and other learning materials, aides, etc. The list could go on but would essentially consist of a finite set of resources required to initiate the program.

A second way of measuring costs would be to formulate and describe one or more ways of meeting the same educational need. In the example of a reading deficiency identified at a particular grade level, alternatives to the installation of a new reading program might be the employment of extra reading teachers plus special supplemental reading materials, hiring several teacher aids along with a different set of reading materials, etc. For each alternative way of meeting the same educational need, it should be possible to identify the resources involved.

Going one step further, one could try to estimate the value of each alternative way of meeting the identified need. The value of an alternative is not merely a dollar cost: each alternative would have associated with it a constellation of advantages and disadvantages. These would have to be assessed; the difference between the two would constitute the net value of an alternative. The cost of adopting the alternative with the highest net value would, in economic terms, be the value of the next highest alternative. This procedure produces a measure of a choice's opportunity costs since it provides an estimate of the program benefits foregone.

The difficulty and complexity of the above procedure, here only briefly sketched, should not be underestimated. In attempting to calculate the value of a particular way of meeting an educational need, one must be able to express each advantage and disadvantage on some common scale. For some elements of an alternative this is fairly easy to do. Teacher salaries and benefits can be reckoned fairly easily; so can the cost of materials and supplies. On the other hand, the effect on teacher morale of adopting a particular course of action, or the enhancement of a learner's self-esteem by achieving a higher level of proficiency, cannot be estimated with the same facility. There is no educational calculus that allows one to make such determinations. While economists recommend trying to measure costs through estimation of the value of alternative ways of dealing with a particular set of educational needs, this goal is not easily met in most educational situations. As a result, evaluation workers may be forced to limit their efforts to trying to attach a dollar value to two or three choices. This should be done with the realization that such a procedure does not do full justice to the situation. There can often be nondollar costs associated with a course of action. If these cannot be estimated, they should at least be acknowledged.

It is important to recognize that the estimation of costs cannot be full and complete, but it is imperative that evaluation specialists try as best they can to at least estimate the dollar costs of educational courses, programs, and curricula. Failure to do this is a serious omission of an important aspect of the evaluation enterprise.

COST PROCEDURES

While evaluation specialists will quickly realize the limitations inherent in cost estimation, the task must be undertaken even at the risk of considerable imprecision. There are procedures to follow that should prove helpful. Unfortunately, the tendency in many costing exercises is to begin considering matters of procedural detail before the larger issues are resolved. To become embroiled in details about how to estimate overhead costs of a program before the decision alternatives have been formulated is not only inadvisable; in some cases, as will be shown later, it can be a wasted effort.

The first step in estimating costs associated with educational decisions is to establish the alternative courses of action available. The particular course, program, or curriculum under consideration is, of course, one alternative. There are, however, probably several other alternative courses of action in the situation, including doing nothing. Identification of one or two realistic alternatives in a situation is not a task that an evaluation specialist can undertake singlehandedly. Usually it requires an interplay between the evaluation specialist and other educational personnel such as curriculum workers and administrators. Some discussion is required to identify possible alternative courses of action.

It is quite possible that educational decision makers will be reluctant to consider alternative ways of meeting a particular educational need. If the decision maker has a particularly strong commitment to trying out a certain program, even on a pilot basis, serious consideration of alternative ways of meeting the educational need may be impossible. This phenomenon has been described by

Campbell (1969) who characterized such decision makers as "trapped administrators." In contrast, "experimental administrators" (Campbell, 1969) relate a particular program to the problem being addressed and not to their beliefs about a particular solution. They are committed to going on to other potential solutions if the first one fails. The task for the evaluation specialist is to assist the administrator in focusing on the problem, or educational need, being addressed and to explicate alternatives as fully and clearly as possible.

Once a set of decision alternatives has been formulated, it is necessary to ascertain the outcomes or benefits that the administrator sees accruing from each alternative. These will normally be expressed in rather general terms. While one would like to obtain as clear and specific information as possible about the goals expected to be attained by following a particular course of action, it may not be possible to do so. Sometimes the professional staff connected with a program is in a better position to enumerate the benefits attached to an alternative than an administrator. However, by focusing an administrator's attention on the benefits associated with each alternative, the relationship between costs and benefits is more clearly seen.

The benefits that one can expect to attain by choosing an alternative are embodied in the objectives of a course, program, or curriculum. For purposes of cost estimation, the general objectives should suffice. Formulating a set of specific objectives for every decision alternative would require too much time and effort. Resources for evaluation can be used more productively elsewhere. It may even be possible to use the short expository statement that describes a program instead of a list of general objectives, but this will vary from situation to situation. The essential requirement remains: one must be able to formulate a reasonably clear, if not specific, statement of claimed benefits for each decision alternative. Once this is done, a list of activities needed to achieve the benefits envisaged for each decision alternative should be developed. The list will furnish a basis for further cost work.

The second step in conducting a cost estimation is developing a framework for estimating the costs associated with each alternative. It is not possible at once to estimate the total cost associated with a decision alternative. First, a set of cost categories should be formulated, then estimates made within each category. Finally, costs within each category are combined, and a total cost can be estimated. The system of categories used for this purpose is referred to as an *input structure*. An input structure that has particular relevance for educational enterprises uses the following categories:

1. *Time* (of teachers, extraclass professional staff, administrators, students, etc.)
2. *Space* (classrooms, offices, etc.)
3. *Equipment* (movie projectors, tape recorders, microcomputers, etc.)
4. *Supplies* (paper, pencils, paints, etc.)

Since education is a labor-intensive activity, the time category will usually involve the greatest costs, supplies, normally the least. It is useful to keep in mind the general magnitude of each category of costs since, for example, fairly large errors in estimating supplies will probably have a negligible effect on the total estimated cost of a program, whereas relatively small errors of estimation in the time category can affect the total cost figure considerably.

Each of the above four categories of costs occurs over a period of time. From the time an educational need or problem is identified until the time an operational program is dispensed after an appropriate trial, a variety of costs can be incurred within each category. One way of breaking down this temporal dimension is in terms of the three major stages of an educational program: (1) planning and development, (2) implementation, and (3) operation. The first stage, planning and development, includes activities defining the educational need with sufficient precision, formulating the general and specific objectives and selecting or developing the learning experiences, including associated instructional materials. The second stage, implementation, involves the costs of installing the program in the educational setting for the intended beneficiaries. The costs of teacher workshops and other in-service activities, equipment purchases and so on, would be covered in this stage. The third stage, operation, includes those costs needed to keep the treatment going, for example, maintenance, whatever in-service activities may be needed to keep teacher performance at a desired level of proficiency, induct new teachers into service to the program, and pay salaries, and other ongoing costs. Spread sheet programs that have been developed for microcomputers can be quite useful for recording the costs of decision alternatives (Levin, 1986, p. 96).

None of the stages is discrete from the others. In fact, it is usually desirable for them to overlap. Some implementation costs will undoubtedly be incurred while a program is still in the planning and development stage. Similarly, operational costs will accumulate while the program is in the state of implementation. It is not inconceivable, and it may be desirable, that costs associated with planning and development, for example, for some revision of the program, be incurred while the program is in an operational stage. Thus, while the basic input structure for cost reckoning may look tidy on paper, the reality is apt to be far messier. But this is no cause for concern. Questions can be expected to arise as to whether a certain cost should be classified as planning and development or implementation; the important thing is to make sure it is classified at some stage and not omitted. Similarly, one may face problems deciding whether an item is an equipment or supply cost. Such decisions should not take up much time, simply make sure that the item is included somewhere.

An unresolved issue in cost reckoning is whether to count student time as a cost. On the one hand, educational treatments intended for learners within the period of compulsory schooling can be considered cost-free since learners are obliged to be in school for a certain number of hours each day and a certain number of days each year. If a particular program is not implemented, it is unlikely that student instruction time will decrease. In this sense student time is not a cost. On the other hand, applying the economic notion of a cost to student learning, the time spent in a particular learning situation means that the learner is not learning something else. If an extended reading program were introduced, for example, the learner would have less time to learn mathematics or science. In this sense the introduction of a new program creates a learning foregone situation and consequently involves a cost. Though it may be difficult to attach a value to student time, its cost must be recognized. As one moves from compulsory to noncompulsory schooling, the case for including learner time as a clear cost becomes stronger. Here one must consider the alternate uses of the individual's time. This is what was done in one landmark study (Schultz, 1953). How one treats learner time in a particular evaluation situation will doubtless depend on a number of situation specific factors. The purpose of raising the issue is to alert the reader. At present, there is no clear solution to the problem.

The last major step in cost reckoning is to measure current costs and estimate the future costs associated with decision alternatives. The input structure discussed in the previous step should furnish the framework for organizing cost data. However, before proceeding it is necessary to make several distinctions between different kinds of costs, some of which should be excluded.

SOME TYPES OF COSTS

Basic and Additional Program Costs

If a particular program is carried on in an elementary school, cost estimates derived from the school budget can be misleadingly high because of the inclusion of a number of fixed costs. Consider, for example, a nutrition education program that takes up 10 percent of the school day. The total annual school budget is, let us say, $750,000. If there are five hundred learners in the school, the annual per-learner cost of education is $1,500. Since 10 percent of the school day is devoted to nutrition education, one might divide the per-learner cost of education by ten, the proportion of time devoted to nutrition education, to obtain a cost of $150 per learner. This is a rather high figure. It is worth examining what it includes.

By starting with the total annual school budget in the cost reckoning, all expenditures of school operation are included. Some of these items are payments of principal and interest costs on the building, heat, light, administration, grounds keeping expenses, as well as costs associated with instruction. The $150 figure of per-learner cost of nutrition education includes a number of basic program costs for the school which are passed on to the program by this method of reckoning.

A different way of reckoning the cost of the program is to examine the additional costs associated with the program. Additional program costs are based on the presumption that if the nutrition education program did not take up 10 percent of the school day, then some other activity would. Educators do not curtail the school day if a particular program is eliminated; they either replace it with something else or increase the time allocation for the remaining learner activities. In reckoning additional program costs, one asks what the additional costs are associated with having the nutrition education program. Fixed costs such as building, heat, light, grounds keeping expenses, etc., will be excluded, since they would have to be paid no matter what was taught in the 10 percent block of time allotted to nutrition education. Furthermore, if the nutrition education program is taught by the regular classroom teacher rather than specially hired ones, there is no additional cost for teachers' salaries. In fact, the only additional costs associated with the program may be those that involve learning materials (books, pamphlets, filmstrips, etc.). Let us say this cost averages out to ten dollars per learner, a total vastly different from the $150 per learner reckoned previously.

Recurring and Nonrecurring Costs

Another distinction that needs to be made in cost reckoning is between recurring and nonrecurring costs. Recurring costs are those that are incurred with each administration of a program. For example, if a consumable workbook is used in the above nutrition education program, the workbook constitutes a recurring cost since each entering learner must be supplied with one. A textbook, on the other hand, is a nonrecurring cost since it can be used by successive groups of learners. To take our present example, it may be that, of the ten dollars per learner additional cost of the nutrition education program, only two dollars (the cost of the workbook) is a recurring cost, while eight dollars (textbooks, filmstrips, etc.) is nonrecurring. Thus, the administrator responsible for the program may need to spend only two dollars per learner in the second year of the program. This is quite different from the ten dollar expenditure in the first year and a far cry from the originally estimated basic program cost of $150 per learner.

Sunk and Incremental Costs

Sunk costs refer to expenditures made in the past and consequently are of no concern in estimating the cost of decision alternatives that lie in the future. The construction of a school building is a clear example. If the building was constructed at some prior time, it cannot be considered in estimating the cost of some decision alternative lying in the future; consequently, it should be excluded from cost reckoning. On the other hand, if a contemplated program will require alterations to the building (new electrical wiring to accommodate microcomputers seems to be the fashion these days), this would be regarded as an *incremental* cost since it lies in the future. It should therefore be included in cost estimation.

One complicating factor in cost estimation that arises from the above distinction is that while a particular cost may be sunk, for example, the building, there are future consequences: there may be principal and interest payments on the building that will continue for years. There will be costs involved in heating, lighting, and maintaining the building. How are these treated? Strictly speaking, such costs are incremental ones, since they will occur in the future. They are considered, however, to be fixed. They will be incurred as long as some use is made of the building space. Thus, they would add a constant amount to each decision alternative. Whether one should include them or not is a somewhat open question. From the point of view of decision making, it is probably not pertinent, since one is apt to be concerned with the differences in cost between decision alternatives. Thus, the addition of a constant value to each alternative is not likely to influence the outcome of a decision. On the other hand, from a bookkeeping point of view, such costs are real and should be assigned on a pro rata basis to all activities carried out within the building. The important consideration in handling such fixed costs, it would seem, is to be consistent with regard to each decision alternative. Thus, if fixed costs of operating a building are assigned to a contemplated program, then they should be assigned to all other decision alternatives.

Hidden Costs

There are often hidden costs in the introduction of educational undertakings. For example, a reading consultant may be engaged as part of a new reading program. The salary of the reading consultant is readily identifiable and will probably be routinely included in cost estimation. Less apparent are the additional costs involved. To begin with, the consultant will probably receive a set of fringe benefits, including medical and life insurance, retirement, etc., which may add between 20 and 40 percent to the actual salary cost. In addition, accommodations will have to be found for the reading consultant. An office may be needed or even an additional classroom. Failure to consider such costs can result in seriously underestimating the cost of decision alternatives. The object should be clear: try to identify hidden costs and include them in cost estimation.

ASSEMBLING COST INFORMATION

With these distinctions in mind, one can proceed to the task of estimating and projecting costs of decision alternatives. In doing so, the evaluation specialist must be consistent in following the procedures that are adopted.

Economists generally recognize four types of costs that should be considered in trying to evaluate decision alternatives (Haller, 1974). They are (1) costs that can be measured in dollar expenditures, (2) costs that can reasonably be measured in dollar expenditures, though they are not reflected in expenditures, (3) costs that are quantifiable, and (4) costs that are not quantifiable. While economists emphasize the importance of all four types and stress the necessity of gathering information about each, this chapter will deal only with the first three kinds. There are two reasons for this. First, one of the major themes of the next chapter is nonquantifiable costs and, accordingly, is addressed there. Second, while economists quite properly stress the importance of information regarding psychic costs (and benefits), the methods and procedures for assessing them are far more developed in the field of educational and psychological measurement than in economics.

Costs that can be measured in dollar expenditures, the first type of cost, have been discussed already. With the previously given caveats in mind, the estimation of such costs within the input structure already set forth should present no unusual problems. It is important to make sure that all costs associated with a decision alternative are identified and included in the input structure. Errors of omission constitute the greatest danger in this area. The second type of cost, costs that can reasonably be measured in dollar expenditures, should also present no special problems. Included here would be depreciation of equipment and textbooks and estimated dollar costs of space. The third kind of cost involves time, primarily that of students and other nonsalaried personnel such as volunteer aides and assistants. For example, in a learner tutorial program where older learners are used to tutor younger ones, the time of both would need to be included. Such costs cannot generally be expressed in dollars. However, they usually can be expressed in time. The extent of the time commitment required by learners and other nonsalaried personnel should be estimated. In compulsory schooling, learner time cannot be expressed in dollars and is therefore properly treated in this third type of cost. In other areas of education where learners receive stipends for participating in training programs, learner time can be expressed in dollar expenditures and would therefore be included in the first type of cost. The total time commitment required on the part of learners is an important component of a program's costs.

In developing cost estimates of various decision alternatives, the evaluation specialist will quickly realize that costs in the near future will be far easier to estimate than costs in the distant future. Near future costs can be measured with reasonable accuracy. For example, the cost of a set of textbooks could be quickly obtained from a publisher's catalogue. The same is true of teachers' salaries for the coming year; there is undoubtedly a salary schedule that can be readily consulted. Costs that are further in the future will be estimated with far less precision. No one can say how much a publisher is going to raise book prices, nor can one predict the outcome of negotiations that will result in a new salary schedule for teachers several years hence. As the evaluation specialists attempt to estimate costs further into the future, the confidence in such estimates will decrease substantially. This, of course, poses a dilemma for the evaluation specialist who is conscientious about estimating costs. The more exhaustive he or she tries to be, especially with regard to time, the more imprecise the estimates will be. This raises the issue of how far into the future cost estimates should be taken. There is, of course, no definitive answer but for many educational programs, the life of a textbook, roughly three to five years, should be of sufficient duration to provide some guidance with respect to projected costs. As long as each decision alternative is estimated for the same length of time, there is little likelihood that the procedure will yield grossly erroneous results.

COMPARING COSTS

The fourth major step in the consideration of costs involves the comparison of costs of different decision alternatives. Assuming that the necessary information has been gathered, or estimated, in the previous step, there are three basic ways that comparisons can be made.

The first way that costs can be compared is in terms of the total costs of various decision alternatives over a specified period of time. For example, the cost of a particular health education program can be estimated, year by year, in terms of dollar costs and nondollar student time. Estimates of various alternatives, including a decision not to adopt a program, can be estimated and compared with the costs of the contemplated program. Comparisons like these can be helpful, and sometimes decisive, when considering adoption of a program. If money is tight, cost considerations may have a determining influence.

If the decision alternatives being considered involve different ways of meeting the same set of educational needs, then a comparison of average costs is helpful. This is a second way that costs can be compared. Average costs are determined by dividing the total costs of a decision alternative by the number of learner hours involved so as to obtain a cost per learner instructional hour. The numerator of the equation has been discussed previously. The denominator, number of learner hours, must be carefully reckoned. There can be a considerable difference between the number of learners who begin a program and the number who actually complete it. If dropout rates are substantial, it would seem wiser to use the number of learners completing a program in calculating average costs, since they, presumably, are the only ones who have received the program benefits.

Nevertheless, the number of learners completing the program can ordinarily be used to establish the number of learner hours involved. For example, if one hundred learners complete a program that meets for one hour a day for each of the 180 days in a school year, the number of learner hours involved is 18,000 (100 x 180). This would serve as the denominator of the equation to establish the average cost per learner instructional hour.

The third way of comparing the cost of decision alternatives involves marginal costs. A marginal cost is the cost required to provide one additional unit of some benefit. In educational settings, this would involve enrolling an additional learner in a particular course, program, or curriculum. Marginal costs are useful to decision makers when expansion or contraction of a service is being contemplated. There are, however, substantial problems in estimating costs this way. It may be easy to accommodate an additional learner in an existing program. The marginal costs may, in fact, be negligible, perhaps an extra book. However, if an extra one hundred learners are to be served by a program, the costs involved may be substantial. New teachers will have to be hired, accommodations provided, materials obtained, etc. It would seem that only when a sizable venture is being contemplated should marginal costs be considered. For example, if it is decided to quadruple the day care facilities in a community, then the calculation of marginal costs should be undertaken. In such a situation, however, it would seem worthwhile to secure the services of a highly trained cost specialist.

For most evaluation situations, the estimation of average costs should be sufficient. Since total costs are calculated as one step in the estimation of average costs, these too can be reported. Only infrequently will it be necessary to consider estimating marginal costs.

The last step in the cost estimation process will be considered only briefly here since it will be dealt with at length in chapter twelve and is not the exclusive concern of economics. This last step involves the cost-benefit comparisons of decision alternatives. A mere comparison of the costs of different courses of action can be justified on two grounds. It is either important to know what the projected cost of various decision alternatives will be, so that prohibitive alternatives can be immediately excluded, or the benefits of various decision alternatives are presumed to be equal. The first justification, elimination of utterly unrealistic alternatives, is self-evident. In fact, it may not even be necessary to carry through a cost estimation to see that a particular alternative is too costly to seriously consider. Sometimes only a few minutes of systematic costing suffice to expose the fruitlessness of a course of action. (Interactive, computer-based instructional programs in public school settings are often cited as examples of a prohibitive decision alternative.) The other basis for carrying out cost comparison without regard to benefits, when the benefits of various decision alternatives are presumed equal, is not acceptable. Evaluation studies are undertaken largely to find out what the actual benefits of a course, program, or curriculum are. Presuming that the benefits of various decision alternatives are equal is the last thing a responsible evaluation specialist or educator would want to do. It is necessary to systematically relate costs to the benefits of various decision alternatives.

A straight comparison of the costs of several decision alternatives can only be done when the outcomes are quite similar. Straight cost comparisons cannot be done meaningfully when outcomes are dissimilar. Consider two programs that have been developed to teach beginning reading. Imagine that one program has a moderate average cost while the other program has a low average cost. However, it might be that the program with the low average cost is ineffective in getting students to learn how to read while the program with the moderate cost is quite effective. Clearly, one needs to take into account program outcomes in making comparisons. Comparisons of costs alone are insufficient.

The incorporation of outcome information along with costs in program comparisons leads to two types of studies. The first is *cost-benefit analysis* while the second is *cost-effectiveness analysis*. Cost-benefit analysis can be undertaken when program outcomes can be translated into monetary terms. Levin (1986) cites, "educational and training programs that are designed to improve employment and earnings or reduce poverty ... " (p. 84) as examples that lend themselves to the use of a cost-benefit approach. The ability to express outcomes in monetary terms makes possible the comparison of programs that may be quite dissimilar, for example, health, education, criminal justice, and public assistance programs.

Many programs, however, are not characterized by outcomes that can be readily converted to monetary values. A school reading program, for example, may not allow for the expression of student achievement in dollar values (in fact, a unit of increase in reading performance may have very different values at different points along a scale of reading achievement). It can even be argued that the outcomes of most educational programs cannot be translated into monetary terms. In such cases, a cost-effectiveness analysis can be undertaken. Effectiveness is determined by the use of the kinds of techniques described throughout this book for comparing programs that have common goals. In such cases, alternatives with the same goals can be compared according to their costs and effectiveness (see especially chapter eleven). Those alternatives with the lowest cost-effectiveness ratios would be the most promising with respect to the use of an institution's resources.

A major problem in conducting a cost-effectiveness analysis is obtaining an overall measure of program effectiveness. Considering that five major classes of information have been presented that can be gathered about a program, several subclasses of information and multiple objectives within one class of information, combining such a large amount of information into a composite measure of effectiveness is a formidable challenge. Some suggestions have been offered as to how this might be done (Keeney and Raiffa, 1976; Nagel, 1983). To date, there is no generally accepted solution to this problem.

While a single overall estimate of a program's benefits seems unlikely, at least for the near future, much can still be done. Chapter twelve is devoted to the task of using evidence for the purpose of decision making. The process is slow and painstaking. Unfortunately, there is no alternative at present.

Making cost-benefit or cost-effectiveness comparisons on the basis of evidence or estimates has traditionally been the province of economists. There are understandable, if unacceptable, reasons for this. Economists have developed techniques for relating costs to benefits in highly systematic ways. The arsenal of quantitative techniques is impressive and, it is hoped, they will be employed more widely in the future. The glaring deficiency of traditional cost-benefit comparisons is in the measurement and estimation of benefits. This is precisely the area where evaluation specialists and educators are strongest. Much evaluation work consists of identifying and measuring the benefits, for example, learner achievement, attitudes, etc., that constitute the outcomes of educational enterprises. The difficulties and complexities of such work are considerable and should not be underestimated. This work, however, is the responsibility of educators and evaluation specialists. Highly trained as economists may be, they are rarely in a good position to estimate benefits. For example, in one cost-benefit analysis of a public health program to eradicate syphilis in the United States, the "stigma" of syphilis was estimated to be 1.3 billion dollars (Mishan, 1975). This estimate is, of course, utterly arbitrary. In another study of the economics of the family, sex was lightly treated as a "nonmarketable household commodity"!

It is unlikely that the estimation of benefits in educational situations will be readily quantifiable, although efforts in that direction are to be encouraged and should be instructive. For the foreseeable future it is likely educational decision makers will continue to decide educational questions in a judgmental fashion. Cost-benefit and cost-effectiveness comparisons can undoubtedly contribute to such decision making. It is highly questionable, however, whether cost-benefit, cost-effectiveness comparisons, or the decision-making process will ever be quantitatively tractable. Nonquantifiable costs and benefits will be involved along with value positions. Since this is an extremely complex issue and goes far beyond the scope of the estimation of costs, it is treated in two separate chapters (chapters eleven and twelve).

SUMMARY

This chapter attempted to introduce the reader to some of the basic considerations involved in determining costs associated with an educational treatment. The definition of a cost is the one generally accepted by economists, namely, a benefit foregone. A number of implications stem from this definition. One is that costs occur in the future. Identifying what benefits are foregone in selecting an alternative is an important step in cost determination. Other steps involve the formulation of an input structure that consists of a set of cost categories for planning and development, implementation, and operation of a decision alternative. Such a structure should facilitate cost estimation. Whether learner time is to be considered as a cost is an unresolved issue at present.

The determination of costs for various decision alternatives should not present any unusual problems. Nevertheless, distinctions between various kinds of costs were made: basic vs. additional, recurring vs. nonrecurring, and sunk vs. incremental costs. Some are included in cost determination while others are not. The important point is to be consistent in estimating costs of each decision alternative.

Once costs have been estimated, comparisons can be made in several ways. Of these, average cost per learner seems preferable. Obviously, very high cost decision alternatives can be quickly eliminated from further consideration. While cost comparisons can be made, comparisons in relation to attained benefits would appear to be considerably more important. This topic is treated in later chapters.

References

Campbell, D. T. 1969. "Reforms as Experiments." *American Psychologist* 24: 409–29.

Haller, E. J. 1974. "Cost Analysis for Program Evaluation." In *Educational Evaluation: Current Applications*, edited by W. J. Popham, pp. 401–50. Berkeley, CA: McCutchan Publishing Corporation.

Keeney, R., and Raiffa, H. 1976. *Decisions with Multiple Objectives: Preferences and Value Tradeoffs*. New York: Wiley.

Levin, H. M. 1983. *Cost-Effectiveness: A Primer*. Beverly Hills, CA: Sage.

Levin, H. M. 1986. "Cost-Benefit and Cost-Effectiveness Analyses." In *Evaluation Practice in Review*, edited by D. S. Corday et al., pp. 83–99. San Francisco: Jossey-Bass.

Mishan, E. 1975. *Cost-benefit Analysis*. New York: Praeger Publishers.

Nagel, S. 1983. "Nonmonetary Variables in Benefit-Cost Analysis." *Evaluation Review*, Vol. 7, pp. 37–64.

Schultz, T. 1953. *The Economic Value of Education*. New York: Columbia University Press.

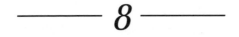

8

GATHERING SUPPLEMENTAL INFORMATION

It should be clear by now that the evaluation of educational courses, programs, and curricula involves the systematic collection of a number of kinds of information, the analysis and interpretation of that information, judgments about the worth of the enterprise, and decisions about future actions. Learner-performance information at the beginning and after some period of treatment, the extent to which the designed program has been carried out, and costs are all necessary classes of information. They are not, however, sufficient. There is one additional major class of information that needs to be considered. Since this last class covers several different kinds of information, it has been named "supplemental." This does not mean that the information is in any way less important than those previously presented. It may, in fact, be decisive in judging the worth of an educational venture. It is simply that the kinds of information to be dealt with in this chapter are somewhat diverse. They have not generally received the attention accorded learner-performance information in relation to objectives.

The three categories of supplemental information that will be covered are views and opinions of individuals and groups, learner performance not covered by program objectives, and unintended effects of instruction. Each category could perhaps legitimately be treated as a separate class of information since the links between them are tenuous at best. To do so, however, would mean having seven major classes of information, an undesirable outcome since it would result in a more cumbersome framework. One of the criteria of the framework for evaluation advocated in this book is that it should be succinct. In any case, the weights assigned to various kinds of information in judging the worth of an educational enterprise need not be equal. Thus the inclusion of views-opinion information as a category of supplemental information does not mean it has less inherent weight than any other class of information. Also, the existence of a class of information termed "supplemental" indicates a certain fluidity which should allow for the accommodation of new kinds of information.

VIEWS AND OPINIONS

The solicitation of the views and opinions of individuals who have had some contact with an educational venture has been undertaken occasionally in connection with evaluation efforts. The reception accorded such information has been mixed. In many cases, the views and opinions of participants, teachers, administrators, and others have been judged self-serving and not much above the level of testimonials. Undoubtedly, there is some basis for this contention: individuals with some investment in a venture are apt to want to see it judged in a favorable light. Such a disposition may or may not be consciously felt. Whatever the reason, the views and opinions of individuals associated with a program have often not been given much weight in judging educational work. Program personnel, on the other hand, frequently give undue prominence to such information.

The schism over how much attention should be accorded information about the views and opinions of persons associated with an educational enterprise is unfortunate. The views and opinions of various groups can be critical in the evaluation of an educational program. Consider the case of a new English program that uses writings by contemporary American authors. Some parents and community members might feel that certain reading selections contain language that they consider offensive and this feeling could swamp all the positive features of the program. This may seem trivial, but it is precisely the stuff out of which school controversies are often made. Similarly, an after-school art program showing somewhat meager results may not only be gratefully received by learners but enthusiastically endorsed by working mothers who no longer have to worry about what is happening to their children between the close of school and the time they arrive home from work. Unless some systematic attempt is made to solicit the views and opinions of persons who have some connection with a program, valuable information may be missed, resulting in incomplete or even erroneous judgments about a program's worth.

In order for information about the views and opinions of persons associated with a course, program, or curriculum to be useful in an evaluation study, several conditions need to be met. First, the kind of information sought needs to be carefully specified. This includes identifying what information will be gathered and what will not. For example, in a number of attempts to solicit student evaluations of courses at the college and high-school levels, learners are occasionally asked to judge the teacher's knowledge of the subject. This question is quite often inappropriate since the learner is usually in no position to make such a judgment. The use of inappropriate items not only produces highly questionable data but can often cast doubt on the rest of the results obtained by the use of the instrument. It is necessary, therefore, to specify carefully what will be asked of whom.

The second step in obtaining the views and opinions of persons associated with an educational enterprise is to formulate one or more questions about each aspect of the enterprise for which information is sought. Initially, the questions can be in an open-ended form, unless they immediately lend themselves to an alternative response format. Maxims for the development of such questions exist in several places and can be readily consulted (Noelle Neuman, 1970; Wolf, 1985). A set of questions, once developed, should be tried out informally. Ideally, the questions would be tried in an interview with a small but variable sample of individuals belonging to the group from which information is being sought. In an informal interview situation it should be possible to obtain an indication as to whether the respondents understand the questions and can supply clear, responsive answers. Ideas for additional questions and ways to improve the initial set of questions should result from a small number of informal interviews. In conducting these interviews, the tryout nature of questions needs to be carefully explained and a clearly stated guarantee of anonymity, especially to learners, needs to be made so that resistance to giving frank answers can be minimized. On the basis of information so obtained it should be possible to (1) revise the questions so that they elicit the desired information, and (2) develop response categories for those questions for which a closed-end format is considered desirable.

While a few informal interviews would be an ideal way to proceed, there may not be enough time or personnel available for even this modest undertaking. An acceptable though less desirable approach would be to administer the tryout set of items to a small group of individuals in questionnaire form, asking them not only to respond to the items but also to comment on them. Again, the items should be asked in open-ended form where possible. The data yielded by the tryout should enable one to revise the questions and formulate response categories for those items for which a closed-end format is desirable. In formulating the response categories, one should be heavily guided by the responses of individuals who were presented with the questions in an open-ended form.

The above discussion has been procedural in nature. Specific questions one would ask of learners, teachers, administrators, parents, and others will, of course, depend on the enterprise being evaluated. Generally, however, one wants to know how the program was received. Did learners feel they benefited from the course, program, or curriculum? What did they see as its major strengths and weaknesses? What particular activities were most beneficial? What suggestions can be offered for improvement? How helpful were the learning materials? Did the expectations and standards seem realistic and fair? Somewhat different questions would be asked of teachers. For example, how did teachers view the organization of the program? Were the objectives and learning experiences appropriate for the learners being served? What were the strengths and weaknesses in the program and materials? How should the program be modified? What objectives should be revised or eliminated? What new objectives and learning experiences should be added? Which instructional materials worked out well; which ones did not? Separate lists of questions can be formulated for administrators, parents, and any others connected with the program.

In obtaining the views and opinions of various groups, dramatic results are not to be expected. It is more likely that somewhat conflicting results will be found. For example, in a study that sought reactions to a number of features of a statistics course, one-fourth of the learners thought the textbook used was too hard, one-half said it was just about right, and one-fourth felt it was too easy. This is quite understandable. Unanimity is not to be expected in most matters, and evaluation is no exception. Generally, however, one tends to find a fair degree of agreement among the members of a particular group. More weight, of course, should be given to such results. If, for example, a clear majority of parents of learners felt that not enough homework was assigned, this finding would warrant close examination. On the other hand, if parents were about evenly split with regard to the amount of homework, somewhat less weight would be given to the finding. Since one is dealing with views and opinions, the resulting data will have a validity of its own which may not fully accord with the facts of the situation. One cannot ignore such findings, however.

Just as it was possible to divide a large number of questions measuring learner proficiency with regard to objectives into groups, so that each learner responded to only a fraction of the total set, it is possible to divide views-and-opinions questions and items in a similar way. An evaluation worker need not feel constrained from developing a substantial number of such questions and items for use with learners if he or she follows this procedure. Specific details on how to do this are given in chapter ten. The solicitation of such information from teachers and administrators, however, is a different matter: ordinarily, the number of teachers and administrators involved will be quite small compared to the number of learners.

In most cases it is not worth the effort to develop questionnaires for teachers and administrators. Interviews should be sufficient for obtaining all the information required. These can be conducted individually in an informal manner in offices, classrooms, or even teachers' lounges (the latter is not a recommended site because of possible lack of privacy). In all cases it is necessary to provide guarantees of anonymity. This may not mean much if only one or two teachers are involved. In such cases it may be necessary to assure respondents they will have the opportunity to review and approve the draft of sections of any written report containing their views and opinions. Evaluation workers may be reluctant to furnish such assurances if it appears to be a constraint on their freedom to do their job as they see fit. This is not the case, however; evaluation workers are not being asked to compromise their integrity. It is the way that information is to be handled and, more important, expressed, that is at issue. Protection must be given to those whose cooperation is being solicited. In most cases, anonymity assurance or the right of review will be sufficient to get respondents to state their views and opinions candidly.

Soliciting the views and opinions of parents and other adults associated with a program can be handled in a way similar to that recommended for learners. That is, several questionnaire forms can be employed so that the burden of responding is minimized. This is especially important in obtaining parents' views and opinions. As a rule of thumb no more than five to ten minutes of time should be requested from parents. Tryouts of questionnaires, to determine the amount of time required to answer, are vital. Also, parents should be specifically instructed not to give their names, so that anonymity is assured. Finally, in the course of seeking parents' views and opinions, one must be prepared for the fact that many parents either possess insufficient information to have formed definite, let alone strong, views and opinions about a particular program, or, having been informed, they do not develop strong feelings. Accordingly, instruments designed to elicit their views and opinions and those of others not closely associated with a program must provide an opportunity for them to indicate that they have no definite opinions or feel they possess insufficient information to judge. Introductory statements and directions for responding must clearly state that these responses are acceptable. Response categories, including "no opinion or don't know," should be included for every item. If a considerable number of parents accept a program or even are acquiescent, this is important to know. What needs to be avoided is any subtle (or not so subtle) structuring of questions that tends to distort responses or force reactions. The notion that if one is not for something he has to be against it may hold for certain political situations, but it is not at all pertinent to the evaluation of educational programs.

SUPPLEMENTAL LEARNINGS

The second major type of supplemental information consists of learner-performance information not explicitly called for by the objectives of the course, program, or curriculum. This reflects an unsettled issue in educational evaluation. Some writers would exclude any assessment of learner performance not directly specified in the objectives on the ground that it is inappropriate. For example, in a program of mathematics instruction that purports to develop mathematical reasoning and problem-solving abilities of learners, is it fair to test the computational proficiency of learners in the program if this area is even specifically eschewed? On the other hand, writers like Cronbach (1963) argue that it is not only proper but necessary to inquire how well a course, program, or curriculum serves the larger national interest. The position advocated here is that it is legitimate and important to gather learner-performance information going beyond the stated objectives of a program in a comprehensive evaluation, but the analysis and interpretation of such information should be handled separately from information that bears directly on the objectives. This is the reason for including such information under the heading "supplemental."

What kind of additional learner performance information should be gathered and what should be done with it? These, of course, are the critical questions and satisfactory, if not definitive, answers must be found. The additional learner-performance information can be based on an examination of other courses, programs, and curricula in the same area as the one under study. Inspection of guides, syllabi, textbooks, and tests should produce a considerable body of material about the outcomes being promoted by alternative programs. Statements by specialists in the field to which the program under study belongs may also be helpful in identifying areas of learner performance that may be examined. Even a cursory study should produce some ideas about areas that might be examined. The generation of material on which to assess learner proficiency is not the problem; it is the selection of material that constitutes the challenge. On the one hand, one wishes to obtain as comprehensive a picture as possible about what learners know and can do as a result of a set of educational experiences; on the other hand, one cannot go off in every possible direction. Judgments and compromises must be made.

In deciding what to study it is useful to examine those aspects of learner performance that are emphasized in more than one alternative program. The purpose here is simply to avoid the idiosyncratic. For example, if several alternative chemistry courses stress the importance of balancing chemical equations while the course under study does not, it would be worthwhile including questions testing this competency. Thus, one guide to deciding what to test for is frequency of occurrence of proficiencies not included in the program under study.

Another way of deciding what kind of information to gather is to exclude from study those learnings that are too clearly based on the content or terminology of a particular alternative program. Every educational program has its own specific content and terminology. To test learners on the details of an alternative program is clearly unfair. For example, in the elementary-school social studies program "Man: A Course of Study," learners devote considerable time to studying the life cycle of the salmon and the culture of the Netsilik Eskimos. The purpose of such study is not to master the details but to raise a number of fundamental questions and issues about man. In this context, asking learners in another program to answer questions about the life cycle of the salmon or the Netsilik Eskimos would be highly inappropriate; such information would be too content-specific to its program. One should avoid the specific content of an alternative program as much as possible and rather focus on the processes, skills, and generalized proficiencies emphasized by alternative programs. In some cases, this may simply involve eliminating highly specific and detailed questions from tests used in alternative programs; in others it may require modification or adaptation of questions to make them suitable for learners in the program being evaluated. Whatever course is followed, one would want to include a variety of questions dealing with a range of outcomes that are emphasized in at least several alternative programs.

The administration of questions, items, and exercises measuring competencies not specifically emphasized in a particular program is a somewhat delicate undertaking. If included as part of the regular collection of learner performance information, such supplemental testing material could be strongly resented by learners and teachers. The material is likely to be considered unfair, especially if it is testing objectives not emphasized in instruction. Consequently, it is recommended that the additional testing material be put into a separate section of an instrument and be preceded with special instructions, emphasizing that the questions, items, and exercises are not designed to assess the objectives of the program but, rather, some general outcomes. A frank and honest explanation of the purpose of such testing material with a request for the learners' cooperation and best effort in responding is probably the best approach to the situation. Assurance should also be given that the response information will in no way affect the learners' grades or other appraisal of their work.

The potential resistance to answering such supplemental questions, items, and exercises can be reduced considerably by following the same sampling procedures suggested for gathering information about learner performance in relation to the stated objectives. That is, the total collection of testing material can be randomly divided into a number of different forms, each requiring about the same amount of time to answer, and distributed at random to the learners in the program to complete. The double randomization should serve to insure that the results from each form can be used to characterize all the learners in the program. The administration of the supplemental material can immediately follow the collection of learner-performance information relative to the stated objectives. In this way, if the collection of the supplemental performance information meets with a hostile reaction, it will have no influence on the other important part of the evaluation: the assessment of learner performance in relation to the objectives of the program.

Just as the collection of supplemental performance information must be separated from the collection of performance information in relation to the objectives, the analysis and interpretation of the resultant data must also be clearly separated. With this single proviso in mind, there are a number of ways of handling such supplemental information. The first step, no matter what follows, is to score the questions, items, and exercises. In addition to examining the correct answers, it may be useful to study the kinds of wrong answers learners make in order to determine if the course, program, or curriculum is systematically producing certain kinds of misinformation, that is, incorrect ways of attacking and handling certain issues or phenomena. Generally it is undesirable to try to aggregate all of the learner-performance information into a total or overall score. Such scores usually conceal more than they reveal. If one of the goals of the evaluation is program improvement, it will be worthwhile to report results item by item, including the most popular wrong answers. In this way, program developers may get useful clues for program revision. If the purpose of the evaluation is more summative in nature, it may be worthwhile to develop scores based on clusters of items that purportedly measure the same kinds of proficiencies. There would appear to be a number of ways that such supplemental performance information could be examined, and at least several should be tried. The object in analyzing and interpreting such information is to achieve as complete a description as possible about what learners know and can do as a result of a set of educational experiences.

The timing of the administration of such supplemental assessment material has already been mentioned. It should be done in a posttesting situation, that is, after some period of instruction. Whether supplemental material should be administered before instruction begins is a different problem. The answer seems to depend on how specialized the course, program, or curriculum is. For example, in a first course in neuroanatomy in a medical school, the material may be so specialized that testing prior to instruction is a waste of time. Virtually all learners can be safely presumed to be ignorant about the subject. On the other hand, in a high school course in government and politics, learners may possess considerable prior knowledge, experience, attitudes, and dispositions. Any failure to carefully assess as much of this as possible would be a gross oversight. Thus, whether instruments to measure learner proficiencies not embodied in the objectives are used on a pretest basis will depend largely on the judged likelihood of the previous exposure of the learners to the material. One will have to rely on the judgment and experience of others when deciding whether to use instruments designed to measure proficiencies not stated in the objectives of a program.

UNINTENDED EFFECTS

A third kind of supplemental information is the unintended effects of a course, program, or curriculum. This is unquestionably the most difficult kind of information to gather since, unlike the other kinds of information, one usually has no clear idea what to look for. Educational programs are usually developed with some set of intentions in mind, and much of evaluation consists of assessing the extent to which those intentions have been realized. It is becoming increasingly clear in education that the adoption of a particular course of action can result in consequences that are not intended. Chapter two, for example, cited the adoption of a rigorous academic high-school physics program that adversely affected learner interest in taking additional course work in physics. It is but one example out of many that could be given of educational programs that had unintentional effects.

It is the responsibility of evaluation specialists to try to assess the unintended effects of a course, program, or curriculum. They may not always succeed. Limitations of time and resources, coupled with the difficulty and complexity of the task, may prevent the evaluator from accomplishing as much as he or she would like. Nevertheless, the effort must be made if the evaluation is to be comprehensive.

The assessment of unintended effects is not merely a negative matter. That is, adverse effects of educational programs are not the sole object of the search for unintended effects. Positive outcomes are also of interest. For example, a mathematics program that eschews computational proficiency because of a concern for the development of mathematical reasoning ability and problem solving may produce learners who are actually superior in computational ability. If so, this is important to know. Similarly, a program in social studies that strives to have learners acquire content knowledge may show that learners are also developing proficiencies in work study skills, report writing, and the like. Again, this is important to know. The goal of assessing unintended effects is to identify as many outcomes as possible, both positive and negative, that appear to be due to the treatment being evaluated.

The assessment of unintended effects has been likened to the search for a black cat in a dark room on a moonless night. In many ways it is. One often has no clear idea of what is being sought. This means that formal information-gathering devices such as tests, scales, and questionnaires have little or no value since their use depends on having a rather clear notion of what one is looking for. Consequently, one must use less formal procedures for detecting unintended effects. The main ones are observation, loosely structured interviews, and small and large group discussions. A considerable amount of sensitivity is required in these procedures. The evaluation specialist must try to place himself in the role of an anthropologist who is trying to understand a different culture whose ways are largely unknown, when gathering information about unintended effects.

It is useful for the specialist to spend some time observing a program in action so that he can steep himself in the culture of the learning situation. This can be done in connection with the observations necessary to determine whether the intended learning experiences are being carried out. Evaluation workers should consciously set aside a certain amount of time that will not be devoted to assessing whether the intended learning activities are occurring; instead, they should try to observe the situation to see what is happening. In carrying out such loosely structured observations, the evaluation worker's focus is not on what is happening in terms of the program's objectives, but rather on the ongoing activities, the relationships among learners, and the interactions between teacher and learners. The evaluation workers should be trying to function much as a cultural anthropologist would in a field setting. After several such observations, the evaluation worker should be able to form some ideas about what might be happening to learners that was not intended as part of the program.

While observational procedures are employed to generate ideas about possible unintended effects, it is necessary to study them further and to test them somewhat systematically before one can conclude, even presumptively, that a program is having a particular unintended effect. For example, in evaluating a science program that was developed in the United Kingdom and was being used in a developing country, several of the consultants brought in to help install the program noted that learners seemed uninvolved with the program. This was puzzling since the learners were the most able ones in the country, were highly motivated to do well in school, and were in fact learning the material in the program, as judged by the results of achievement tests. The condition persisted: while the learners continued to perform well, there remained a strange kind of lethargy on the part of the learners. What is more, this phenomenon did not occur in other courses.

The consultant team was able to confirm this apparent disinterest on the part of the learners through their own observations, although the reasons were not at all clear. The consultants, however, were able to talk with the program's teachers and shared their observations with them. The teachers agreed about the detachment but could offer no explanations. They were not sure if the detachment was due to the program or to some extraneous factor instead. The consultants persevered. At least the teachers confirmed what they had noted, even if they were not able to provide reasons for it. The consultants then arranged to meet with two class groups. They told the learners what they had observed as simply as they could and invited comments. The learners agreed with the observation. Further discussion revealed, somewhat surprisingly, that the feeling of distance was greater when the learners were in a laboratory situation than in a regular class situation. This feeling of detachment, the learners agreed, was not characteristic of their other studies. When asked to suggest reasons for this widely held feeling, one learner volunteered that he did not become highly engaged in the study of science because, after completing the required amount of study, he doubted he would ever study the subject again. Other learners concurred.

The consultants were somewhat bewildered by the learner's reason for feeling detached and gently pressed further. Did they (the learners) see no value in studying science? If the consultants felt that the learners were like C. P. Snow's humanists caught in the two-cultures dilemma, they were to be disappointed. The learners indicated that they regarded science as vitally important to their nation's development, and they wished they could contribute. The consultants asked them why they felt that they might not be able to. It was then that one learner expressed the idea that science was a "rich man's" study and that since he came from a home of limited means, he would not be able to afford to engage in the study of science as fully as the subject required.

The quickness with which the others endorsed this statement indicated to the consultants that they were on to something. They continued to gently probe the learners' feelings. The study of science, the learners felt, required considerable resources. Laboratory equipment, apparatus, and supplies cost a lot of money and, without such resources, one could not properly study science. The reason for this feeling, the consultants soon learned, stemmed from the fact that the science program brought from the United Kingdom relied heavily on the use of elaborate equipment and supplies. The learners clearly felt that unless one had special resources or was so talented that he or she could gain them through merit, the study of science on any serious basis was beyond the reach of the great majority of learners.

The consultants left the meeting with much to ponder. The science program clearly used elaborate apparatus, equipment and supplies. This, in fact, had been one of the attractive features of the program, and the decision to adopt it by officials in the Ministry of Education was based in some measure on furnishing learners with the opportunity to work with the best materials and equipment available. It had been a costly decision. The consequences were clearly different from what had been hoped for. Instead of luring learners deeper into the study of science, the elaborate equipment and apparatus had served to convince them that science could be learned only at great expense, which placed it beyond the reach of all but the richest or most talented. Subsequent interviews with other learners and discussions with other classes confirmed this finding.

The reason for devoting so much attention to this unintended effect of instruction is to show the procedures that were used to identify, refine, and test it. Initially, casual observation was employed to sense the unintended effect, which was itself only dimly perceived. Second, discussions with teachers served to verify the observations but the meaning of these observations was still unclear. Third, discussions with a group of learners served to define the unintended effect. Fourth, further discussion with the learners resulted in a hypothesis linking an aspect of the program, that is, the apparatus, equipment and materials, with the unintended effect. Last, the hypothesis was tested in two ways with new groups in both interview and discussion settings.

All the steps in the above procedure were important. What is particularly critical in the identification of unintended effects is the sensitivity required to be able to identify and define such effects. It may be that evaluation specialists, chiefly concerned with determining the extent to which stated objectives are being achieved, may not be able to sense unintended effects. If this is the case, then it is the responsibility of the evaluation specialists to get others to observe and report what they see happening. Persons knowledgeable about curriculum in general or the subject being studied and who have had considerable experience could be wisely used in this capacity. Specialists in the use of ethnographic methods may also be suitable for such a task. Whether they should be informed about the stated objectives so that they know what not to look for is an unresolved issue. If time and resources permitted, some observers could be informed about the objectives and others not. The results of the two groups of observers could then be compared to see if it made a difference to inform observers about the program's intentions in other than a cursory way. More important, the observation notes of these external observers should provide a fruitful list of possible unintended effects.

The identification of unintended effects is extremely delicate. It is for this reason that loose and informal methods must be used. Observations of the learning situation are highly recommended as an initial step. Loosely structured interviews with teachers and learners can also be used to identify and define what appear to be unintended effects. Discussions with groups of learners and teachers can also play a part. The object of this activity is to search out what might be happening that was not part of the program's intentions. But once identified, it will be necessary to use more systematic procedures to establish that what was thought to be an unintended effect really was. As in most validation studies, it will be necessary to establish that the unintended effect that occurred with one group of learners occurs with another. This is essential, for it may be that a particular outcome or set of outcomes, characteristic of a certain group of learners or a single teacher, is not a program effect at all. This requires considerable perspicacity. If an effect arises out of the peculiarities of a single situation, it would be a grave disservice to attribute it to the program. Identifying the effect in one situation and then systematically trying to test for its existence in another is one of the best ways to avoid jumping to conclusions.

If a program, course, or curriculum is limited to a single group of learners, there is no easy way to establish the existence of an unintended effect. The evaluation specialist has no option but to wait for the next group of learners in order to verify the existence of the unintended effect in question. This could easily require waiting a semester or even a year. If the effect is considered to be particularly noxious, such a delay may be unacceptable. One would wish to take corrective action before the evidence can clearly establish that the unintended effect is, in fact, due to something in the program rather than arising out of specific situational factors. Such judgments and actions typically come under the heading of formative evaluation, and they present problems. Certainly, if there is something unwholesome in an educational situation, it should be remedied as quickly as possible. Such actions are clearly the responsibility of teachers and administrators. The evaluation specialist, on the other hand, has a more difficult task, namely, to assess whether the effect is due to something in the program or to something in the specifics of a particular situation or, as sometimes happens, to both.

An example of both program and situational factors producing an unintended effect occurred several years ago in a reading program for retarded readers at the seventh-grade level. Extensive and careful testing had been done to establish a class group of average and above average ability learners who were more than two years below grade-level in reading achievement. While the class was known to contain some learners with histories of behavior problems, it seemed to exhibit more discipline problems than had been expected. At first it was believed that assembling a number of learners with behavior problems explained the phenomenon, but continued investigation revealed that the learners were offended by the use of certain reading materials that, while appropriate for their reading level, were far below their interest level. Learner comments about much of the reading material being "babyish" was the critical incident that revealed the program defect. Fortunately, it was possible to secure some high interest, low readability materials fairly quickly. Once these were introduced, discipline problems declined substantially.

The use of observations, loosely structured interviews with learners and teachers, and discussions with both are ways of detecting unintended effects of a newly instituted program. The information thus obtained can be used in a formative way to remedy obvious program defects. The evaluation specialist will want to know whether such effects are due to the program or arise from a particular group of learners and/or teachers. Hence the need for independent verification with another group. If the enterprise being evaluated is one that involves several schools or several class groups, this is not a problem. Effects can be searched for in one set of schools or class groups and checked out in another. If the program is limited to a single class group, one will have to wait until another occasion for study arises with a subsequent group. This may involve a considerable delay but cannot be avoided. The evaluation worker should delay ascribing a particular effect to a program until there has been an opportunity to verify it independently. Even if verification with a subsequent group of learners is undertaken, there will still be the possibility that the effect might be due to the teacher. While learners change from semester to semester or from year to year, the same teachers may remain in the situation. Only close study of a situation, coupled with sensitive judgment, can lead to a proper ascription of a particular unintended effect.

The procedures described above are intended to ascertain unintended effects of educational programs on a prospective basis. A retrospective approach may also be used. Teachers who receive learners into the next level of an institution may be informally questioned and asked to comment on the notable strengths and weaknesses among the incoming learners. The learners themselves can also be asked to offer their reflections on the program they have just come through. The resultant information may offer clues about possible unintended effects. The danger in using such retrospective accounts even as a means of generating hypotheses about unintended effects is that individuals may in retrospect see the program differently from the way it actually was. One must be prepared to accept the fact that a number of false leads might emanate from these accounts. Learners, for example, might be unduly harsh or lenient in their view of the program they have just been through. Teachers may ascribe all sorts of inadequacies to the program that are, possibly, more a reflection of the teacher's idealized expectations than a function of the program. One must, of course, be as sensitive as possible in trying to detect possible unintended effects yet alert enough to realize that not every possible criticism or plaudit is true, or, if it is, it might not be a consequence of the program. The need for independent checking will be even greater if the hypotheses about unintended effects originates from retrospective accounts about a program.

The dangers of using retrospective accounts to investigate hypotheses about such program effects should be clear. The advantage they offer is that hypotheses can be checked out almost immediately. That is, if a group of learners are questioned about a program they have just come through and the teachers who receive them supply observations and comments that lead to hypotheses about possible unintended effects, these can be checked out on the current version of the program. Since there is often some degree of independence between the program under study and the next set of learning experiences, one can conduct such investigations with a reasonable degree of confidence. If the program being studied is a terminal one, that is, attended by graduating seniors, then obtaining retrospective accounts becomes exceedingly difficult. First, there is no single group of teachers to query about possible unintended effects. Second, the learners who have graduated from the program may be widely dispersed. Polling them about their views and reactions to the program being evaluated is difficult to do since one would almost surely have to rely on a questionnaire. A questionnaire consisting of a list of general questions and a few extended written responses may be the best one can do in such a situation to generate hypotheses about unintended program effects.

Formal follow-up studies and longitudinal studies of learners have been advocated as one way of generating hypotheses about the effects of programs. Such studies, as research undertakings, have considerable merit. They increase our knowledge about what happens to learners as they move through an educational system; as such, they are strongly recommended. How much they can contribute to the evaluation of specific courses, programs, and curricula is less clear. The number and variety of influences on learners that determine an individual's status on any number of variables at a particular moment is only dimly perceived. To ascribe a particular effect to a particular program is an exceedingly difficult task, considering all the influences learners are exposed to not only in school but out. Multivariate statistical procedures have been recommended as a way of identifying and isolating the effects of various variables, but the results to date have not been encouraging enough to view such proposals with much confidence. Further, such studies require careful specification and measurement of all relevant variables. Unfortunately, the current knowledge base does not permit this, as witnessed by the fact that a number of major studies of school effects have not been too successful in establishing relationships between variables.

The search for unintended effects is an enormously complex affair and can easily consume a major portion of the resources allotted to evaluation. This should not be permitted to happen. The main concern in evaluation is first to establish whether a program was carried out as intended, how successful it was in achieving its stated objectives, and how well the need that served as the basis for having the program was being met. The solicitation of views and opinions of learners, teachers, and others associated with the program may suggest unintended effects worth further study. Likewise, the measurement of learner achievement in the subject not explicitly covered by the objectives may indicate unintended program effects in the achievement area. The accumulated information from the solicitation of views and opinions, supplemental achievement data, and the deliberate search for unintended program effects will, it is hoped, produce what is sought. There are no guarantees, however, because of the uncertain and often elusive nature of unintended effects.

How far one should carry the search for unintended program effects is an open issue. As noted earlier, one does not wish to channel too large a proportion of the resources for evaluation into a single activity that might have an extremely limited payoff. The major resource required for the identification and assessment of such effects is the time of professional personnel. Carefully designed and elaborate instrumentation is not required and would in fact be self-defeating. How far one can afford to search for unintended effects will be largely conditioned by the available time of professional personnel for the task. Possibly, additional evaluation workers or knowledgeable consultants could be specially engaged for the task. If the latter are used, their main job would be to identify the possible unintended effects that could then be checked out more systematically by the evaluation workers. The amount of time and number of available personnel will limit the extensiveness of the search.

Even with considerable resources available to search for unintended effects, there are reasonable limits as to how far the search should be carried. It would seem unlikely that program effects that are extremely subtle and escape detection by procedures recommended in this chapter will have a strong influence on learners. A long, if sometimes undistinguished, history of research in education has failed to reveal variables with such profound influences. If the evaluation worker has made a reasonable search for such effects and failed to uncover them, the most likely explanation is that they do not exist. The somewhat dramatic side effects cited in this chapter are undoubtedly the exception rather than the rule. Hardly anyone would expect the evaluation specialist to be able to show a series of profound side effects each time a course, program, or curriculum is evaluated. All that is expected is that evaluation workers make a reasonable effort in this direction.

SUMMARY

This chapter dealt with the collection of several kinds of information that are supplemental to the main activities of an evaluation study. Supplemental, however, does not mean unimportant. In some cases the information may be of such importance as to be given an overriding weight in judging the worth of an enterprise. Three main types of supplemental information to be gathered were presented and discussed. The first consists of the views, reactions, and opinions of learners, teachers, and others associated with a program. Ways in which such information can be gathered efficiently and economically were presented. The second type of supplemental information discussed was learner proficiency not covered by the stated objectives of the program. The importance of such information (along with some caveats about it) was dealt with, and procedures for gathering it were described. Matters of administration and timing were also discussed. The third type of supplemental information consists of unintended effects of educational ventures. The difficulties in this area were treated at some length. The lack of a single search mode to guide one in identifying this kind of information was stressed, and suggestions were made as to how the job could best be approached.

How great a role supplemental information will play in any particular evaluation study will undoubtedly be a joint function of the program studied, the learners to be served, and local circumstances. No one can speak with any assurance before the fact. Nevertheless, it would seem that any evaluation study seeking to be comprehensive cannot ignore the need to obtain the kinds of information described in this chapter.

References

Cronbach, L. J. 1963. "Course Improvement through Evaluation." *Teachers College Record* 64: 672–83.

Noelle-Neuman, E. 1970. "Wanted. Rules for Wording Structured Questionnaires." *Public Opinion Quarterly* 34: 191–201.

Wolf, R. 1985. "Questionnaires." In *International Encyclopedia of Education,* edited by T. Husen and T. N. Postlethwaite. Oxford, England: Pergamon.

Additional Readings

Anderson, L. W. 1981. *Assessing Affective Characteristics in the Schools.* Boston: Allyn and Bacon.

Henderson, M. et al., 1978. *How to Measure Attitudes* . Beverly Hills, Ca.: Sage.

Sudman, S. and Bradburn, N. M. 1982. *Asking Questions: A Practical Guide to Questionnaire Design.* San Francisco: Jossey-Bass.

9

DESIGN AND CONDUCT OF EVALUATION STUDIES

INTRODUCTION

This chapter attempts to integrate previously presented information about the design and conduct of evaluation studies into a formal presentation of design considerations. The purpose of the presentation is to inform the reader about a number of factors to be taken into account when planning and conducting evaluation studies. It is not intended as a substitute for a thorough grounding in the principles and procedures of experimental design, the field from which much of evaluation design is derived.

Evaluation design refers to the scheduling of learners, treatments, and observations in order to obtain answers to evaluation questions. Generally, these questions center around the effects that educational treatments are having on learners. How the evaluation specialist is able to arrange or, at the very least, have a hand in arranging the conditions under which treatments are scheduled and deciding how and when learners are exposed to these treatments and when observations and measurements are secured will largely determine whether statements about the treatment effectiveness vis-à-vis learner behavior can be legitimately made. Failure to adhere to a carefully worked out design can easily result in a mass of information that could be useless for judging the effectiveness of a program. One of an evaluation worker's major responsibilities is to work out (often with others) the basic plan for the conduct of an evaluation study. Sometimes the planning operation is straightforward and simple. More often, however, it is quite complex. The reason for this is that educational environments are designed to serve the needs of learners, not evaluation workers. This is perfectly understandable. An educational institution was never intended to resemble a laboratory setting where an investigator had complete control of the situation and could assign individuals to groups, groups to treatments, and treatments to schedules, on the basis of a table of random numbers.

The absence of such control requires evaluation workers to carefully plan studies within the constraints of a particular situation so that a maximum amount of information can be obtained bearing directly on the effectiveness of a course, program, or curriculum. Balancing the two—a study design intended to yield unequivocal results about a program's effectiveness and the practical constraints that exist in a particular situation—constitutes a formidable challenge to the evaluation worker. Sometimes the two requirements are virtually irreconcilable. In other cases, admittedly rare, they present no problem at all. In most instances, however, there will be some tension between the two, and the evaluation worker's task is to find some way to resolve them. This doubtless involves some compromise but should not result in sacrificing the aims of the study: it is one of the keenest challenges that the evaluation specialist has to deal with. While much is made of the technical aspects of the design of studies, finding a way to resolve the tension between considerations of design and the hard realities of an operational situation often requires considerable ingenuity and diplomacy, if not outright creativity.

What makes for a good design? This question has been a central concern of researchers and evaluation specialists for some time. Essentially, a good design is one that allows clear and unequivocal interpretation of the results of a study. This does not mean establishing the effectiveness of a particular educational treatment; it may as easily mean clearly establishing that a program was not effective. What is important is that the evaluation specialist be in a position to state unequivocally that a program did or did not have certain effects on the learners who were exposed to it.

SOURCES OF INVALIDITY

Being in a position to say something about the effect of an educational treatment means that detected effects can be ascribed to the treatment and not to something else. What might this "something else" be? D. T. Campbell and J. Stanley in a famous chapter on design for research on teaching (1963) point out two sets of factors that can jeopardize the validity of experimental studies in education. The first set deals with *internal validity* and constitutes the basic minima without which the results of any study are uninterpretable. The second deals with *external validity* and relates to the generalizability of results from a particular situation to different samples, populations, settings, treatment variables, and measuring instruments. The question of external validity presents special problems in inductive inference and is never completely answerable. It is also of no real concern in evaluation studies where the goal of an investigation is to establish what effect a course, program, or curriculum is having in a particular situation and not in general. Factors relating to internal validity, however, are critical and must be dealt with. The best way of doing this is to control them through careful planning and control. This is not always possible in evaluation studies so they may have to be handled in other, less desirable ways.

Ten major factors, singly or in combination, can jeopardize the internal validity of an evaluation study and prevent any meaningful interpretation of results. The reader will need to be familiar with each factor and consider it when attempting to interpret the results of a particular study. The factors, identified by Campbell and Stanley (1963) and elaborated by Cook and Campbell (1979), are presented below.

1. *History* refers to the influence of events that are not a part of educational treatment under study but occur at the same time. For example, an in-service workshop to improve the knowledge and proficiency of reading teachers may be undertaken by a local school district. At the same time, some of the teachers may be enrolled in graduate programs leading to an advanced degree. As part of the program, these teachers may be taking a course in the teaching of reading. It may be possible to assess the teachers' knowledge and proficiency in the teaching of reading at the end of the workshop in a variety of ways, but one would be hard pressed to determine how much of the teachers' performance is due to the in-service workshop and how much to their enrollment in the graduate course in the teaching of reading. In fact, the task is virtually impossible. The evaluation specialist, seeking to interpret the results of any study, needs to consider alternative explanations for his results. The influence of variables that are not a part of the treatment under study is a prime candidate for an alternative explanation.

2. *Maturation* refers to normal growth processes that occur while an educational treatment is in progress and not to the influence of specific events. The growth processes can be biological, psychological, or even a combination of the two. Learners growing up in a culture are exposed to a variety of stimuli and learn a great deal simply as a result of such exposures. For example, learners at the third-grade level, who have mastered some of the rudiments of reading, will undoubtedly improve in their reading ability simply as a result of being confronted with printed material in a variety of situations—road signs, magazines, newspapers, television advertisements, etc. The problem for the evaluation specialist is to determine to what extent reading improvement for such learners is due to the effects of instruction and to what extent it is due to growing up in a culture where one is constantly exposed to reading material.

3. *Testing* refers to the effect that readministering a test has on the scores of a second testing. If one administers a test to a group of learners and then readministers the test at a later time, the second set of scores will typically be higher. Having taken the test before can account for part of this score rise. The effect of retesting can be reduced by making sure that learners are given a different set of questions to answer when a test is readministered. There are two ways to eliminate a testing effect. The first would be to only test once, at the

completion of instruction. This would be unacceptable since it would deprive the evaluation worker of an important class of information, namely, learner performance before instruction. The second way to eliminate a testing effect is to randomly divide a group of learners in half and administer the test to one-half of the group before instruction and the other half after the period of instruction. Such a plan would require having a fairly sizable group of learners, say, forty or more.

4. *Instrumentation* deals with changes that can occur as a result of changes in the calibration of a measuring instrument or changes in the observers or scorers. At the simplest level, if the scorers of, say, essay tests change from pretest to posttest, differences in grades given to learners' essays may arise out of the different standards used by the two sets of scorers. If the scorers of the pretest essays are particularly stringent in grading while the scorers of the posttests are lenient, then score differences may reflect changes in the standards of the scorers more than changes in learner performance. The same situation may hold for more objective measures of learner performance too. One may simply ask easier questions on a posttest than on a pretest. This is one reason for trying to use the same instruments from one testing to another, a task that can be readily accomplished if each learner is presented with a different sample of questions at each testing but the same total set of questions is used.

There is a further problem, however. The amount of proficiency required to go from, for example, a score of six to twelve may be different from the amount required to go from twelve to eighteen. Yet scores typically are treated as if the difference between score points is uniform throughout the test. The evaluation worker should be particularly sensitive to the nature of the instruments employed and the units of measurement that express performance.

5. *Statistical regression* arises when one deliberately seeks to select individuals on the basis of extreme scores. Later testing invariably will show that such individuals, on average, perform somewhat closer to the average for all learners. This phenomenon was noted by Terman in his studies of gifted children over half a century ago. Terman sought to identify a group of clearly gifted children. His major criterion for classifying them as gifted was the score obtained on the Stanford-Binet. Obviously, the higher—that is, the more extreme—the score, the greater likelihood that the child was gifted. As part of his initial follow-up, Terman had all members of his gifted group retested and found to his surprise that the average I.Q. had regressed rather dramatically (specifically, 8 I.Q. points) toward the average.

More recently, educational programs have been undertaken to help disadvantaged learners. A common practice in such programs is to select individuals who score extremely low on some measure. On later testing, these learners invariably show a higher average level of performance. While some increment in performance may have occurred, much of the apparent improvement is simply due to statistical regression: in this case the direction is upward instead of downward, as in the case of Terman's classic studies of gifted children. In both cases the phenomenon is the same: individuals initially selected on the basis of extreme scores will, on retesting, show less extreme scores.

6. *Selection* refers to the employment of different criteria in the establishment of groups to be compared after a period of instruction. The employment of differential criteria can result in biases in the selection of learners, particularly for those in the comparison groups. For example, if selection into an experimental program was voluntary, then it can be expected that those learners who did not volunteer, and consequently served as a comparison group, could differ both initially and subsequently from those in the experimental program. Similarly, if teachers volunteer to teach in an experimental program, they can differ considerably from teachers who opt to continue teaching in a conventional program. In this case, the act of volunteering may indicate that the volunteer teachers are looking for new challenges and may approach the teaching function with greater zeal. If differences favoring the experimental program are found, one faces the task of trying to decide how much such results reflect the effects of the program and how much the dedication of the teachers.

7. *Mortality* refers to the differential dropout rates of learners from groups being studied. Obviously, if care has been taken to establish groups that are comparable to begin with, yet one group incurs a loss of low-performing learners during the course of the program, that group's average performance level will increase, regardless of the effectiveness of the program to which it was exposed. When schooling is no longer compulsory, the effect of learner mortality or attrition can be considerable. Even in compulsory schooling it is wise to determine how much mortality has occurred to insure that inherently unequal groups are not being compared.

8. *Interactions* of some of the previously mentioned factors can occur in certain designs involving comparisons between different groups. The joint operation of several factors can lead one to conclude erroneously that a program has been effective. For example, the first year of evaluation of "Sesame Street" used four different groups to judge the instructional effects of the program. The groups were established on the basis of the time spent in watching "Sesame Street." This ranged from rarely or never watching the program to viewing it more than five times a week. Scores on the "Sesame Street" pretests were found to be highly related to the amount of time spent viewing the program (Ball and Bogatz, 1970). That is, the higher the initial score the more time was spent in watching the program. Scores on the posttest, and hence the gains, were in the same way highly related to the time spent viewing the program. The combination of initial status and self-selection into viewing category made it impossible to assess the effectiveness of "Sesame Street" from the data. (Fortunately, this flaw was not repeated in the second-year evaluation of the program.)

9. *Diffusion or Imitation of Treatments* can occur when programs involve the dissemination of information, for example, particular subject matter con-

tent, and when the learners in the treatment group can communicate with those who are in groups receiving alternate treatments. The learners in one group may learn the information intended for those in the other group. Thus, the study may become invalid because there are, in fact, no real differences between supposedly different groups. This problem can be particularly acute in situations where different groups are physically close enough to communicate. While it may not be possible to control such contact in some instances, the monitoring of program implementation in both the group receiving a particular treatment and the group not receiving the treatment should reveal how likely a threat diffusion or imitation of treatments is to the validity of the study.

10. *Resentful Demoralization of Learners Receiving Less Desirable Treatments* can arise when the members of a group not receiving the treatment that is being evaluated perceive that they are in an inferior status group and either "lose heart" or become angry and "act up". This could lead to an after treatment difference between groups that may not be a consequence of treatment effectiveness but rather of resentful demoralization by the learners in the alternate treatment program. Some monitoring of the group receiving the alternate treatment should quickly reveal how plausible this threat to validity is. The threat can be controlled somewhat by planning that separates the group receiving the treatment of interest from the group receiving the alternate treatment in either time or space. Alternatively, arrangements can be made to enliven or "spice up" the alternative treatment so that is appears as desirable as possible to participating learners. This issue will be dealt with at length in the next section of this chapter.

The presence of the factors listed above, singly or in combination, can make it impossible to determine whether learner performance is due to the effect of an educational treatment or to something else. A major goal of the evaluation studies is to interpret results meaningfully so that a clear determination of the source of an effect can be made. Failure occurs when the evaluation worker cannot say whether a particular level of learner performance was due to the effectiveness of a program, maturation on the part of the learners involved, other experiences that the learner had, or something else.

COMPARISON AND CONTROL GROUPS

One of the dominant influences on educational evaluation has been the area of method called experimental design. The origins of that field, at least in education, can be traced to W. A. McCall's *How to Experiment in Education*, published in 1923. This book preceded R. A. Fisher's *Statistical Methods for Research Workers* by two years and introduced educators to a number of important concepts in experimental design, among them control groups and randomization. In many respects, subsequent work in the field has consisted of refinements and extensions of McCall's basic ideas. Campbell and Stanley (1963, p. 171) in a now standard work acknowledge their debt to McCall by noting that their chapter "aspires to achieve an up-to-date representation of the interests and considerations of that book."

One of the major ideas introduced by McCall and emphasized ever since was the employment of equivalent groups in educational experiments. Equivalent groups were to be established by chance, that is, learners were to be assigned to instructional groups on a random basis. Such assignment, McCall stated and subsequent writers have echoed, would insure the establishment of comparable groups. In an experiment, comparable groups are established by random assignment and a random procedure is used to determine which group will receive the experimental treatment and which the alternate treatment. In the vocabulary of experimental design, the group receiving the alternate treatment is called the control group. This designation is based partly on its receipt of the alternative treatment but, equally important, partly on the way that it was established. Only the use of randomization in the assignment of learners to groups permits one to legitimately use the term "control" to the group receiving the alternative treatment.

There have been experiments in education that have employed control groups. The number of such studies is small, however, in relation to studies using groups not established on the basis of the application of the principles of randomization. Such nonrandomly established groups are called "comparison," or "contrast," groups. Ideally, comparative studies in education should employ control groups. In many cases, however, this is not possible. The obstacles to the use of randomization can be formidable, and heroic efforts are required to establish comparable groups on a random basis. The reasons for the objections to randomization in educational studies are generally well known. Resistance, on the part of parents, teachers, and other school officials, is deep-seated and widespread. Often there is a genuine concern for the welfare of the individual learner. School policies with regard to grouping of students often specify that instructional groups are to be established on the basis of ability, previous achievement, or other criteria. Considerable time and effort is expended in setting up groups that are anything but random, and professionals in the schools see this as one of their important responsibilities. None of this is intended as criticism of teachers and administrators. They are clearly trying to fulfill what they feel is an important professional function. It does, however, make it difficult to establish comparable groups for purposes of evaluating the effects of different educational treatments.

The evaluation worker typically faces a dilemma. On the one hand, the use of control groups offers the best prospect for obtaining meaningful answers to evaluation questions, but the realities of educational institutions often prevent this. How the evaluation worker resolves this dilemma is often critical to the success of his or her efforts. Accordingly, the issue needs to be discussed at some length.

There are occasions when it is possible to employ strict randomization in establishing equivalent groups for evaluation studies. Such occasions are rare. Usually, they involve dispensing treatment that does not require disruption of existing schedules, groupings, and other arrangements. A notable example is

Page's study of teachers' comments on students' papers (1958). Page was able to assign students, at random, to one of three treatment groups within each of seventy-four classrooms. The study was conducted without the students' knowledge that they were in a particular treatment group. In fact, the students were not even aware that a study was being conducted. Admittedly, the Page study is an example of educational research and not educational evaluation. In evaluation, the educational treatment being dispensed is, and should be, clearly known. It will typically be a course, program, or an entire curriculum. In contrast, the variables examined in a research study can be subtle and rather unobtrusive, such as the comments bestowed on student papers or other similar variables.

In some situations, the evaluation worker may have no power to influence the establishment of class groups, but he or she may be able to decide which groups receive which treatment. One such study involved the use of a synthetic alphabet in the teaching of beginning reading. First-grade teachers from twelve elementary schools in a midwestern city were invited to participate in a study, but no details were given. Two teachers in each school were selected from among those who volunteered. Class groups in all schools were set up according to the usual procedures followed in the school. Once established, however, it was possible, through a flip of a coin, to decide which group and teacher would receive the new reading program and which would get the regular program. The study had a number of other interesting features, some of which will be described later. For now, the important point is that while there was no random assignment of learners to groups, it was possible to randomly assign the groups to treatments. Thus, it was possible to preserve the integrity of the notion of a control group.

In the above example, the class group served as the basic unit of assignment. Already established class groups were assigned, on a random basis, to one treatment or another. This is not only acceptable but often highly desirable (Poyner, 1974). The study as carried out ranged over twelve schools with each classroom contributing one item of information, the class average, to the data collection for each variable studied.

There are a number of special features about this design that employed the class group as the basic unit of assignment and, consequently, the unit of analysis. Some of these features will be discussed in chapter eleven in connection with data analysis. The point is that, unlike conventional experiments in which *individuals* are randomly assigned to treatment groups, it is possible and sometimes desirable to randomly assign intact *class groups* to treatments. In terms of experimental design principles, it makes no difference whatever whether individuals or class groups serve as the basic experimental unit. It may even be desirable to use the group as the basic unit if the treatment that is dispensed is uniform for the group.

In the above example, randomization was employed as the means for assigning units (groups or individuals) to treatments. There is much to be said for randomization. It is the only way to insure the establishment of equivalent groups. Such equivalency is critical if one is seeking to compare groups with respect to performance after a period of instruction. Any other way of establishing equivalent groups is inferior and carries no assurance that groups can be considered equal before instruction commences.

While randomization is a sine qua non for conducting experimental studies, it frequently cannot be used in evaluation studies. The obstacles in a particular setting may prohibit randomization. This can occur in a number of ways. There may be only a single treatment being studied, and all eligible learners are automatically assigned to it. For example, a local school may set up a special program to provide instruction for all learners found to be weak in reading. Withholding the program from some eligible learners may be considered administratively and politically impossible as well as educationally undesirable. Also, it may be that the total number of learners involved at any level is so small that even the use of randomization procedures is not sufficient to guarantee equivalency of groups. This would appear to contradict earlier statements about randomization providing assurance that groups are equivalent at the beginning of instruction. There is no essential conflict between the statements when one realizes that for randomization to be effective, there must be a sufficient number of units to be randomly assigned. For example, if there are only four learners who are eligible for a program, randomization will probably not result in the establishment of two equivalent groups of two learners each. A pool of only four learners to be assigned to two groups is just too few for randomization to offer assurance of equivalency. Normally, one would hope to have an initial pool of at least thirty. This point will be discussed in some detail in chapter ten. Another obstacle to randomization may occur if some measure of choice is permitted to learners or, in some cases, to their parents in deciding which program the learner may enroll in. One can assume with some confidence that groups will not be equivalent if a free, or even restricted, choice is given. There are also situations arising with teachers that can undermine an experimental study. Teachers may be unwilling to participate in a study for a variety of reasons. In such situations, forced participation, even where possible, is likely to produce worthless, or at best questionable, results, if those who are responsible for giving instruction are reluctant recruits.

It may not be possible to arrange and conduct a true experiment. Faced with such a prospect, what is the evaluation worker to do? Assuming that the evaluation worker will not abandon the enterprise because of an inability to conduct a true experiment, quasi-experimental procedures must be used. Quasi-experimental studies not only sound less desirable than true experimental studies, they actually are. However, while quasi-experimental studies can be somewhat hazardous undertakings, they are not necessarily doomed to fail.

The chief difference between true experiments and quasi-experiments is that the former, properly designed and executed, contain all the necessary safeguards with regard to those factors influencing the internal validity of the results, while the latter do not. Thus, in carrying out comparative studies using quasi-experimental procedures, the evaluation worker must be extremely careful to evaluate the likelihood of each possible source of bias. This requires a considerable amount of perspicacity on the part of the evaluation specialist as well as the assistance of others knowledgeable about the program under study. Nonetheless, the conclusions drawn from such studies, although often presumptive, are clearly superior to no conclusions at all. Thus, the evaluation worker is urged to undertake comparative studies using quasi-experimental designs when the conduct of true experiments is not possible (Cook and Campbell, 1979).

In a true experimental study, two or more groups are studied. The group receiving the major treatment under investigation is referred to as the *experimental group*, while the group, or groups, not receiving that treatment, or treatments, is referred to as the *control group* . The term "control group" can cover either an untreated group or a group receiving an alternate treatment. In pharmaceutical studies, for example, a control group will receive no medication at all, an alternate medication or, more likely, a placebo. In educational studies, the usual practice is to have a control group receive a conventional or traditional program, while the experimental group receives some innovative one. Withholding any treatment from the control group, equivalent to discontinuing schooling, is not a realistic, or in most cases, even a legal alternative. Thus, in a typical true experiment, the experimental group receives some innovative treatment while the control group receives a conventional one. "Control group" is also used to denote a group that has been established on the basis of randomization. Comparative studies that are true experiments always use control groups. Groups receiving alternative treatments in quasi-experimental studies are called "comparison" or "contrast" groups. This shift in terminology is sometimes ignored in the literature but will be strictly followed here so that the reader will be constantly aware of whether a particular design being considered is an experimental or quasi-experimental one.

One of the major obstacles that an evaluation specialist faces in designing a comparative study is to locate suitable comparison groups. If, as often happens, a program is instituted in a particular setting and administered to all eligible learners, there is no readily available comparison group. The options available to the evaluation specialist in such a situation are limited and not particularly appealing. However, since the concern here is with doing the best job possible under the circumstances rather than the best possible job, the courses of action that are available will be considered. The first possibility is to use a previously enrolled group in the same institution as a comparison group. If an innovative program is to be installed in the fifth grade of a school, let us say in 1989-90, and this is known far enough in advance, it should be possible to use learners enrolled in the school in 1988-89 as the contrast group. This can be quite acceptable as long as there is no fundamental change in the nature of the school population from one year to the next. In most cases, dramatic shifts in the nature of the institution's population do not occur from year to year. The major requirements for using a previous cohort of learners as a comparison group are (1) sufficient information about learner performance can be obtained, either through direct evidence-gathering efforts or through resurrection of information from files, and (2) the learner population is reasonably stable from year to year.

A second source of groups that might be used for contrast purposes may exist in neighboring institutions. This is a somewhat risky venture and should be undertaken only if other attempts at securing a comparison group are not successful. The advantages of using a group in a neighboring institution for comparison purposes are (1) diffusion or imitation of treatments is not likely to occur, (2) little likelihood of resentful demoralization of learners, and (3) evidence-gathering activities can proceed concurrently for all groups being studied. The latter advantage has considerable appeal since the various measures to be used in the data collection may not be completed until the new program is about to be initiated. There are several disadvantages in using groups in neighboring institutions for comparison purposes that need to be carefully considered before deciding to use them. Unquestionably, the greatest disadvantage in using groups from neighboring institutions (either within the same school district or outside) is that they may not be comparable. If the school undertaking an innovative program is located in a middle-class neighborhood and an available contrast group is located in a school drawing learners from a lower-class neighborhood, the two groups are fundamentally incomparable. No amount of statistical manipulation and adjustment can compensate for the fact that the groups come from basically different populations. A sizable social class difference is fairly obvious and easily detected.

There are other ways in which groups from different institutions can differ, many of them subtle. One school may have a more transient group of learners than another. Teachers in one school may exercise fairly tight control over learners while the teachers in another may place a greater emphasis on learners' independent activities. All of these often subtle differences may make it difficult, if not impossible, to obtain meaningful comparisons between groups with regard to program effects. The evaluation worker will have to work hard to get reasonable assurance that groups in different institutions are basically comparable before instruction commences. Another major disadvantage in using groups from neighboring institutions in comparative studies is that the evaluation worker is in a poor position to exercise control over the groups receiving the alternative treatment. Usually, the evaluation worker is selected to serve a particular institution. The control he can exercise over groups located in neighboring institutions is quite limited. At best, he or she will be able to observe groups receiving the alternative treatment and offer suggestions with regard to maintaining a certain operational program. At worst, he may be barred from entering the institution except to deliver and collect testing material. This would indeed be an unfortunate state of affairs. If the evaluation worker is not in a position to describe the nature of the alternative treatment being dispensed, he or she will be severely hampered when it comes to interpreting the results of the evaluation study. If the prospect for cooperation is low, the evaluation worker should seriously consider not using groups from such institutions.

A corollary of the above disadvantage of lack of control is that the neighboring institution may decide to withdraw from the project at any time but particularly at the most critical point, when information needs to be gathered. It has not infrequently happened that a school, hard pressed by various demands, decides to drop an end-of-year testing. The plight of the evaluation worker in such a situation is obvious and painful. Although evidence-gathering requirements can often be reduced to a bare minimum by judicious sampling and scheduling of data collection, this may still be too much of a burden for a participating institution. It would be desirable to extract a commitment, preferably in writing, from the institutions furnishing comparison groups guaranteeing their participation in the study for a specified period of time. Such a written commitment would probably not be enforceable, but it might serve as an ethical reminder.

When trying to secure the cooperation of neighboring institutions participating in evaluation studies, the evaluation worker is normally restricted to the use of persuasion. While appeals to professionalism and the importance of conducting evaluation studies in education may help secure participation, the prospect of more tangible benefits is likely to have a greater effect. Normally, each participating institution should be promised a full set of results and the opportunity to review and discuss them. The framework for evaluation advocated in this book, and the wide array of information to be gathered, should insure that institutions furnishing comparison groups will receive useful information about the functioning of their programs. Of course, the confidentiality of all information that is gathered must be assured. This means that no individual learner or teacher be identified by name and, if requested, names of cooperating institutions must not be revealed. Such guarantees, once given, must be honored. The use of groups from neighboring institutions for comparison purposes in evaluation studies is a risky venture. It also entails considerable time and effort. It is not a first choice but it should at least be considered if there are no better alternatives.

The third source for constrast groups is riskier than the second and even more restricted in application. The use of standardized tests in educational settings carries with it an implied contrast group, namely, the norm group on which the test was standardized. Thus, if a program seeks to improve the reading proficiency of a group of learners, administration of a standardized test at the beginning of the program and again after a period of instruction allows the possibility of making estimates of program effectiveness on the basis of changes in test scores. The risks in using the norm group for a standardized test for comparison purposes are considerable. First there is the matter of finding a standardized test that is relevant to the objectives of the program being evaluated. This is not particularly difficult in reading and mathematics, but it can be quite problematic in other areas. If so, this approach would have to be abandoned. Second, the group receiving the course, program, or curriculum under study must be similar to the one on which the test is normed. If it is not, the use of a norm group for comparison purposes is inappropriate. For example, a reading improvement program may be initiated for disadvantaged learners, yet every eligible standardized test of reading is based on samples of *all* learners at a particular grade level throughout the country. Unless there are special norms for disadvantaged groups, the use of the norm group for the test (for contrast purposes) would not be correct. There are several reasons for this—not the least of which might be the phenomenon of regression toward the mean discussed earlier. The test, of course, could be used in connection with the evaluation of the program, but the interpretation of results, in terms of published norms, would present special problems.

The use of the norm group for a standardized test for contrast purposes is a somewhat unappealing compromise that should probably be used only as a last resort. In a hierarchy of ways to secure a comparison group in an evaluation study it probably ranks at the bottom. The best solution from a design point of view is to use control groups in connection with true experiments. The second-best is to use a contrast group from the same institution but from a different year. A somewhat less desirable procedure is to use an existing group in the same institution at the same time. The use of a group from a neighboring institution is a more undesirable practice because of possible incomparability and lack of control. Using norm groups from standardized tests is an even less desirable approach but may be applicable in certain limited situations. Another alternative is to employ no comparison groups whatsoever. In the remainder of this chapter, where particular designs are considered, the question of which approach should be followed in the selection of groups for purposes of comparison will be specifically addressed.

EVALUATION DESIGNS

In this section a number of designs that can be employed in studies of educational treatments will be covered. Each has certain features that warrant its use under specific conditions. In choosing a particular design, the evaluation worker will need to consider not only its special features but also the conditions under which it will be used. Frequently, this will mean that a design that is theoretically less than desirable may be used because local conditions prevent the use of a more desirable one. What is important for the evaluation worker to bear in mind is that each design has certain strengths and weaknesses. Knowledge of them is important, and adequate provision for dealing with the weakness inherent in a particular design is critical to the success of an evaluation study.

The designs to be presented have been drawn from Campbell and Stanley's well-known chapter (1963) and from an extension of that work by Campbell (Campbell and Stanley, 1963; Campbell, 1969) and by Cook and Campbell (1979). Though the designs were developed primarily for research studies on teaching, their use in evaluation studies, with some modification, is clearly warranted. The reader should be familiar with the original Campbell and Stanley chapter, especially the tables listing the sources of invalidity of various designs. The symbolism employed in the presentations of various designs for evaluation studies departs slightly from that used by Campbell and Stanley. The symbols that will be used here are:

R = Random assignment of units (individuals or class groups) to treatment groups.

T_1 = Treatment (a course, program, curriculum, organizational pattern, etc.). The subscript will denote a particular treatment. For most studies, at least two alternative treatments are studied, that is, T_1 and T_2. However, in some studies there may be only a single treatment under consideration.

P = Performance measure. This refers to some measure of learner performance. It includes measures related to specific program objectives as well as supplemental performance measures. By rights, there should be a subscript after the symbol, for example, P_i, $i = 1, k$, denoting that there are a number of performance measures (in this case k of them). However, for the sake of brevity, the nonsubscripted P will be used. This implies that analyses will be carried out on *all* performance measures.

Pretest-Posttest Control Group Design

The classic true experimental design is the pretest-posttest control group design. It can be symbolized as follows:

Group 1 $R\ P\ T_1\ P$

Group 2 $R\ P\ T_2\ P$

The design is interpreted in the following way, reading from left to right. Random assignment is used to assign units to groups and groups to treatments. (In the above schema, only two treaments are being compared. However, the design could easily be extended to additional treatments by adding more lines, one for T_3, T_4, etc. Each additional line would also contain R, P, and P.) The first P denotes that pretesting occurs before the treatment while the second denotes testing after a period of instruction. Usually, such posttesting occurs at the conclusion of the treatment period, but this may not always be the case. When the posttesting occurs will depend largely on the purposes of the evaluation, but may be influenced by other factors. For example, while one may wish to conduct posttesting at the conclusion of the treatment period, the need to decide about future action may require that testing be done some-time earlier. This is not wholly satisfactory but, if the results of the evaluation study are to be used in planning future action, incomplete information may be far better than no information at all.

The pretest-posttest control groups design is generally considered to be a highly acceptable design for evaluation studies. The chief reason is that it provides the basic comparability required to meaningfully interpret results. The use of randomization, provided that there are enough units, serves as an assurance that the groups receiving the different treatments are equal to begin with. The collection of pretest data serves two purposes. First, it provides information about the initial status of the groups before treatment commences, thus furnishing one of the major classes of information required in evaluation studies. Second, the pretest information can be used in the analysis of the data to increase precision. This point will be discussed in some detail in chapter eleven. The equal distances between the letters in the same lines denote that the treatment period is the same for all groups. In analyzing the data from the above study, the essential comparisons involve the posttest performance between the two groups after adjusting for whatever pretest performance differences there are.

Interpretation of results produced by the pretest-posttest control group design is straightforward. The use of randomization serves to eliminate history, instrumentation, statistical regression, selection, mortality, and interactions of various variables as possible explanations for whatever results are obtained; at the same time, using two or more groups eliminates maturation as a possible cause of the results. On the face of it, the design would appear to be admirably suited for determining the comparative effectiveness of alternative treatments, and, for the most part, it is. There are, however, two qualifications. First, if the study consists of two class groups and their teachers, it is possible that any differential effectiveness might be due to the teachers instead of the treatment—materials, learning experiences, etc. The employment of randomization to establish equivalent groups of learners has nothing to do with the teachers. Even if two volunteer teachers are used, with the flip of an honest coin deciding which teacher is assigned to each treatment, one cannot be sure that any differential performance between groups might not be due to the teachers involved. An investigation of the teachers themselves would have to be made to eliminate differential teacher effectiveness as the source of differential learner proficiency. Such a study would involve examination of the teachers' backgrounds, training, experience, and observed classroom performances. If one can satisfy oneself that the teachers do not differ appreciably then the teachers can be eliminated as the sole source of differences between groups.

The second qualification centers on the treatments being compared. If one treatment is an innovative program involving new materials and equipment while the other is a conventional one involving used textbooks, run-of-the-mill materials and the like, it is possible that learners in the first program might outperform learners in the second because they feel they are a part of something special. Improved performance due to a feeling of being specially chosen is referred to as the Hawthorne effect (after the now famous experiments conducted at that site for the Western Electric Company). The possibility of a Hawthorne effect in evaluation studies is very real, especially when an innovative treatment is being compared with a conventional one. There is no easy way to eliminate it: if a program is truly innovative and requires new materials, learning experiences, and the like, then these need to be present. Of course, one can wait several years until the novelty of the innovative program wears off and it comes to be viewed simply as an alternative program. However, few administrators and policymakers can be expected to wait that long. Usually, administrators want to know about a program's effectiveness four months ago, not four years hence. A rather different approach is to attempt to equalize all treatments under study with respect to a possible Hawthorne effect. For example, in the previously mentioned study on the teaching of beginning reading using a synthetic alphabet, it was clear from the outset that the innovative program required new books, special in-service training for the teachers using the synthetic alphabet, and a variety of collateral materials. The novelty of the approach simply could not be avoided. To counter this, it was decided to provide teachers using the conventional approach, basal reader and associated workbooks, with additional materials, and an equal amount of in-service training, so as to make maximally effective use of the regular materials. Through an arrangement with the publisher of the basal reading series it was possible to secure the services of the publisher's consultants and a variety of supplemental materials. By the time the study began, both groups of teachers had equal amounts of in-service training and had their classrooms bedecked with fresh and appealing new materials. In contrast, other teachers in the school who were following the conventional program had to get along with the same materials and no special help or extra in-service training.

In retrospect, it would have been desirable to include the balance of the teachers as a second comparison group. A comparison between the synthetic alphabet classes and the conventional classes, in which the teachers received supplemental materials and additional training, afforded an estimate of the differential effectiveness of the treatments. A comparison between the specially treated conventional classes and the untreated conventional classes, on the other hand, could have provided some estimate of the extent of a Hawthorne effect. Unfortunately, the investigators did not have the foresight to build this into their study. They did, however, anticipate the possible influence of a Hawthorne effect and took active steps to control it by equalizing innovative and conventional classes with respect to it.

The above qualifications to the pretest-posttest control group design are technical ones. They can be dealt with in a number of ways, some of which have been described above. From the standpoint of the evaluation worker who must organize and conduct the study in a particular situation, there are apt to be practical obstacles to a pretest-posttest control group design. It may not be possible to assign units randomly to groups and groups to treatments, although every attempt should be made. It is also possible that there may not be a treatment alternative available for a comparative study. In such cases, the evaluation worker will need to consider another design.

The final qualification to the pretest-posttest control group design is more basic. Experimental designs are comparative in nature. That is, the difference in performance between groups is used as the basis for judging the efficacy of a treatment. This is not good enough for an evaluation study where the attainment of objectives is of paramount concern. Thus, an innovative instructional program may outperform another one, but if both fail to meet program objectives, what value should be accorded the new program? This point will be discussed further in chapter eleven.

Posttest Only Control Group Design

The posttest only control group design is also a true experiment and is symbolized:

Group 1 $R \; T_1 \; P$

Group 2 $R \; T_2 \; P$

The difference between this design and the previous one is the absence of the pretest measure. This design is considered acceptable from the point of view of specialists in experimental design since it controls for all major sources of invalidity. It is not, however, acceptable from the standpoint of educational evaluation advanced in this book. This is due to the absence of the pretest, considered crucial to a comprehensive evaluation study. It is quite possible, for example, that learners in both treatment groups had already learned what they were supposed to or were well on their way to doing so when instruction commenced. The posttest only control group design does not permit one to determine this. Without such information, the evaluation worker is in no position to distinguish between what learners have acquired as a result of exposure to the treatment under study and what they knew and could do before instruction began. Thus, while the above design would satisfy specialists in experimental design, it should be avoided by evaluation specialists, unless one is prepared to assume that learners knew virtually nothing about what they were supposed to learn before treatment began.

This is a reasonable assumption in certain situations. When the course, program, or curriculum being evaluated involves highly specialized knowledge or competencies that are quite novel, there is little to be gained by using pretests. For example, in a first course in a foreign language, it seems highly unlikely that entering learners possess much, if any, proficiency. The same may hold true in a first course in algebra, biology, chemistry, or physics. On the other hand, courses in reading, English, general mathematics, social studies, and even general science are more developmental in nature and an assumption of low-to-nonexistent initial proficiency is highly questionable.

Popham (1988, p. 191) has introduced a modification of the posttest only control group design that is intended to overcome the hazard of not pretesting learners. This modification assumes that the treatment to be dispensed is of relatively short durations, for example, a unit of instruction, and that while all learners are to receive it, there is no requirement that they all receive it simultaneously. Random assignment is used to establish equivalent groups, and the flip of a coin can decide the order of presentation. The design is symbolized as follows:

Group1 $R\ T_1\ T_1\ T_2\ T_2$

Group 2 $R\ T_2\ P_2\ P_1\ T_1$

Treatment 1 and Treatment 2 refer to different units of instruction while P_1 and P_2 refer to measures of learners' proficiency associated with each unit. Random assignment and scheduling of treatments serve to establish the basic equivalency of the groups. Note also that all learners receive both treatments. The comparisons that Popham recommends are as indicated:

Group 1 $R\quad T_1\quad \textcircled{P_1}\ \textcircled{P_2}\quad T_2$

Group 2 $R\quad T_2\quad \textcircled{P_2}\ \textcircled{P_1}\quad T_1$

Insofar as the first treatment (T_1) is concerned, the estimate of its effectiveness comes from comparing Group 1's posttest performance with Group 2's pretest performance. For the second treatment (T_2), the situation is reversed. It would appear that the basic comparability for a clear and meaningful interpretation of results exists; unfortunately, this is not necessarily so. There would appear to be three possible sources of invalidity in this design. The first would be contamination arising from the close proximity of the two groups. If random assignment has been employed, it is more than likely that the two groups are in reasonably close proximity to one another, usually in the same school, if not the same classroom. Normal contact among members of the two groups could easily result, for example, with members of Group 2 acquiring some information about T_1 from members of Group 1. Thus, when the members of Group 2 are administered the performance measures for the first treatment (T_1), they are not in the naive state that Group 1 members were prior to exposure to treatment (T_1). The comparison between the P_1 measures for the two groups is apt to produce questionable results since the P_1 measures for Group 2 could be misleadingly high because of treatment diffusion. Whatever effect the first treatment (T_1) has will probably be underestimated. The same will be true for the second treatment (T_2).

Another factor that is likely to introduce invalidity into the results is maturation. If the treatments are of any appreciable length—a month or more might make a change—then Group 2's performance on P_1 might also underestimate learner performance prior to treatment, adding to possible underestimation of a treatment effect. The third possible source of invalidity could arise from an interaction between the previously discussed sources of invalidity. Technically, the first source of invalidity discussed, treatment diffusion, would be termed history, the second, maturation. The joint effect of these two sources can only be guessed at. Further work would be needed to estimate its effects. Until such time as the problems surrounding this staggered design can be clarified and resolved, it is recommended that it be avoided.

Nonequivalent Contrast Group Design

The nonequivalent contrast group design is identical to the pretest-posttest control group design in all respects except for the absence of random assignment of units to groups. It is symbolized as follows:

Group 1 $P\ T_1\ P$

Group 2 $P\ T_2\ P$

The absence of randomization immediately raises questions about the equivalence of the groups receiving the different treatments. From the point of view of research design specialists, this design is scientifically unacceptable and does not constitute a true experiment: it is a quasi-experiment. While true experiments are certainly preferable to quasi-experiments, an evaluation worker may have no alternative but to use a quasi-experimental design. The nonequivalent contrast group design may be serviceable. In order to use the design, however, the evaluation worker will have to conduct a number of subsidiary investigations to establish the comparability of the two groups. This is usually accomplished in two ways. First, analysis of the pretest performance measures is carried out. The goal of the analysis is to determine that there are no appreciable performance differences between the two groups. Second, other descriptive information about the two groups will need to be gathered and analyzed with the same goal in mind. Typical variables examined are age, sex, socioeconomic status, previous school performance, and scholastic ability. If the evaluation worker can, using the results of the two kinds of analyses, provide a fairly convincing case that the two groups are quite similar at the outset, then he or she will be in a reasonably good position to draw presumptive conclusions about treatment effects on the basis of the information gathered after a period of instruction.

There are two important features to note about the nonequivalent contrast group design. First, its use is dependent on establishing that groups are comparable. In a true experiment, randomization is a sufficient basis for establishing comparability. In the nonequivalent contrast groups design, additional investigative work is needed to establish that comparability. In some cases, it may be impossible to do so. For example, if a group of poor readers is singled out for treatment, there may be no remaining poor readers to constitute a comparison group. The use of a group of average readers would not satisfy the requirements for an equivalent group; these learners would simply not be comparable. Either another, more suitable comparison group should be identified or a different design will have to be used. The second feature to note about the nonequivalent contrast control group design is that any conclusions drawn from the results are necessarily presumptive. One cannot attribute causality to the treatment with the same degree of confidence as one can in a true experiment. The point of view advocated here, however, is that presumptive conclusions, while inferior to the strong conclusions to be drawn from true experiments, are clearly better than none at all. Furthermore, presumptive conclusions can be useful in assessing the worth of an educational enterprise and planning future action. One must be careful, of course, that the conclusions, albeit presumptive, are warranted. This involves considerable checking to insure the comparability of the groups under study.

The Single Group Pretest-Posttest Design

This design differs from the others that have been considered in that only a single group is involved. It is characterized as follows:

Group 1   *P T P*

Essentially, the design involves identifying a group, pretesting its members, exposing them to a treatment, and testing them again. The difference between the pretest and the posttest measures is intended to estimate the magnitude of the effect of the treatment. However, there are a number of alternative explanations for whatever difference might be found. It may be due simply to maturation. History, instrumentation, statistical regression, selection, mortality, and interactions can also produce the obtained results. Faced with such a variety of competing explanations, specialists in research design generally dismiss the single group pretest-posttest design as useless. The evaluation worker may not be able to do so, because the alternative—no study at all—is unacceptable.

There is little doubt that this design presents formidable problems. If used, no matter how reluctantly, the only course open to the evaluation worker is to systematically eliminate each competing alternative explanation so that the presumptive conclusion of a treatment effect is tenable. The way that competing explanations are eliminated depends on logic and judgment rather than on data analysis. In some cases the possibility of doing this is real and definite; in others not. Consider, for example, a first course in chemistry at the high-school level. It may be possible to establish that entering learners showed a low initial level of proficiency but a high level at the conclusion of the course. Further, it might be possible to demonstrate that there is little chance for learners to acquire competence in chemistry elsewhere. It may also be possible to show that there is little learner mortality, that few students dropped out of the course. The point here is that the evaluation worker must separately consider each alternative explanation for the obtained results and confirm or confute the explanatory power of each. If the explanatory power of each source of invalidity can be confuted, the evaluation worker can presumptively conclude that the obtained results were due to the effect of the treatment.

This judgmental and logical approach to dealing with the possible sources of invalidity presumes that the evaluation worker possesses sufficient knowledge about the details of a particular situation. This is quite correct. The evaluation worker must spend a considerable amount of time in the situation, or have access to those who do, in order to acquire the necessary knowledge to deal with competing explanations.

The above example used a first course in high-school chemistry. This course lends itself to dealing with competing explanations rather well because of its specialized and novel subject matter. In contrast, reading comprehension at the elementary-school level presents special problems since the subject matter is neither specialized nor novel and is readily accessible from a variety of sources. The likelihood of eliminating competing explanations is considerably reduced if not all but eliminated. An evaluation worker would be in an exceedingly difficult position if he tried to conclude that the increase in reading performance from, say, the beginning to the end of the school year was due solely, or even in large measure, to the nature of the reading program.

The foregoing discussion was intended to convey the notion that interpretation of results of an evaluation study is not an antiseptic exercise in which the evaluation worker examines results according to some mechanical procedures and draws inferences about treatment effectiveness. Rather, it is an intellectual exercise that makes heavy demands on the evaluation worker. Cook and Campbell characterize it in the following way:

Estimating the internal validity of a relationship is a deductive process in which the investigator has to systematically think through how each of the internal validity threats may have influenced the data. Then the investigator has to examine the data to test which relevant threats can be ruled out. In all of this process, the researcher has to be his or her own best critic, trenchantly examining all the threats he or she can imagine. When all of the threats can be plausibly eliminated, it is possible to make confident conclusions about whether a relationship is probably causal. When all of them cannot, perhaps because the appropriate data are not available or because the data indicate that a particular threat may indeed have operated, then the investigator has to conclude that a demonstrated relationship between two variables may or may not be causal. Sometimes the alternative interpretations may seem implausible enough to be ignored and the investigator will be inclined to dismiss them. They can be dismissed with a special degree of confidence when the alternative interpretations seem unlikely on the basis of findings from a research tradition with a large number of relevant and replicated findings. (Cook and Campbell, 1979, pp. 55–56)

The One-Shot Case Study

One of the most castigated designs is the one-shot case study. It is frequently presented first in any discussion of study designs and soundly criticized as being scientifically worthless. It is symbolized as follows:

$$T_1 \, P$$

That is, a group, usually not drawn at random from some larger population, is exposed to a treatment, and measures of learner performance are obtained. From a scientific viewpoint, it is impossible to conclude that the level of learner performance is due to the effect of the treatment. History, maturation, selection, and mortality could singly, or in combination, serve to explain the obtained results. After a fairly brief discussion, most specialists dismiss this design as being so fraught with problems as to have no value at all. While not challenging this conclusion from the standpoint of experimental design, there are occasions when the design can be quite serviceable in evaluation studies. However, the conditions under which it should be used are limited, and the interpretations that can be made of the results are restricted.

The one-shot case study design can be employed in two ways. First, the design can be used in connection with small-scale tryouts of program segments to obtain an initial estimate of how particular learning experiences or materials are working. The one-shot case study should be able to provide useful information about how segments of a larger program are functioning, especially in the early stages of development. While no one would wish to draw firm conclusions about a program's effectiveness from such small-scale studies, their use in formative evaluation could be quite helpful, especially to program developers. In fact, a very strong argument could be made for increased use of one-shot case studies during the early stages of the development of courses, program, and curricula.

The second use of the one-shot case study design involves the evaluation of specialized programs where (1) it can be strongly presumed that entering learners are virtually ignorant about what is to be learned, and (2) it is not possible to have a comparison group. A program to train people in welding would be one example where a one-shot case study could be rather serviceable. Entering learners could safely be presumed to lack proficiency in the area. Because of the nature of the program, pretesting would probably not only be a waste of time but potentially dangerous. The program could be initiated as soon as the learners are assembled and testing carried out after a period of time. (In the case of welding, the conventional procedure is to test learners after they have been instructed and have practiced each type of weld. Of course, a single postinstructional test, covering a variety of welds, can also be used.) The likelihood that history and maturation could adequately explain resultant learner proficiency is extremely low and could probably easily be rejected on logical grounds. Learner mortality, however, can easily be checked and, if low, can also be rejected. An examination of the selection procedures can provide information about the type of learners the results might apply to while replication can fortify the validity of the results. In short, what is typically rejected as an unacceptable research design can be a quite serviceable design in an evaluation study.

To be sure, the particular program selected to illustrate the use of the one-shot case study, welding, is admirably suited to this design. The example is not so farfetched, however. Beginning courses in specialized subjects such as algebra, foreign languages, laboratory sciences and special skill courses such as pottery, silk screen printing, automotive repair, and sailing could all use the design. The chief requirements for use of this design are novel and specialized subject matter and learners without proficiency in the subject. While one would wish to see a stronger design employed, it may be reasonable to use a one-shot case study; local circumstances in fact may prevent any other design from being used. It is not a design to be rejected automatically simply because of its disrepute among specialists in research design.

The Interrupted Time-Series Design

The interrupted time-series design is especially useful when a particular treatment is introduced on an across-the-board basis. It is represented as follows:

P P P P T P P P P

Measures are obtained on a regular basis, before the introduction of a treatment and afterwards. Archival data in the form of standardized test results, average daily attendance rates, learner referrals for various purposes and, in the case of morale studies, teacher turnover statistics are examples of information that are gathered on a regular and routine basis, and can be used to estimate the effect of the introduction of a particular treatment. While the procedures for analyzing the data from interrupted time-series studies are somewhat complex (see, for example, Cook and Campbell, 1979) a graphical representation often provides a reasonable basis for judging the efficacy of the treatment. Consider the examples in Figure 9.1.

In the case of Line A, note that there is an increase from Time 4 to Time 5. This coincides with the introduction of the treatment. However, as can readily

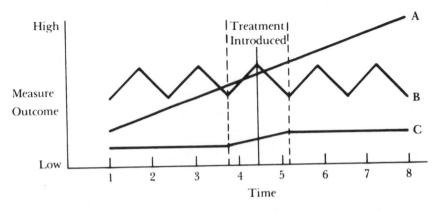

FIGURE 9.1: Possible Outcomes in an Interrupted Time-Series Design

Source: Adapted from D.T. Campbell and J. Stanley, "Experimental and Quasi-experimental Designs for Research on Teaching." In *Handbook of Research on Teaching*, edited by N.L. Gage, pp. 171–246. Chicago: Rand McNally.

be seen, the measure was increasing steadily from Time 1 to Time 4 and also after Time 5. In fact, the various points show a clear upward trend throughout. The introduction of the treatment apparently had no effect on this trend. If inspection of the measure at only Time 4 and Time 5 had been made, one would have been tempted to conclude that the treatment had made an effect insofar as the measure would indicate. However, the longer view, Time 1 through Time 8, refutes this.

Line B also shows an increase on the measure that coincides with the introduction of the treatment. However, when all the measures are considered, it appears that the increase is part of a general bumping along in the level of the measure over time rather than the result of the treatment. In Line C, however, there is evidence for treatment effect. The level of the measure after the introduction of the treatment is higher than before. In this example there is no overlap in the average level of performance before the treatment is introduced and afterward. It would be reasonable to consider the possibility that the treatment did, in fact, result in a higher average level on the measure. This does not, however, mean that the treatment was responsible for the effect. There are at least two other possibilities to consider: namely, history and instrumentation.

It is possible that another event occurred at the same time that the treatment was introduced and was responsible for the increased level on the measure. This, of course, is history, the influence of an extraneous variable. An evaluation specialist would need to carefully check on the likelihood of such an event.

The second alternative explanation, instrumentation, exposes a fundamental flaw in the interrupted time-series design. Educational institutions routinely collect and store all kinds of information. However, there is no guarantee that the procedures used and the information gathered will remain uniform over time; the chances are they will not. Learner attendance data, for example, has been used from time to time as an indirect indicator of a program effect. Changes in state laws with regard to the gathering and reporting of such information do occur, often as a result of political factors. Such changes can result in an apparent treatment effect when, in fact, there was only a change in the way records were kept. A change in data-gathering procedures can also affect the assessment of treatment results: the renorming of an existing test, or the introduction of a new edition of a test, can do it. For example, educational institutions are expected to use tests with up-to-date norms (and usually do). The introduction of a renormed test or a new edition of a test can produce an apparent treatment effect or mask a real one, depending on the relationship between new and old norms. To illustrate, the 1972 renormed Stanford-Binet has a higher set of norms for individuals up to age six and above thirteen than the previous edition; that is, it now takes a higher level of performance to attain an I.Q. of (say) one hundred than it did previously at these age levels. Similarly, the norms for the 1973 edition of the Stanford Achievement Test (Stanford Research Reports, 1973) are higher than the norms for the 1964 edition of the same battery.

A school which routinely installed the 1973 edition as part of its testing program would show a dramatic jump in average performance among its learners, and this higher performance level would continue even if learner performance itself had remained stable. This spurious effect arises solely from the introduction of the new edition of the test. If a new curriculum were instituted at the same time as the changeover in test editions, results would be identical to those shown in Line C in Figure 9.1; this would occur even if the new curriculum had no effect whatsoever on learner performance. The lesson is plain: shifts in instrumentation in an interrupted time-series design can affect results. It can either mask a real treatment effect or produce a spurious one, depending on the nature of the shift. The evaluation worker clearly needs to consider carefully the nature of the instrumentation and the uniformity of procedures employed in gathering data about possible treatment effects.

Three other issues that surround the interrupted time-series design can strongly influence its possible adoption. First, the design assumes that a treatment is instituted at a particular time. In Figure 9.1, this is indicated by the vertical line designating "Treatment Introduced." If this condition is met, the design can be considered for use. If the innovation is introduced over a period of time in phases, then the design is inappropriate, since it will not be possible to separate a treatment effect from whatever secular trends there are in the data. A second major issue that must be dealt with when considering an interrupted time-series design involves the relevance of the measures to be used. While educational institutions routinely collect and store all kinds of information, the relevance of such information to a particular course, program, curriculum, organizational pattern and the like can vary enormously. In some cases, archival data may bear directly on the planned innovation; in other cases they may not. If the information has no relevance to the treatment, the design simply has no attraction. The evaluation worker must carefully study existing data sources, the nature of the treatment to be introduced, the scheduled introduction of the treatment, and the relationship between the treatment and the data sources before deciding to employ an interrupted time-series design. The third issue involves the number of data points available for study. Statistical procedures for analyzing time-series data are somewhat complex. They also require a sizable number of data points in order to model a time series and to estimate the effect of a treatment effect. Current thinking (Cook and Campbell, 1979) suggests that at least fifty observations are needed to adequately analyze data from an interrupted time series. This requirement may preclude the use of this design in some situations in which one would otherwise wish to use it.

Regression Discontinuity Design

The regression discontinuity design most closely resembles the nonequivalent contrast group design with one major exception. In the latter, the two groups are considered to be comparable, while in the former they are not. The regression discontinuity design was developed for use in situations where a treatment is intended for all eligible learners. The treatment could range from a program of remedial instruction to an enrichment curriculum. A regression discontinuity design requires a strict and orderly procedure for assigning all eligible learners to a treatment. For example, all learners at a given grade with test scores below a certain point are assigned to a remedial program. In another situation, all learners above a certain cutting score are given an enrichment program. The ineligible learners constitute a contrast group. Unlike the nonequivalent contrast group design, however, the ineligible learners are not presumed to be directly comparable to those in the treated group. One of the chief differences between the regression discontinuity and the nonequivalent contrast group design lies in the way that the resulting data are analyzed. In the nonequivalent contrast group design, some procedure for comparing the average level of performance between the treatment groups is used. This may involve one of a number of techniques, including the analysis of covariance. In the regression discontinuity design, however, the techniques of regression analysis are used. This is illustrated in Figure 9.2.

As shown in Figure 9.2, all learners were administered a pretest. The resulting scores were strictly used to decide which learners received the treatment and which did not. In that example, the treatment might be a remedial program in reading. After a period of instruction, a posttest was administered to all learners. The regression of posttest scores on pretest scores was calculated for each group separately and the regression lines plotted. The distance

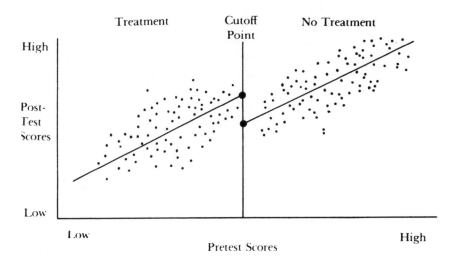

FIGURE 9.2: Regression Discontinuity Design: Genuine Effect

Source: Adapted from D.T. Campbell, "Reforms as Experiments." *American Psychologist* 24, 1969: pp. 409–429.

between the points where the two regression lines intersect the vertical line at the cutoff point line provides an estimate of the treatment effect. The determination of the statistical significance of the distance between the points remains a problem. While no definite procedure has been established, Reichardt (1979) provides some useful guidelines for data analysis. Essentially, Reichardt suggests an analysis of covariance that contains an interaction term for groups to allow the regressions of posttest on pretest scores to differ across groups and an adequate regression model to fit the data. The latter often involves the use of polynomial terms in the analysis. Fortunately, readily available statistical packages for computers can be used to carry out these analyses. The evaluation worker who needs to analyze data from a study that used a regression-discontinuity design would profit from reading Reichardt's discussion of data analysis issues associated with the use of this design (Reichardt, 1979, pp. 202–05).

Obviously, proper execution of a regression discontinuity design requires strict adherence to the use of a cutoff point for selection into treatment. Any fuzziness in the selection procedure will cloud the results. There is also the issue of the relationship between the posttest measure and the pretest measure. It is not obligatory that the pretest and posttest measures be identical, only that they be related. If the relationship between them is high, the regression discontinuity design will be a relatively strong one. If it is low, the design more closely resembles the nonequivalent contrast group design. If the relationship is zero, the design resembles the pretest-posttest control group design.

The regression discontinuity design is a relative newcomer in the field of evaluation. Its origins can be traced to the work of Thistlewaite and Campbell (1960) in attempting to assess the effects of receiving a fellowship. While originally envisaged as a way of estimating a treatment effect through the use of tie-breaking procedures, it has developed into a general approach for the estimation of effects when a scarce boon must be distributed to the most needy or the most meritorious or when all eligible members of a group are to be given a treatment. Quantification of need or merit makes the regression discontinuity design an excellent candidate for evaluation studies. There are, however, a number of outstanding problems with regard to the analysis and interpretation of results. Considerable progress in resolving them can be expected in the near future.

MASTERY LEARNING

There has been a growing interest in mastery learning in recent years. The work of Bloom (1976), Carroll (1963), and others has led to the development of instructional programs in which learners work to accomplish present goals. Such programs differ from conventional ones in that learners work at achieving each instructional goal as long as it takes to reach a specified level of proficiency termed mastery. Once a goal has been attained, the learner then proceeds to the next goal. Learner performance information is binary in nature, either the goal has been achieved or it has not.

Conventional designs are not suited to the evaluation of programs of mastery learning. Such designs presume a fixed treatment period and variable performance. A successful matery learning program will show no variability in performance, that is, all learners achieved all program goals.

A design that is suitable for the evaluation of mastery learning programs uses time as the outcome variable. Thus, there is a fixed level of performance (mastery) and variable time taken to achieve mastery. Such a design requires that careful records be kept of the amount of time taken to achieve mastery. These records are then analyzed separately for treatment and comparison groups. Abrahamson et al. (1969) report the results of a study using this approach to evaluate the use of a computer controlled dummy to train anesthesiologists to perform endotracheal intubations.

REPLICATION

The designs presented above should furnish the evaluation worker with a sufficient array of procedures to effectively study most educational treatments. As noted, each design has its own strengths and weaknesses. Some of these are theoretical, some methodological, and some practical. The evaluation worker will need to consider the nature of the course, program, or curriculum to be evaluated, and the existing conditions in a particular setting, before choosing a particular design. Even after a design has been selected, some modifications may be necessary in order to use it in a specific situation, although modifications may increase invalid results.

One way of improving the validity of evaluation studies is through replication. In evaluation studies, replication can occur in three ways. The most familiar is when a number of learners are exposed to each treatment under study. The presentation of each design routinely referred to groups receiving one or another treatment. Little was made of the fact that each group is composed of a number of individuals and that the purpose of studying a number of individuals is to obtain more precise estimates of treatment effects. Thus, the study of a number of individuals receiving a certain treatment is considered a replication.

There are two other ways that replication can occur. An evaluation study may be carried out with successive cohorts of learners. A program may be initiated one year and evaluated and a second trial and evaluation may be carried out the next year with a new group. The results of the two separate evaluation studies can be compared and judgments and decisions then made. Those responsible for deciding what course of action should be followed are apt to feel more comfortable basing their decisions on the results of separate evaluation studies rather than on a single one. Of course, problems can arise. The results of the two studies may be inconsistent, the program may have been modified from one year to the next, etc. However, these problems can be handled within the context of the framework for evaluation emphasized throughout this work. The framework explicitly includes provisions for monitoring the treatment being dispensed, the learners being served, the objectives being pursued, etc. It seems clear that having two separate evaluation studies as a basis for making judgments and deciding on future action is superior to having the results of only a single study. What is required, however, is that those responsible for deciding on future action willingly postpone such decisions until the needed information is in hand. Decision makers willing and able to postpone such decisions have been termed "experimental administrators" by Campbell (1969). Such administrators have effected a posture that advocates the seriousness of a particular need and persistence in seeking ways to meet it. "Trapped administrators," according to Campbell (p. 409) "fall into the snare of advocating a specific reform as though they were certain to be successful." According to Campbell (p. 410), the experimental administrator says in effect: "This is a serious problem. We propose to initiate Policy A on an experimental basis. If after two years there has been no significant improvement, we will shift to Policy B." Not only will such a posture permit honest evaluation of the outcomes of a treatment—Campbell's main point—but it should buy time for the kind of sequential replication advocated here. A notable example of the use of successive replication can be found in the evaluation studies of Sesame Street. See S. Ball and G. Bogatz, *The First Year of Sesame Street: An Evaluation* (Princeton, N.J.: Educational Testing Service, 1970); and G. Bogatz and S. Ball, *The Second Year of Sesame Street: A Continuing Evaluation*, 2 vols. (Princeton, N.J.: Educational Testing Service, 1971).

The last way that replication can occur is when a treatment is simultaneously introduced into a number of units in an institution and separate evaluations are carried out in each unit. A particular innovation may be introduced into a number of elementary schools in a single district, for example, and separate studies can be conducted in each school. Simultaneous evaluation of a treatment in each of its implementations should produce a series of replications that fortify the validity of results. Furthermore, replication over units should produce a considerable time saving that may be critical if the need for action is acute. Whether an evaluation worker adopts a procedure of replication over time, successive replication, or replication over units, simultaneous replication, will undoubtedly depend on conditions in the local situation. Either procedure is clearly better than a single trial, no matter how elegant the design.

SUMMARY

This chapter has presented a body of information regarding the design and conduct of evaluation studies. While the main source for this topic is the branch of applied statistics called experimental design, some revision has been made to render it suitable for educational evaluation. Accordingly, the treatment here differs somewhat from some of the standard works on the topic.

While differing in a number of details, the general principles of experimental design hold for evaluation studies. The threats to the validity of results in both experimental and evaluation studies are the same: history, maturation, instrumentation, statistical regression, selection, subject mortality, selection-maturation interaction, diffusion or imitation of treatments, and resentful demoralization of learners receiving less desirable treatments. These factors were described and presented and discussed in relation to each design.

The importance of equivalent groups for the purpose of comparison was examined at length. Ideally, procedures of random assignment are employed to establish equivalent comparison groups. In evaluation studies, such procedures are often not feasible, and the problem of locating groups that could be considered equivalent was discussed. Considerable attention was given to the identification of comparison or contrast groups for use in evaluation studies.

Specific designs for evaluation studies were considered in detail, and strengths and weaknesses of each design were noted. The logic of each design was emphasized rather than formal details. Throughout the discussion practical considerations concerning the use of each design in an educational setting were taken up. Finally, the value of replication in evaluation, as a way of fortifying the validity of results, was shown.

References

Abrahamson, S., Denson, J. S. and Wolf, R. M. 1969. "Effectiveness of a Simulator in Training Anesthesiology Residents." *Journal of Medical Education* 44: 515–19.

Ball, S. and Bogatz, G. A. 1970. *The First Year of Sesame Street: An Evaluation*. Princeton: Educational Testing Service.

Bloom, B. S. 1976. *Human Characteristics and School Learning*. New York: McGraw-Hill.

Campbell, D. and Stanley, J. 1963. "Experimental and Quasi-experimental Designs for Research on Teaching." In *Handbook of Research on Teaching*. Edited by N. L. Gage, Chicago: Rand-McNally, pp. 171–246.

Campbell, D. T. 1969. "Reforms as Experiments." *American Psychologist* 24: "Designs for Research on Teaching." In *Handbook of Research on Teaching*, edited by N. L. Gage, pp. 171–246. Chicago: Rand McNally.

Carroll, J. B. 1963. "A Model of School Learning." *Teachers College Record* 64: 723–33.

Cook, T. D. and Campbell, D. T. 1979. *Quasi-experimentation: Design and Analysis Issues for Field Settings*. Chicago: Rand McNally.

Fisher, R. A. 1925. *Statistical Methods for Research Workers*. London: Oliver and Boyd.

McCall, W. 1923. *How to Experiment in Education*. New York: Macmillan.

Page, E. 1958. "Teacher Comments and Student Performance: A Seventy-four Classroom Experiment in School Motivation." *Journal of Educational Psychology* 49: 173–81.

Popham, W. J. 1988. *Educational Evaluation*, 2nd edition. Englewood Cliffs: Prentice-Hall.

Poyner, H. 1974. "Selecting Units of Analysis." In *Evaluating Educational Programs and Products*, edited by G. Borick. Englewood Cliffs: Educational Technology Publications.

Reichardt, C. S. 1979. "The Statistical Analysis of Data from Nonequivalent Group Designs." In *Quasi-experimentation: Design and Analysis Issues for Field Settings*. Chicago: Rand McNally.

Thistlewaite, D. L. and Campbell, D. T. 1960. "Regression-Discontinuity Analysis: An Alternative to the Ex Post Facto Experiment." *Journal of Educational Psychology* 51, 309–17.

Additional Readings

Benson, J. and Michael, W. S. 1987. "Designing Evaluation Studies: A Twenty-Year Perspective," *International Journal of Educational Research* 11, 43–56.

Berk, R. A. (ed.). 1981. *Educational Evaluation Methodology: The State of the Art*. Baltimore: The Johns Hopkins University Press.

Cronbach, L. J. 1982. *Designing Evaluations of Educational Programs*. San Francisco: Jossey-Bass.

10

SAMPLING CONSIDERATIONS

In his primer on sampling (1960), M. Slonim pointed out that anyone who has poured a highball into a potted plant after taking one sip has had an experience in sampling. We are bombarded almost daily with the results of polls that make routine use of sampling procedures. The goal of all sampling is to make accurate and meaningful statements about some group on the basis of a study of a subset of the group. The group may be a collection of individuals (as in a Gallup or Harris poll) or it may be a collection of objects as in an industrial process such as the manufacture of light bulbs. Whether the group consists of individuals or objects is of no consequence; the principles and procedures of sampling remain the same. The object is to select a subset or sample of a group in such a way that it will be representative of the whole.

Sampling is undertaken for several reasons. First, it is usually more economical to study a subset of a group than a total group. Second, it is generally more efficient to examine a sample than a larger group. Third, it is often impractical to study an entire group, especially if it is widely dispersed.

The two key terms in sampling are population and sample. A population, previously referred to as the total group, is defined as a collection of elements (people or objects) having one or more characteristics in common. Typically, a population is defined by specifying those common characteristics. Thus, one can define a population as broadly as "all students, age 13.0 to 14.0, enrolled in full-time schooling in the United States," or as narrowly as "all boys enrolled in the fifth grade in the Watson Elementary School." Both are acceptable definitions of populations. Each defines a population by specifying the characteristics that the members of the population have in common. A sample is a part of the population. In selecting a sample we usually wish to select a part of the population that will be representative of the total population. How this is done to best insure representativeness, at the lowest cost, is the business of sampling.

There are three general types of samples. The first is often referred to as a chunk sample. It involves selection of some fraction of the population for closer study, often on the basis of simple availability or economy. Chunk samples are considered to be scientifically worthless since there is no assurance that the sample is at all representative of the population and usually there is no way to find out. When an investigator chooses to study a group of children because of easy accessibility and tries to draw conclusions from the findings about children in general, he or she is on dangerous ground. This sampling procedure is open to serious criticism: there is nothing about it worth recommending except its convenience. It will sometimes suffice for pilot studies when one is interested in testing out instruments and data collection procedures, but it should not be used as the basis for drawing substantive conclusions about a population.

A second type of sample is the judgment sample. Here, members of the population are selected for inclusion in the sample on the basis of the investigator's judgment. The aim of a judgment sample is to select a subset of the population that will be representative of the total population. A judgment sample may or may not be representative. Unfortunately, there is no way of knowing, and this is the chief weakness of judgment samples, since one must depend solely on the judgment of the person who has selected the sample. In certain instances, judgment sampling may be the best available way of obtaining a representative sample. For example, if resources are extremely limited, forcing the selection of a very small sample, it may be better to use a judgment sample than some other procedure such as random selection. The sample size may not afford enough of an opportunity for a randomization principle to operate. Usually, however, judgment samples should be avoided since there is no way of gauging their accuracy.

The third type of sample is a probability sample. A probability sample is one in which every member of the population has a known and nonzero chance of being included in the sample. There are two general kinds of probability samples: simple and complex. The best known type of simple probability sampling is a simple random sample. Here, each member of the population has an equal chance of being selected for the sample. Simple random samples are selected in one of two equivalent ways. Each member of the population is assigned a unique identification number, and enough members to constitute a sample are selected through a lottery procedure or, more likely, a table of random numbers. Detailed procedures for selecting a simple random sample can be found in the references at the end of this chapter. The most well-known form of sampling is routinely taught in introductory statistics courses and usually is easily understood. How widely simple random sampling is actually used is another matter. In large-scale studies of educational effects of programs such as "Sesame Street" or Harvard Project Physics, simple random sampling could not be used: a single list of all the individuals in the population did not exist, and constructing one would have been an extraordinarily difficult task. Furthermore, even if such a list did exist, it would be highly impractical to use it in selecting a sample. Random selection from such a master list might result in having to test one student in, say, Grand Marais, Minnesota, another in Clarence, New York, another in South Pasadena, California, etc. Resources for data gathering would not likely be available to support such a scheme. Accordingly, a variety of complex sampling procedures have been developed. Despite their complexity, they are highly practical to apply. Among complex sampling procedures there are multistage sampling, either random or with probability proportional to size; stratified sampling; cluster sampling; and sequential sampling. Also, various combinations of complex procedures can be used. Detailed discussions of each procedure can be found in the Kish text (1966) cited at the end of this chapter.

In selecting a sample, there are two major concerns. First, the sample should be representative of the population. If any part of the population has a very low or zero chance of being selected for inclusion in the sample, the sample is likely to be biased. Considerable effort is often made to insure that every segment of the population has a known and nonzero chance of being included in the sample. Sometimes, special provisions are made to insure that groups that make up a very small fraction of the population are included in the sample. Usually this is accomplished through stratification. The second concern in sampling is precision; that is, estimates of characteristics of the population based on sample results should have as small a margin of error as possible. Furthermore, these estimates of error should be known. The two major reasons for using some form of probability sampling are that (1) it offers the best guarantee of obtaining representative samples and (2) it is possible to obtain estimates of the precision of a sample's statistics. We know, for example, that in well-conducted polls by the Gallup or Harris organizations, voter preferences in the sample are likely to be within 2 percent of the population values. In studies of educational effects, it is similarly possible to obtain estimates of the precision of sample statistics.

The precision with which characteristics of a population can be estimated from sample data depends largely on the sample size. The larger the sample, the more precise the estimates of population characteristics. The limiting case occurs when the sample is 100 percent of the population. Sample statistics in that case have zero error, being population values. The important point to note is that of the three major types of samples—chunk, judgment, and probability—only probability sampling offers a way to determine the precision of statistics based on information obtained from a sample. Probability sampling, correctly done, also furnishes the best assurance that the sample selected for study will be representative of the population, that is, free from bias (Ross, 1987).

Sampling is widely used in research. Often it is necessary to obtain information about some large population when exhaustive testing of every member of the population would be prohibitive. In evaluation studies, the situation is often quite different. A course, program, or curriculum has usually been developed for a particular group in a certain institutional setting. A new social studies program, for example, may be introduced at the sixth grade in a school district. Selecting a sample for study would be a questionable undertaking for several reasons. First, all the learners in the program are likely to be available, so sampling is unnecessary. Second, sampling would create administrative problems. For example, if a sample was selected, what would the remaining learners do while data were being gathered? Furthermore, how would the learners feel about selective testing? Administratively, it is easier to treat all learners uniformly. Thus, sampling, in the traditional sense, is not only often unnecessary but is likely to cause administrative problems for the institution.

If sampling in evaluation studies is not used in the traditional way, how is it used? There are two answers. First, a group of learners currently enrolled in an educational program in a particular setting may be regarded as a sample from the population of all learners, current and future, who are to undergo the program. Thus, the present group is used to help make decisions about the program for future cohorts. Sampling per se is not carried out; the current group of learners is assumed to be representative of the population of all learners to be served and, consequently, is used as a basis for inference. This is reasonable as long as there is no substantial change in the learner population from year to year.

The second way that sampling is used in evaluation studies has been suggested previously, and will now be treated in detail. The collection of all information required in an evaluation study could place enormous burdens on learners, teachers, and administrators. It is not unusual to develop a series of data-gathering instruments and procedures that, if fully answered by every learner, would require a number of hours of response time. Since time is a commodity that is usually in short supply, an expectation that every learner would be given every question, item, task, or problem is unrealistic. Accordingly, some sampling scheme must be undertaken. The term for the scheme that is increasingly being used in evaluation studies is *multiple matrix sampling*. Various terms have been used to describe this development, for example, item sampling, item examinee sampling, and matrix sampling. Since the only text in the area uses the term *multiple matrix sampling* (Shoemaker, 1973), and since it seems to be most apt, this term will be used. While originally formulated as an efficient way of developing norms for tests, its use in evaluation studies was recognized early, and considerable developmental work and research have been directed toward its use in evaluation studies. The case for the use of multiple matrix sampling in evaluation studies has been well stated by K. Sirotnik (1974):

If an evaluator wants to examine the effects of an instructional program, there is no reason why every student in the program must answer every item related to the outcomes of the program. In fact, obtaining data from every examinee on every item is often a waste. To make decisions about programs one needs data on the programs. If a population of examinees is exposed to an instructional program and a population of items is developed to assess the effects of that program, then the evaluator needs to know how well the population of examinees does on the population of items. The individual student is important to himself, to his teacher, to his parents and even to the evaluator, but he is not, in this case, the object of the evaluation—the program is.

Sirotnik's statement embodies several important concepts. First, it is not only unnecessary but unwise to have every learner answer every item. Second, in evaluation work, the program is the object of attention. Third, two kinds of sampling can occur in a data-gathering enterprise: sampling of items and sampling of learners. This dual sampling can be represented as shown in Figure 10.1.

Box A in Figure 10.1 represents an item-learner population. If every learner in the population answered every item in the population of items, the cells of the matrix would be filled with the responses. For example, if the item population consisted of questions that were scored as correct (1) and incorrect (0), the matrix would be filled with ones and zeros. Inspection of the matrix would allow one to determine how every learner performed on every item. As noted earlier, such a scheme is highly impractical. In evaluation studies, the situation presented in matrix C is the more likely case. Here, all learners are administered a sample of items to answer. The size of the item sample is usually developed on the basis of the time available for testing. That is, the time available for testing is determined first and enough testing material to fill that time block is generated. Unfortunately, the item sample so developed is often a chunk sample. Whether the item sample is representative of the population of items that could be developed to cover the domain represented by the objectives is, alas, not usually considered.

The situation represented in box B is a theoretical one. A sample of examinees is administered a population of items. This rarely occurs because (1) few investigators have ever developed a population of items and (2) it is typically not possible to administer a population of items to even a single examinee. The reason for this is that a population of items would, by definition, be composed of all possible items measuring an educational outcome. Except for a few extremely limited outcomes—the one hundred basic addition facts would be an example—one usually does not develop a population of items. The notion of a population of test items for even narrowly defined educational goals is almost always a theoretical idea; it is rarely a practicable alternative.

The sampling notions represented in the D and E boxes are especially important for educational evaluation studies. Box E is one example of a multiple matrix sampling scheme. A matrix sample is a representation of the responses of a group of learners to a subset of items. In the example given (Figure 10.2), seven items were administered to ten students and responses were scored as right (1) or wrong (0). The matrix thus contains a total of seventy responses. The procedure is not dependent on item type. One could use essay questions graded on a continuous scale ranging from zero to one hundred, as well as attitudinal items in which learners indicate their degree of endorsement of

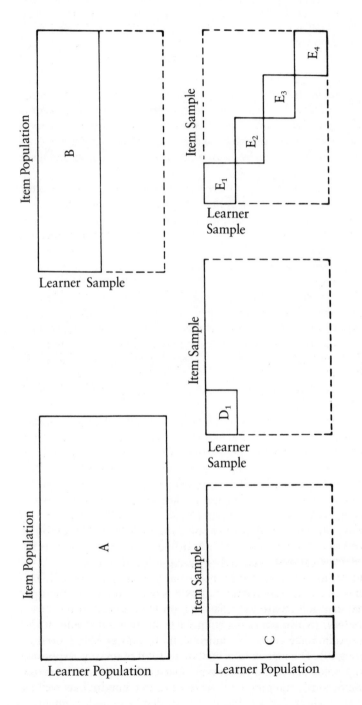

FIGURE 10.1: Sampling Schemes for Items and Examinees

Note: (A = matrix population, B = examinee sample, C = item sample, D = matrix sample, E = multiple matrix sample).
Source: Adapted from K. Sirotnik and R.J. Wellington, "Scrambling Content in Achievement Testing: An Application of Multiple Matrix Sampling in Experimental Design." *Journal of Educational Measurement,* II, no. 3, pp. 179–88.

Learner Sample	Item 1	2	3	4	5	6	7
1	1	1	1	0	1	1	0
2	1	1	0	1	1	1	1
3	1	1	1	1	0	0	0
4	0	1	0	0	1	0	1
5	0	0	1	1	1	1	1
6	0	1	1	0	1	0	1
7	1	1	1	1	0	1	0
8	0	0	0	1	0	1	0
9	1	0	0	0	0	0	1
10	0	0	0	1	1	0	1

FIGURE 10.2: Example of a Matrix Sample

Source: Adapted from D, Sirotnik, "Matrix Sampling for the Practitioner," In *Evaluation in Education: Current Applications,* edited by W.J. Popham, Berkeley: McCutchan Publishing, 1974.

statements, from "strongly agree" to "strongly disagree." The use of items scored right or wrong is only a simple example of a matrix sample.

In a matrix sampling procedure, a sample from a pool of items is administered to a subset of learners. While it would be possible to obtain a score for each examinee, this is rarely done, because the sample of items answered is usually too small to yield a reliable score for an individual. Also, the particular sample of items taken by a learner is an inadequate sample of the total pool of items and, further, it is of no interest for evaluation purposes to know how each learner responds. The program is the object of concern.

The notion of matrix sampling has been considerably extended in the E boxes. In this case, a pool of items has been divided into four sets and each set is administered to a different set of examinees. One obvious advantage of this scheme is that no learner responds to more than 25 percent of the items for the total pool. This represents a considerable savings in testing time, an often critical consideration. A somewhat less obvious feature of the multiple matrix sampling scheme is that it is a rather straightforward matter to estimate the performance for the total group on the basis of the matrix samples. (Detailed procedures, including formulae and computer programs, for estimation of characteristics for the total group are supplied by Shoemaker [1973] and Sirotnik [1974]). That is, the information that would be obtained by the testing scheme represented in box A can be closely approximated by the sampling scheme set forth in box E. What is less apparent is that estimates of a population (box A) based on multiple matrix sampling (box E) will be more precise (less variable) than those based on learner sampling (box B). Yet that is the case. The standard errors obtained with multiple matrix sampling will be less than those obtained with learner sampling.

While the representation of multiple matrix sampling set forth in Figure 10.1 may look complicated, the procedures involved in carrying out such a scheme are straightforward and easily executed. Consider a simple example. An evaluation worker wishes to obtain information on one hundred test questions, dealing with mathematical problem-solving and proficiency, from four hundred learners enrolled in an innovative fifth-grade mathematics program. Time does not permit each learner to respond to all one hundred items. Accordingly, the evaluation worker randomly divides the items into five piles of twenty each. Each pile is organized into a test booklet and assigned a letter A through E. Eighty copies of each booklet are reproduced. An equal number of booklets of each form are given to each classroom teacher who shuffles them and passes them out at random for learners to answer.

The double randomization—random assignment of items to booklets, and random assignment of booklets to learners—insures that the results are unbiased. Each learner answers one-fifth of the total pool of items, an 80 percent saving in testing time. The resulting information can be easily assembled in the form represented in box E in Figure 10.1, the chief difference being that there will be five matrix samples instead of four. Furthermore, if both initial and final levels of proficiency are to be assessed, it is a simple matter to see that the particular form a learner receives at the end of the program is different from the one he or she is given at the beginning. Thus, the likelihood of specific testing effects is minimized, if not eliminated.

There are a number of technical considerations in developing a set of procedures for multiple matrix sampling in a specific situation. These are discussed in considerable detail by Shoemaker (1973) and Sirotnik (1974). Two important questions that need to be dealt with are (1) how many subtests should be assembled from a total pool of items, and (2) how items should be allocated to subtests. In the previous example, random assignment of items to booklets was used, but stratified random assignment could also have been used. Stratification can be done in several ways. The difficulty of the items, the objectives being tested, or a combination of the two can be used to stratify the items. Some considerations in deciding how many subtests to use are: (1) the size of the total pool of items, (2) the amount of time for testing, (3) the size of the learner group to be tested, (4) the expected distribution of scores, and (5) the judged importance of certain items. In the case of the last variable, it may be that certain items in the pool are judged so important that it is decided that the performance of all learners, and not just a sample, be obtained. In that case, such critical items would appear in all test booklets; thus, it will be necessary to reduce the number of remaining items to be used if testing time is to remain constant. Given an item pool of a fixed size and a limited amount of time for testing, the only way this can be done is to increase the number of subtests or booklets. Technically, this procedure, referred to as sampling with replacement, introduces some complications into the multiple matrix sampling procedure that should be considered. It is mentioned to let the reader know that, while multiple matrix sampling is a highly efficient way of gathering information, it is not without problems. Nonetheless, it is a highly useful development and well worth considering in evaluation studies because of the economies it offers.

In addition to these benefits, there are other features to multiple matrix sampling that make it especially attractive for use in evaluation. First, research to date on multiple matrix sampling suggests that scrambling of cognitive test items in a multiple matrix sampling scheme has minimal or no effect on average learner test performance or on any of the statistical estimates obtained from analysis (Sirotnik and Wellington, 1974). The implications of this finding are extremely important for evaluation work. Typically, a program, course, or curriculum consists of a number of objectives, some rather diverse. While multiple matrix sampling was originally developed to be used with tests that were homogeneous with respect to what was being tested and the way it was being tested, the findings of Sirotnik and Wellington and others suggest that the scheme is more robust and can be used with different content, item types, and other context factors. Thus, the evaluation specialist need not be overly concerned that the test forms or booklets administered to learners may be highly varied with regard to what is being tested and the item types employed.

Another benefit of multiple matrix sampling that is not readily apparent is that it can be combined with traditional learner-appraisal procedures so that the twin goals of appraisal and evaluation can be served through the administration of a single instrument. In the International Educational Achievement Association's study of science achievement in nineteen countries, for example, every high school senior tested received one of six booklets (Comber and Keeves, 1973). The first twenty-four test questions were the same in all booklets and were used to obtain a score for each learner. The last six questions, which differed over the six test forms, were used to obtain an estimate of school performance on another thirty-six items covering an additional number of science achievement objectives. Assignment of test forms was carried out at random within each classroom. Since twenty-four items were common to all forms, the random distribution had no effect whatsoever on the measurement of individual learners.

Another benefit of multiple matrix sampling has already been hinted at: it allows for the collection of a maximum amount of information in a minimum amount of testing time. In addition to this obvious economy, multiple matrix sampling makes it possible to gather information with regard to every objective being pursued by a course, program, or curriculum. It was noted earlier that obtaining learner performance information about every objective is important if major judgments and decisions are to be made. Multiple matrix sampling enables the realization of this important goal.

A last benefit is highly practical but not immediately obvious. One of the difficulties in conducting comparative studies in education is obtaining the co-operation of contrast groups. Time demands are made on the contrast groups, and there is no obvious benefit for cooperation. Administrative edicts may produce contrast groups when required, but securing genuine cooperation does not automatically follow. The use of multiple matrix sampling with contrast groups may not generate enthusiasm, but it can minimize the intrusiveness of the data-gathering effort by reducing the time demand to a level deemed tolerable by the members of the comparison group, notably the teachers. While "hit and run" data collection procedures are not generally recommended in any educational study, consideration should be shown to the groups that are used for purposes of comparison. One way of doing so is by keeping the time demands of data-gathering down to a minimum. Multiple matrix sampling meets this requirement admirably.

LIMITATIONS OF MULTIPLE MATRIX SAMPLING

While the benefits of multiple matrix sampling far outweigh its limitations, limitations do exist and should be noted. The most serious has already been mentioned: multiple matrix sampling does not produce scores for individual learners; only estimates for groups are obtained. Individual learner appraisal must either be undertaken separately or, as described earlier, in connection with a multiple matrix sampling scheme. A second limitation is that there are no theoretical guidelines for determining the most efficient multiple matrix sampling design for a particular situation. There is, however, a growing body of evidence, based on empirical studies and simulation work, that is being used to establish guidelines for an evaluation worker to follow (Sirotnik, 1974). Recently, Chartock (1980) conducted a series of simulations of various multiple matrix sampling plans and concluded that the division of a total set of items into four or five subtests was most efficacious in estimating the mean and standard deviation for a variety of distributions.

Three other limitations are more specific in nature. First, multiple matrix sampling does not seem to be appropriate for highly speeded tests. A learner's responses are not independent of the context of the set of items he or she is answering, and estimates of group performance will not be valid when tests are speeded. Second, multiple matrix sampling cannot be used with orally administered tests, unless learners are segregated by test forms. To do this would, at minimum, require that learners be randomly assigned to test forms, segregated into different rooms, and an administrator would be needed in each room to carry out the testing procedure. Such an arrangement can pose serious logistical problems. On the other hand, if the different forms consisted of written tests, there would be little problem in giving general directions to a class of learners and setting them to work, even though different learners answered different questions. Finally, the testing of reading comprehension poses some interesting problems in multiple matrix sampling. Typically, a reading comprehension test is composed of a number of passages, each followed by questions. Random assignment of questions to test forms would be highly inefficient: it would probably result in one, or at most, two items being included in the same test form. The learner would have to read an entire passage to answer one or two questions, a rather inefficient use of learner time. This can be overcome by using the passage and associated questions as the unit to be assigned to a form. Whether this produces a particular context effect, undermining the estimation procedures of multiple matrix sampling, is not known at present, and requires further study.

In recent years, two new approaches for testing purposes have been developed. The first, BIB spiralling (Messick, 1985), was developed for use with the National Assessment of Educational Progress (NAEP). BIB stands for balanced incomplete block. It refers to the fractionalization of a large body of testing material into blocks of items requiring about fifteen minutes of learner response time. Three blocks of such material are typically taken by each learner. One advantage of this design is that, by exhaustive pairing of each block with each other block, it is possible to estimate the correlations among various outcomes as well as with background variables. While important in some contexts, the estimation of correlations does not seem particularly important in evaluation work. The second development, the duplex design (Bock and Mislevy, 1988), was developed as a way of furnishing learner performance information for a number of uses at different educational levels as well as being able to scale performance in relation to external measures of performance such as the NAEP measures. By judicious item arrangement, such testing requires no more testing time than a conventional achievement test.

SPECIAL SAMPLING CONSIDERATIONS FOR EVALUATION STUDIES

The preceding presentation has tried to indicate how sampling activities in evaluation studies differ, often markedly, from sampling procedures used in conventional research studies. Since evaluation studies are normally undertaken to assess the worth of a particular program in a certain setting, the production of generalizable knowledge is often of no concern. Furthermore, since the group of learners enrolled in a program, course, or curriculum are generally available to participate in data-gathering activities, there is no reason to exclude any of them. Generally, it is better to have information about all members of a group than a part, no matter how carefully selected. There are also good practical reasons for testing every learner enrolled in a program. If some selection process is used, those chosen for testing may wonder why they have been chosen; those who have not may also wonder. A uniform treatment is likely to arouse the least amount of questioning or resistance. Selective testing could lead those chosen to put forth less than their best efforts. Also, selecting some learners for testing would require segregating them for the testing period, and the administrative and logistical arrangements involved might be considerable. Consequently, it is better, for theoretical, methodological, and practical reasons, to test all learners enrolled in a program rather than draw a sample.

The testing of all currently enrolled learners is highly desirable for evaluation purposes. The group, however, is not a population. It is a sample of all learners who have or will be exposed to the program. Thus, the testing of a cohort of learners in one academic year is used as the basis for estimating the present effects of a program so that judgments and decisions with regard to the program's future operation can be made. Any subdivision of the cohort enrolled in a single year is made to improve the efficiency of the data-gathering operation. Random distribution of testing forms to learners (as in the case of multiple matrix sampling) is not a sampling exercise but an assignment one. The clear intention is to test all available learners at any point in time.

If the sampling of learners is not a major consideration in evaluation studies, what is the major sampling consideration? The answer, usually only dimly realized, is the domain of learning outcomes. Virtually every data-gathering enterprise involves sampling. A ninth-grade mathematics program, for example, may include among its objectives the ability to solve two simultaneous equations involving two unknowns. Teachers or evaluation workers may construct a series of problems testing learner ability to solve for the two unknowns. A set of such problems would constitute an extremely small sample of all problems that could be formulated to test this proficiency. It should be clear that it is not possible to ask a learner every question that could be generated for even a single objective. The sole exception would be in connection with an extremely narrow and limited objective, such as the one hundred basic addition facts or the names of the fifty state capitals. For most objectives, however, only a limited sample of items can be asked.

Yet the concept of a population of items or questions testing a single objective or domain exists. It is in fact one of the basic tenets of testing theory. Testing practice, however, does not generally follow testing theory. That is, we do not usually define a domain with clarity and precision, generate an exhaustive list of problems, tasks, or questions testing competency in that domain, and then select a sample of these to administer to our learners. There are good practical reasons for not doing so. It would be a waste of time and effort to produce a wealth of testing material and use only a tiny fraction in an actual testing situation. Even in multiple matrix sampling, which allows for a broader sampling of each objective, the number of items that can be administered for each objective is extremely small compared with the number of items that can be produced.

It is in this respect that the notion of sampling must be carefully examined. The set of items administered to a learner in a testing situation is considered to be a sample from the population of items that could be asked. It is also considered to be a representative sample. Yet how is this sample of items determined? The answer is clear: it is a judgment sample. Test developers, working from a set of specifications, produce test items that, in their judgment or the judgment of specialists in the subject, measure the outcomes included in a given objective or set of objectives. Sometimes test items and test specifications are compared to assess the content validity of the test material, sometimes not. Even when a systematic comparison is carried out, it is usually confined to determining whether the test items fall within the domain specified by the objectives and test specifications. Usually, little attention is devoted to the issue of the representativeness of the items.

The evaluation worker must be particularly sensitive to the relationship between items, questions, tasks, and problems used to obtain information regarding the attainment of educational objectives, and the objectives themselves. In earlier chapters, attention was given to the need for careful specification of objectives and to the importance of selecting appropriate evidence-gathering procedures. In this chapter, the importance of sampling, or more accurately, the production of testing exercises that provide a representative estimate of learner performance in the domain specified by an objective, was stressed. Unfortunately, there is no well-developed set of procedures that assures representativeness. Unlike the sampling of individuals from a population, the sampling, or production, of items from a domain remains largely a judgmental matter and open to considerable subjectivity. Cronbach (1971) has addressed a number of these issues and has proposed procedures for test validation that could lead to improvements in test development. While many of Cronbach's proposals are rather technical and would involve extensive and intensive investigations, there is a heightened recognition of the importance of judgment in the process of test development. It involves an explication of the types of judgments to be made at each step in the process, identification of the information needed to form such judgments, and the development of principles for making such judgments.

Much work, of course, remains to be done. The evaluation worker may feel uncomfortable with the knowledge that the sampling or generation of items for assessing the attainment of objectives is a somewhat haphazard and unscientific affair that may remain so for some time to come. Such discomfort will be a good thing if it results in greater attentiveness to the development of test items and exercises for evaluation studies and to the development and use of procedures that yield the best judgment of representativeness. Judgment sampling, as noted previously, may be very good or very bad. Steps to insure that it is good must be carefully and deliberately taken. This means that the production of item pools for objectives must be carried out with extreme care and constant checking must be the order of the day. Once a pool of items is developed for an objective, however, the same procedures used for random assignment of learners to forms can be used to assign items to forms in a multiple matrix sampling scheme.

Multiple matrix sampling was originally developed as an efficient way of norming tests of ability and achievement. Its obvious attractiveness in evaluation work was recognized fairly early, and a great deal of important work has already been done to establish its utility. While the notable accomplishments to date have been in the area of achievement testing, there are no conceptual reasons why the procedure cannot be extended to the assessment of affective outcomes of educational endeavors and the collection of background information. Attitude scales, opinion polling, and questionnaires of one form or another can be accommodated within the framework of multiple matrix sampling. In addition to the obvious economies and efficiencies, there may be sound theoretical and methodological reasons for doing so. For example, in the testing of affective outcomes, various biases are known to influence responses. By exposing individuals to only a fraction of the items normally responded to, and mixing them up with items measuring other outcomes, it may be possible to considerably reduce certain kinds of response bias frequently encountered in assessing affective states. Obviously, more research and development work needs to be done with multiple matrix sampling. Fortunately, interest in this relatively new development is running high, and the prospects for the needed work getting done appear good. In the meantime, multiple matrix sampling can be used in most cognitive areas where speed is not a major consideration. Of course, when individual appraisals are needed for grading, certification, and licensure, conventional testing procedures must be employed.

SUMMARY

This chapter introduced the reader to a number of concepts associated with sampling and for their use in evaluation work. The traditional notion of sampling, for the purpose of estimating population parameters, does not generally apply in evaluation work the same way it does in research studies because of the extremely limited generalizability associated with evaluation studies. In addition, the limited scope of such studies often makes sampling of individuals not only unnecessary but, for practical reasons, undesirable.

The dimension of sampling that often does not receive adequate attention in educational studies deals with the sampling of items from domains of interest. In educational studies these domains of interest are the objectives of the program, course, or curriculum under study. The large role of judgment in this area was stressed.

Multiple matrix sampling is presented as an efficient, economical, and practical way of gathering learner-response information in evaluation studies. Its advantages are stressed, its limitations noted. While originally evolved as a means of developing test norms, multiple matrix sampling serves as a highly useful assignment vehicle for gathering a broad range of information in a minimum amount of time. Formulas for estimating program effects are readily available in standard works on the subject.

References

Bock, R. D. and Mislevy, R. J. 1988. "Comprehensive Educational Assessment for the States: The Duplex Design." *Educational Evaluation and Policy Analysis* 10, no. 2: 89–105.

Chartok, P. 1980. "The Effect of Item Discrimination on the Precision of Estimates of the Population Mean and Variance for Non-overlapping Multiple Matrix Sampling Plans." Unpublished Ph.D. Dissertation. Columbia University, New York.

Comber, L. C. and Keeves, J. P. 1973. *Science Education in Nineteen Countries*. New York: Halstead Press (John Wiley).

Cronbach, L. I. 1971. "Test Validation." In *Educational Measurement*, edited by R. L.Thorndike. Washington, D.C.: American Council on Education.

Kish, L. 1966. *Survey Sampling*. New York: Halstead Press (John Wiley).

Messick, S. 1985. "Response to Changing Assessment Needs: Redesign of the National Assessment of Educational Progress." *American Journal of Education* 94, no. 1: 90–104.

Ross, K. N. 1987. "Sample Design." *International Journal of Educational Research* 11, no. 1: 57–75.

Shoemaker, D. 1973. *Principles and Procedures of Multiple Matrix Sampling*. Cambridge, Mass.: Ballinger.

Sirotnik, K. 1974. "Matrix Sampling for the Practitioner." In *Evaluation in Education: Current Applications*, edited by W. I. Popham. Berkeley: McCutchan Publishing.

Sirotnik, K. and Wellington, R. I. 1974. "Scrambling Content in Achievement Testing: An Application of Multiple Matrix Sampling in Experimental Design." *Journal of Educational Measurement* 11, no. 3: 179–88.

Slonim, M. 1960. *Sampling*. New York: Simon and Schuster.

11

ANALYZING AND INTERPRETING EVALUATIONAL INFORMATION

An evaluation study involves the collection of a sizable body of information. The emphasis thus far in this work has been on the classes of information needed for a comprehensive evaluation of educational courses, programs, and curricula. Considerable attention has also been given to the procedures for gathering such information. In this chapter, attention will be paid to the organization, summarization, analysis and interpretation of this information. While a number of excursions into statistical issues will be made, the central objective of data analysis must not get lost, namely, to obtain answers about questions of educational worth.

This material focuses on the analysis and interpretation of information gathered in evaluation studies. A strong emphasis is placed on the logic of analyzing and interpreting such information, but relatively little attention is given to statistics per se. There are so many textual treatments of statistical procedures available that it would be not only wasteful to repeat standard presentations but also somewhat distracting. (The reader who does require knowledge about standard statistical techniques can find them in the references listed at the end of the chapter.)

The first step in the analysis and interpretation of evaluation information is the organization and summarization of data. In the conduct of a study, information about a large number of variables will be gathered in each of five major classes. These must be organized and summarized one variable at a time. Many of the variables are quantitative, or readily quantifiable. For example, age and sex of learners, scores on various tests and scales, cost information, ratings, opinions and reactions, and attitudinal responses can be readily classified into categories, organized into frequency distributions and, in some cases, averages and measures of variability can be computed. The nature of the scale of measurement underlying each variable will determine what statistical operations can be used. For nominal scale variables, a count of the number of individuals in various categories can be sufficient; percentages in each category can then be easily determined. For example, if learners have been categorized in terms of the type of program they are pursuing (academic, vocational, or general), simple counts and percentages in each category can readily be made.

Data for ordinal scale variables such as socioeconomic status can be organized in the same way. In addition, the median of such an ordered distribution can be computed along with the interquartile or semi-interquartile range as a measure of dispersion. For variables measured on an interval scale, the mean and standard deviation can be computed. It is generally wise, however, to obtain a frequency distribution for every quantitative variable included in an evaluation study as well as for every variable that can be quantified without undue difficulty. For example, learners may be judged according to whether they meet the highest, second, third, or lowest level of proficiency of some desired educational outcome. The number of learners in each category can readily be determined and a frequency distribution generated.

It is expected that all variables in the first two major classes of information, initial and later status of learners, can be quantified without undue difficulty. It may not be easy to quantify all variables in these two categories, especially when the variables of interest are highly qualitative in nature, but research, experience, and a vast history of previous practice indicates that it can generally be done. Ratings of the quality of learner products such as essays, term projects, and oral presentations can and are made routinely. Similarly, the quality of a process can be observed and rated.

The summarization of information about the way that a course, program, or curriculum has been carried out will undoubtedly have to be handled differently from the summarization of learner-performance information. Much of the information about the execution of the program will probably come from observation and will be in the form of written descriptions. These should be summarized into short essays about the main features of the treatment as executed. Statements about the organization, relative frequency of various instructional procedures and the quality of execution of each, the kinds of learner assignments, rapport between teacher and learners, and other salient aspects of the learning experience will need to be covered. Since much information will be based on observational information that cannot be easily quantified, verbal summaries and analyses will need to be made. If descriptive scales have been employed, however, it is possible to summarize the information from them quantitatively. The summarization of such information is treated differently than that of learner-performance information. In the latter case, the mean or median serves as the best summary of learner performance and the standard deviation or semi-interquartile range, as a description of learner variability. In the case of items from descriptive scales, the standard deviation or interquartile range provides important information bearing on the quality of the information obtained. If a high degree of agreement in the program is achieved, for example, the use of multiple texts vs. a single text, then one can have much more confidence in the obtained results than in the absence of such agreement. On dichotomously scored items, for example, Pace has recommended two-thirds agreement as a rule of thumb for assessing learner responses (1969). That is, unless two-thirds of the learners enrolled in a particular institution, curriculum, program, or course agree about the presence or absence of a particular feature, one would not report the result in the same way that other results are reported. If more than two-thirds agreement is found, then the modal response would be reported. Even if descriptive scales of the kind developed by Pace, Stern, and the International Educational Achievement Project are used, it is expected that observational information about the execution of the program will also be obtained. Both qualitative and quantitative information need to be aggregated into a written summarization about program execution.

The presentation of cost information can also be treated discursively, although considerable financial information would necessarily be included. Tables, setting forth expenses by category, can be produced, and estimates of costs associated with alternative means of meeting the need that the program was developed to address can be included. As noted earlier, estimates of basic and additional program costs, fixed and variable costs, as well as other kinds of costs, can be presented. The goal, as in all presentations of information, is to provide as complete a picture as possible about the treatment.

The presentation of data from the class of supplemental information can be handled rather straightforwardly. Information about opinions, views, reactions, and attitudes toward the program by various groups can be summarized and presented either in terms of measures of central tendency and variability or in percentage form, expressing the extent of endorsement or rejection. Obviously, the form of presentation will depend to a large extent on how the data were gathered. If particular scales were used, then summary statistics would be appropriate; if single items about particular features of the program were asked, then percentage responses could be computed, and results reported in the same way that opinion-poll results are presented in newspapers and magazines.

Information about learner performance not covered in the stated objectives of the program can be summarized and presented in several ways. The choice of procedure will depend largely on how questions and items were framed and asked. If items can be grouped into clusters that define a particular proficiency, then reporting them in this way would be suitable. Thus, if a mathematics program aspiring to develop learners' concepts and problem-solving abilities paid little attention to computational abilities and supplemental learner proficiency data were gathered in this area, it would be quite natural to report performance on each of the four major computational processes—for whole numbers, fractions, and decimals—if these were frequently taught in other programs at the same grade level.

Besides reporting information by item clusters, it may even be worthwhile reporting results for individual items. Some specialists, notably Cronbach, recommend doing so. The reason for presenting results for individual items is that it provides the reader with a fairly clear picture of how well learners are succeeding at various tasks. On the negative side, it is often hard to digest the mass of information generated by presentation of individual item results. There is no easy way to resolve the issue. Item results may furnish clues as to what proficiencies are being developed in an educational venture, but wholesale reporting of such results may be unproductive. They should be obtained and studied; reporting, however, should probably be selective or presented in a separate document of appendix. The chief beneficiaries of such information may be program personnel who may find it instructive for purposes of program improvement.

Information bearing on unintended program effects is apt to be the most limited section of any evaluation report. Reasons for this have been discussed earlier. Paramount are lack of any clear idea of what to look for, limited resources to spend on searching for such effects, and the fact that such effects may not become apparent until some later time. Few evaluation enterprises can afford to wait around to detect such effects. Thus, any section on side effects of educational programs is apt to be extremely restricted. Nevertheless, whatever can be done should be.

PRESENTATION OF DESCRIPTIVE INFORMATION

The presentation of information about an educational program, course, or curriculum is a rather knotty problem. The goal is to provide a reader not only the main results of an evaluation study but the full range of findings. A full disclosure policy is important for two reasons. First, if various consumers of evaluation reports disagree with the conclusions and judgments of the evaluation specialist, they should have available an information base that permits them to draw different conclusions. Second, a policy of full disclosure minimizes the likelihood of a loss of credibility in the evaluation specialist's work. Educational evaluation is a field of specialization that is struggling to establish itself. Every evaluation worker should contribute to the establishment of the field by seeing to it that work is reported as fully and accurately as possible. Anything less is apt to raise doubts in the minds of other educators and the public.

While full and accurate reporting is critical in evaluation studies, complete reporting is not without its problems. The chief pitfall to avoid is burying the reader in a mass of results. Unfortunately, there is no easy solution to this problem. Judicious organization and presentation of results can help considerably, however. For example, while questions, items, and exercises may be administered in a haphazard fashion to learners, it is important to report learner-

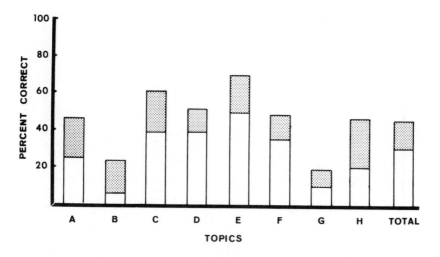

FIGURE 11.1: Pretest and Gains on Number Subtests and Number Total Test for Sesame Street

Source: Adapted from G. Bogatz and S. Ball, *The Second Year of Sesame Street: A Continuing Look,* vol. 2. Princeton: Educational Testing Service, 1971.

performance information by objective. Further, information on a number of specific objectives coming under a general objective should be grouped and presented together. Such organization can greatly assist the reader in digesting a large body of results. In addition, if information bearing on initial and later performance of learners are combined and presented together, it will provide the reader with a more comprehensible picture of learner progress.

The manner of presentation of results is critical. Generally, graphical presentations are preferable to tabular ones. They are easily understood by those who constitute the audience for evaluation reports. Tabular presentations more properly belong in technical appendixes where the quantitatively minded reader can seek them out. Two major types of graphical presentations that can convey considerable information are bar graphs and line graphs. Examples of each (for the same set of results) are presented in Figure 11.1 and Figure 11.2. The results were taken from a numbers test administered to learners before and after a year of viewing "Sesame Street" (Bogatz and Ball, 1971). The eight subtests asked different kinds of questions. To present the results in a meaningful and comparable way, group means were transformed into percentage-correct scores. For each subtest, average initial and final performance levels are given.

In Figure 11.1, the unshaded section of each bar represents initial performance; the shaded portion, the increment from initial to end-of-year performance. The height of each bar represents the final level of achievement on each

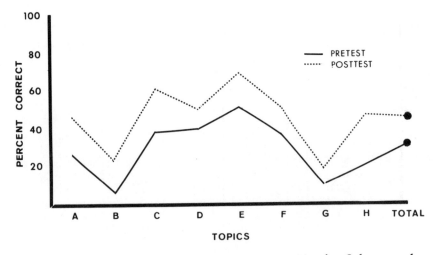

FIGURE 11.2: Pretest and Posttest Performance on Number Subtests and Number Total Tests

Source: Adapted from G. Bogatz and S. Ball, *The Second Year of Sesame Street: A Continuing Look*, vol. 2. Princeton: Educational Testing Service, 1971.

topic. In Figure 11.2 the same information is presented in a slightly different manner. Here, the solid line describes average beginning-of-year performance on each topic, while the broken line describes average end-of-year performance. The distance between the lines for each topic represents the gain. In both graphs, a single presentation describes initial and final learner performance for all specific objectives (as well as the general objective) for a major outcome of "Sesame Street." Even a relatively unsophisticated reader would encounter little difficulty in reading and digesting the results in Figure 11.1 and Figure 11.2.

The graphical presentations of these figures can be easily expanded to accommodate results for both a treated group and a comparison group. In the "Sesame Street" study, for example, one group was encouraged to watch "Sesame Street" and one was not. The latter served as a comparison group. Figure 11.1 and Figure 11.2 present results for the treated group only. Figure 11.3 presents results for both groups.

Figure 11.3 is instructive for several reasons. First, the general closeness of the two groups with regard to initial performance on most objectives furnishes some assurance that the groups could be considered comparable at the outset. Second, the greater increment in performance for the encouraged group is suggestive of the effectiveness of "Sesame Street" in teaching number concepts (the actual evaluation of differences between groups will be treated later). Third, the failure of the encouraged group's performance to shoot up

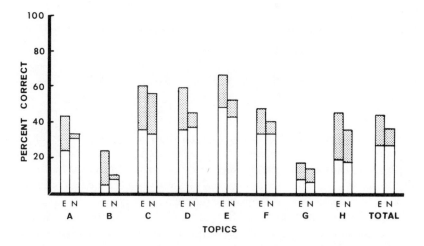

FIGURE 11.3: Pretest and Gains on Number Subtests and Number Total Test for Encouraged and Non-encouraged Viewing Groups: Sesame Street

Source: Adapted from G. Bogatz and S. Ball, *The Second Year of Sesame Street: A Continuing Look,* vol. 2. Princeton: Educational Testing Service, 1971.

to near 100 percent after viewing the program is tempered somewhat by viewing the increment in the contrast group. In summary, the graphical presentation of results shown in Figure 11.3 can present a considerable amount of information. In this figure alone, initial performance, gain, and final performance for both an experimental and control group on eight specific objectives and a general objective are displayed. Most readers would have little difficulty understanding such presentations.

A series of line graphs (see Figure 11.2) can communicate a considerable amount of information in a fairly small amount of space. One procedure, used with considerable effectiveness, is to construct one graph for each objective. Each graph presents results for a general objective and all associated specific objectives. A summary graph is then developed that contains the results for the various general objectives of the program. It would represent the most compact summarization of learner performance with regard to the attainment of the objectives of the program, course, or curriculum.

One of the limitations of the line and bar graphs presented in Figure 11.1 to Figure 11.3 is that they do not convey anything about the shape of a distribution, most notably, the variability. One only gets a sense of the average level of performance for a group. If it is desired to communicate the shape of a distribution, the box and whisker plot can be used. It too is a graphical representation of a distribution of scores but it can convey considerable information. The basic box and whisker plot appears as follows:

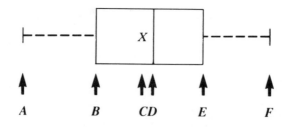

The general shape of the plot is a box with a whisker (broken line) emanating from each end. The arithmetic mean is designated the vertical line (at D) inside the box, usually near the middle. The median is represented by the X inside the box (C). Any difference between the mean and the median is an indication of lopsidedness. The greater the difference, the greater the lopsidedness. The ends of the box (at B and E) indicate the twenty-fifth and seventy-fifth percentile points, respectively. Thus, the box reflects the middle 50 percent of the cases. The wider the box, the more the scores are spread out. Likewise, the narrower the box, the more compact the scores. Finally, the ends of the whiskers (at A and F) usually reflect the fifth and ninety-fifth percentile points, respectively. Again, the shorter the whiskers are, the more compact the scores are while the longer the whiskers, the more spread out the scores.

An interesting use of box and whisker plots is presented in Figure 11.4. This figure is drawn from a report of science achievement in seventeen countries conducted by the International Association for the Evaluation of Educational Achievement (IEA, 1987). The figure presents the results on a science achievement test for ninth graders in seventeen countries. Note how much information is conveyed in a single figure.

While graphs of the sort described above provide a wealth of information about what happened to learners in an educational treatment, they need to be supplemented by other kinds of information. Similar kinds of graphs can and should be developed to summarize the views, reactions, and opinions of learners and others. Information about other kinds of learning, not specified in the objectives, may also be summarized in rather similar ways. Observational information about program execution, supplemented by summarizing expository statements, will also be needed if results are to be correctly interpreted. Finally, cost information needs to be reported, usually in tabular or expository form. There are two goals for all such reporting activities. The first is to describe what was found, and such descriptions should be as clear and as cogent as possible. The second goal is to make the presentation of information as comprehensive as possible.

ANALYSIS AND INTERPRETATION

The previous section focused on description. In this section, attention is directed to the analysis and interpretation of information produced in evalua-

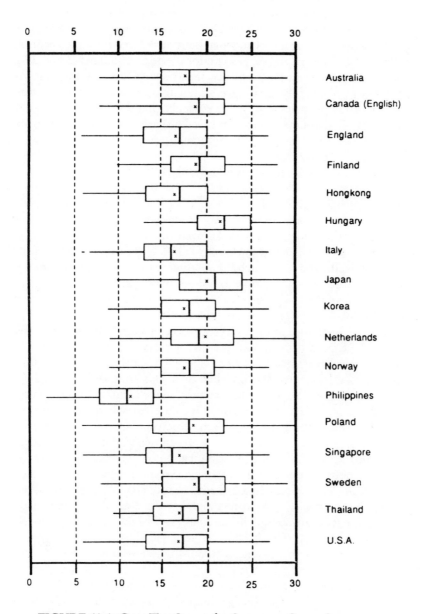

FIGURE 11.4: Core Test Scores for Seventeen Countries

tion studies. This involves both statistical and judgmental considerations. To illustrate something of what is involved, the results for the total score on the Numbers Test in the study of encouraged versus nonencouraged children viewing "Sesame Street" will be analyzed and interpreted. Inspection of Figure 11.3 shows that the initial and final performance levels for the encouraged group were 27 percent and 42 percent, for the nonencouraged group, 27 percent and 35 percent. Initial performance levels were identical for both. As to the matter of whether the groups were equal to begin with, other information from the study provides convincing evidence that the groups were, in fact, comparable. Some of that evidence is based on background information about the individuals in the groups but, more important, on how children were assigned to a particular treatment.

The first question to answer is whether the difference in final performance for the two groups could have occurred by chance or not. This question is answered by using a statistical procedure to test for the significance of the difference between the final performance levels for the two groups. Since the evaluation report provides (1) the mean performance for each group, (2) the number of individuals in the two groups (130 in the encouraged, 153 in the nonencouraged), and (3) enough information to estimate the standard deviation for each group, it is possible to test the significance of the difference between means for the two groups. The statistical procedure for doing this is the *t* test. Formulas for the *t* test are available in many statistical texts. In the present case, the use of the *t* test produced a *t* value of 4.35. Reference to a table of percentiles of the distribution in a standard statistical textbook will quickly show that the chances of obtaining a value of 4.35 purely by chance, with 283 participants, is less than one in one thousand. This is usually expressed by the representation $p < .001$, or by the statement in the text that the difference between the means is significant beyond the .001 level. Whatever the manner of expression, the meaning is the same: the difference between the means is too great to be attributed to chance alone at the chosen level of significance.

In comparative studies, it is important to know whether the performance differences between one group receiving a certain treatment and another receiving an alternate one can be ascribed to chance or not. This is not sufficient, however. It is necessary to go further and determine whether an obtained difference, once its statistical significance has been established, has practical educational importance. This is largely a judgmental matter, although quantitative procedures can be used to assist one in reaching a judgment.

There are two approaches to judging the importance of statistically significant results. The first involves the calculation of an effect size [ES] and the second the calculation of ω^2 (omega squared). Each approach yields a statistic that can assist one in making judgments about the educational importance of statistically significant results (one would not calculate an effect size or ω^2 if there were no statistically significant results. Such an undertaking would be an exercise in triviality).

The effect size has been popularized by Glass and his co-workers (Glass, 1976; Glass, McGaw, and Smith, 1981) in connection with their work in meta-analysis. In comparative studies where performance measures are obtained after a treatment period, the effect size [ES] is calculated as follows:

$$ES = \frac{\overline{X}_T - \overline{X}_C}{S_C}$$

where: X_T = mean posttest score of group receiving treatment
X_C = mean posttest score of group not receiving treatment (comparison or control)
S_C = standard deviation of group not receiving treatment

The formula expresses the difference between group means in terms of the standard deviation of the control or comparison group. Educational methodologists generally regard an effect size of 0.3 or greater as indicative of a meaningful difference. To interpret this effect somewhat more, it is useful to refer to areas of the standard normal curve. Using this guideline, an effect size of 0.3 indicates that the members of the treated group performed at the sixty-second percentile while those of the group not receiving the treatment performed at the fiftieth percentile.

A somewhat different position has been taken by Cohen (1977) who argues that effect sizes of less than 0.8 should be regarded as small. Cohen's background, however, is in psychology where there is an experimental tradition of having a treatment and a nontreatment group. In education, on the other hand, there is hardly ever a no-treatment condition. Usually, there is some alternate treatment. For example, a new approach to the teaching of chemistry is tried out with a group of high school students. The comparison group for such a study would consist of students enrolled in a conventional or traditional chemistry course rather than a group of students not studying chemistry at all. Consequently, Cohen's advocacy that an effect size of 0.8 or greater be regarded as important appears inappropriate for educational situations where a new program is being compared to an alternate program.

Effect sizes have been calculated for the Sesame Street Number Test Results and are reported in Table 11.1. Unfortunately, the authors of this study did not report the standard deviations for the nonencouraged group. They did, however, report the standard deviations for the total group (encouraged and nonencouraged combined). These are undoubtedly greater than the standard deviations for the nonencouraged group with the consequent effect that the effect sizes are probably underestimated. Inspection of Table 11.1 shows that five of the nine effect sizes are less than 0.3. The highest effect size (0.62) is for naming numbers, a proficiency that one suspects can be readily imparted via television. In all, the results are not overly impressive.

The second approach to judging the meaningfulness of statistically significant results is ω^2. (For extended discussions of strength of association mea-

TABLE 11.1: Evaluation of Sesame Street Numbers Test Results

Variables	Max. Poss. Score	Chance Score	Experimental Encouraged Group (N = 153)					
			Pretest			Gain		
			Mean	%	S.D.	Mean	%	S.D.
A. Recognizing Numbers	4	1.0	0.9	23	1.0	0.8	20	1.4
B. Naming Numbers	6	—	0.3	5	0.9	1.0	17	1.7
C. Enumeration	7	0.5	2.5	36	2.0	1.7	24	2.0
D. Conservation	7	2.3	2.5	36	1.5	0.9	13	2.0
E. Counting Strategies	8	—	3.8	48	2.5	1.4	18	2.8
F. Number/ Numerical Agreement	3	0.8	1.0	33	1.0	0.4	14	1.2
G. Addition & Subtraction	13	—	1.1	8	1.8	1.2	9	2.0
H. Counting	30	—	5.5	18	6.9	7.7	26	7.4
Numbers Total	54	5.4	14.6	27	8.3	8.0	15	8.7

Comparison Not Encouraged									
(N = 130)									
Pretest			Gain						
Mean	%	S.D.	Mean	%	S.D.	F†	ES††	2	Comment
1.2	30	1.1	0.1	3	1.3	11.5*	0.33	0.036	Significant but not important
0.5	8	1.3	0.2	73	1.3	18.6*	0.62	0.058	Significant but not very important
2.3	33	2.0	1.5	21	2.3	3.3	0.20	0.009	Non-significant
2.6	37	1.5	0.5	7	2.0	2.4	0.20	0.004	Non-significant
3.4	43	2.4	0.8	10	2.9	12.9	0.42	0.041	Significant but not very important
1.0	33	0.9	0.2	7	1.2	4.8*	0.20	0.013	Significant but not important
0.9	7	1.5	0.9	7	2.0	4.4*	0.22	0.012	Significant but not important
5.2	17	7.0	5.7	19	7.7	6.8*	0.26	0.020	Significant but not important
14.5	27	· 7.6	4.4	8	7.6	18.9*	0.42	0.060	Significant but not very impressive

* Probability: $p < .05$

† These are univariate F ratios for analysis of covariance, using pretest scores on Sesame Street tests, Peabody Picture Vocabulary test, and socioeconomic status as covariates.

†† The effect sizes [ES] have been computed using the standard deviations of the combined group (all subjects) and not the not-encouraged group since those data were not available.

sures, see W. I. Hays, *Statistics for Psychologists*, 2nd ed. [New York: Holt, Rinehart and Winston, 1973] and E. A. Haggard, *Intraclass Correlation and the Analysis of Variance* [New York: Dryden Press, 1958]). Through the use of ω^2, it is possible to estimate the strength of association between being in a particular group (encouraged or nonencouraged) and achieving a certain level of performance on the test. The computed value of ω^2 ranges from zero to one and is interpreted as the proportion of variation in the performance scores that can be accounted for by group membership. For the above "Sesame Street" results, the appropriate formula for ω^2 is:

$$\omega^2 = \frac{t^2 - 1}{t^2 + N_1 + N_2 - 1}$$

where: t^2 = the square of the computed value (4.35 in the "Sesame Street" results)

N_1 and N_2 = the size of the two groups involved (130 and 153 in the present case)

Substituting the values for t, N_1, and N_2 in the above formula yields a value of 0.06 for ω^2. This can be interpreted as meaning that 6 percent of the variation in the test scores can be attributed to the treatment effect, the remaining 93 percent to individual differences among learners. Thus, while there is a statistically significant difference between groups, the strength of the relationship between being in a particular treatment group and achieving a particular score on the Numbers Test is small.

As W. Hays notes (1963, pp. 328–29):

Statistical significance is not the only, or even the best evidence for a strong statistical association. A significant result implies that it is safe to say some association exists but the estimate of ω^2 tells how strong that association appears to be. It seems far more reasonable to decide to follow up a finding that is *both* significant and indicates a strong degree of association than to tie this course of action to significance level alone. . . . In most experimental problems we want to find and refine relationships that "pay off," that actually increase our ability to predict behavior. When the results of an experiment suggest that the strength of an association is low, then perhaps the experimenter should ask himself whether this matter is worth pursuing after all, regardless of the statistical significance he may obtain by increased sample size or other refinements of the experiment.

The use of a measure of strength of association can help the evaluation worker judge the efficacy of treatment effects. There are, however, two additional data analytic considerations in evaluation studies, one conceptual and the other statistical. The conceptual issue is well illustrated in the Sesame Street Numbers Test results. While the encouraged group outperformed the nonencouraged, neither group's performance was particularly noteworthy. Considering that the test questions were specially designed to measure the instructional effects of "Sesame Street," the average performance level of the encouraged group is, at best, unimpressive. That is, an overall level of achievement of 42 percent is not at all high. Presumably, the developers of the Numbers Tests had high expectations about learner performance when they developed their tests. Failure to achieve a high level of performance in the experimental group, no matter how much it exceeds the performance of a comparison group, is noteworthy.

In evaluation studies one is particularly concerned with whether a treatment succeeds in achieving its objectives. If it fails to do so, the fact that it outperforms some alternative may not be important. While comparisons between one program and another may be useful, one must also attend to the level of performance achieved by learners exposed to a program being evaluated. One may also wish to extend one's analyses by examining the performance of various subgroups of learners. For example, how does the program succeed with the most and least able learners; do learners of one sex respond differently to the program than members of the opposite sex? Such analyses are examples of attempts to examine trait-treatment interactions and may provide fruitful leads about how a program is working with particular kinds of learners (Berliner and Cohen, 1973; Cronbach and Snow, 1977). While there may not be a clearly defined level of performance to be achieved, it should be possible to make some judgment about whether a program is succeeding in what it set out to accomplish. Such a judgment is critical, and the evaluation worker, using what assistance he or she can get, will need to render such a judgment. If previously set levels of performance have been specified, the task will be considerably easier. In most instances, however, this will not be the case. Nevertheless, the necessity for making a judgment remains. While comparisons with alternatives and measures of effect size and strength of association can be determined, they are only a means to an end. The end is a judgment about the effectiveness of a program, course, or curriculum. Statistical analyses can and should inform one's judgment; they cannot replace it. In arriving at such a judgment, the level of achieved performance will be a crucial consideration. In the case of the "Sesame Street" results described above, the generally low level of achievement, relating to numbers, seems of greater importance than the performance differential between the experimental and comparison groups.

A second issue frequently faced in evaluation studies involves the number of comparisons to be made. Throughout this book, gathering evidence about a large number of outcomes has been stressed. General and specific objectives, attitudes, views and reactions of learners, teachers, administrators and others associated with educational programs all have been emphasized. Each element can involve a number of comparisons, especially if one uses clusters of items and single items, as well as total scores in analyses of evaluation data. One hazard in making a large number of comparisons is that some may turn out to be statistically significant simply through chance. For example, if one hundred comparisons are made between an innovative and a conventional program, some of the differences can achieve statistical significance through chance factors only. This hazard can be avoided by employing multivariate statistical procedures, which allow for a large number of comparisons but contain appropriate safeguards against false significance. In the "Sesame Street" evaluation study, the investigators employed multivariate analysis of variance and covariance to test their hypotheses of program effectiveness. These were appropriate procedures since dozens of comparisons were involved. It may be necessary to seek statistical counsel in analyzing data from evaluation studies, and it is almost certain that computers will need to be used, if multivariate procedures are employed, because of the complex calculations. A relatively modest investment in such services is strongly advised, and the earlier one can plan for such assistance the better. Ideally, plans for data analysis should precede data collection. If this admonition is followed, many problems associated with data analysis can be avoided.

Some comments about the interpretation of results of data analysis have already been made. Statistical significance, by itself, is not a major consideration. A measure of the magnitude of a treatment effect (effect size) or strength of association between treatment and performance is likely to be useful in judging the importance of results since there is a certain arbitrariness in all such procedures (Cohen, 1977, p. 101). Judgment, however, is necessary. Such judgment will involve a comparison between an achieved level of performance and an expectation about performance. Obviously, the clearer one's expectation about how learners should be performing after a period of instruction, the easier it will be to judge the adequacy of performance. There are, however, a few simple procedures that should facilitate the judgmental process. First, all evidence bearing on a single general objective should be brought together. A single table is generally sufficient to accommodate means, standard deviations, number of items and/or percentage correct of all items, as well as t or F ratios and a measure of effect, size, and/or strength of association, for each specific objective for a single general objective. It is also useful to leave some room for comments. Table 11.1 contains an example of such a summarization for the Sesame Street Numbers Test results.

The table indicates that significant gains were made by the encouraged group in six of the eight subtests as well as on the Number Test total score. Five of the effect sizes are below 0.3 and only one is above 0.5. The ω^2 values are generally unimpressive, with only two exceeding 0.05. Further, inspection of Figure 11.3 shows that the encouraged group exceeded a 60 percent mastery level on only one subtest: counting strategies. The Number Test total score for the encouraged group represented a percentage mastery of only 42 percent, which, while significantly higher than that achieved by the nonencouraged group, is hardly striking. One would reluctantly conclude that, despite statistically significant results, the program did not produce notable final levels of performance on the kinds of numerical proficiencies stressed in the program. This conclusion may seem somewhat harsh, since the groups that were studied included three-, four- and five-year-olds. Inspection of results for each age group, however, indicates that none of the groups of encouraged learners achieved even 50 percent on the Numbers Total.

This conclusion, while informed by the results of the analyses, is not a statistical statement but a judgmental one. Statistical analyses and interpretations can carry one only so far. Judgment must enter the scene at some point. In the above example, the critical judgments were based on gains in performance, final level of performance, F ratios, and the values of the effect sizes and ω^2. Taken together, the relatively unimpressive final levels of achievement, the moderate gains, the moderate effect sizes, and the generally low strength of relationship between treatment and performance were the determiners of the judgment of an absence of strong program effects.

In the Sesame Street Numbers Test a total score could be used to help make a judgment about the attainment of the general objective of number proficiency. This is not always the case. If evidence from several sources is obtained bearing on a general objective, it may not be possible to combine them into a total score. In that event, it will be necessary to proceed through the specific objectives and then arrive at an overall judgment about the extent to which the general objective has been attained. Such a judgment is more difficult to make because of the increased inferential demands.

Judgments about the attainment of objectives are facilitated when a comparison group is available, but, as noted in chapter nine, comparison groups are not always necessary. The absence of a comparison group does present some difficulties which, however, are not insurmountable. The bases for judgment would be limited to the increment in performance and the final level of performance that was achieved. To get some idea as to how this might be attained, the reader is again referred to Table 11.1. Inspection of the pretest and gain results for the encouraged groups does furnish information that can serve as a basis for a judgment about the relatively low level of success in attaining the objectives relating to numerical proficiencies.

If a program, course, or curriculum has been initiated with a single group of learners, and neither a comparison group nor information about the initial status of learners is available, judgments about the attainment of objectives are exceedingly difficult to make. Many researchers with an experimental orientation would argue that no valid conclusions can be drawn. In some cases this may be so. If, however, the treatment to be evaluated is so novel that the initial status of learners, and the likelihood that external events will influence learner performance, can virtually be ignored, then presumptive conclusions can be drawn on the basis of learner performance after a period of instruction. In such cases, judgments about the attainment of program objectives will contain a high degree of presumption. However, the alternative in the situation— no judgment at all—may not be acceptable if a decision must be made. Pre-

sumptive conclusions and judgments will be quite tentative and highly qualified, and it may be that the best use for them is for formative evaluation. Major
decisions about continuation or abolition of a program should probably be
postponed until more and/or better information is obtained. Nevertheless, the
need for some sort of judgment about how well a program is succeeding is
needed; if the evaluation worker fails to make it, chances are that someone else
who is less informed will do so. In such situations Watson-Watt's advice is still
pertinent: "Give them the third best to go on. The best never comes and the
second best comes too late."

TREATMENT OF OTHER INFORMATION

The preceding section, devoted to the analysis and interpretation of learner-
performance information in terms of course, program, or curriculum objectives, covers the first two classes of information needed in the framework for
evaluation recommended in this book. It is now necessary to describe the procedures for the treatment of information in the remaining three classes:
namely, execution of the program, costs, and supplemental information.

Information about the execution of a program usually takes one of three
forms. The first is narrative material, collected on the basis of periodic visits
to the program. The second, ratings, is provided by external observers, usually
members of an evaluation team. The third is program descriptions obtained
through the use of descriptive scales. Whatever form the information may take
(hopefully at least two will be gathered), the evaluation worker must (1) determine what actually occurred in the execution of the program, and (2) compare this with statements of intentions about what was supposed to occur.
These are important tasks.

The procedures for determining what actually occurred will depend largely
on the form of the information. For narrative material, it will be necessary to
compare the reports of each visit and summarize this information as succinctly as possible. Consistencies and inconsistencies in the execution of the
program will need to be noted. Obviously, such comparisons and summarization will be qualitative in nature. For information in the form of ratings,
summarizations of each feature will need to be made. Averages will be useful
in describing the general level of operation of the program, but standard deviations will be equally important, since they will allow one to determine how
"on target" instruction was. The greater the standard deviation for a particular feature of a program over observations, the greater the variability in the
execution of the program. If descriptive scales have been completed by the
learners themselves, it will be necessary to obtain the extent of agreement
among learners as well as the estimates of what actually occurred. Procedures
for estimating the concurrence among learners have been proposed by Pace
(1969). Once it has been established that the learners essentially agree about

what occurred, one can compute averages or proportions describing features of the program as executed.

The analysis of such information can be handled in various ways. For continuous variables, averages and standard deviations can be computed and reported. For categorical information, frequencies and proportions can be obtained. Historically, such data have not been subjected to much analysis. Occasionally, chi-square procedures have been used. More recently, fairly powerful methods have been developed for further analysis. The general approach involves the use of log-linear models and is ably presented by Kennedy (1983).

Whatever the form of treatment, the outcome is a characterization of the program in operation. This then will need to be compared to statements about what was supposed to occur. Again, this is largely a judgmental matter and will probably require some assistance from those in daily contact with the program. For example, if a science program calls for considerable laboratory experience and the available evidence indicates that little was provided, it would be important to check with the teachers and find out, if possible, why it did not occur. The purpose of this is to characterize what actually happened, compare it with what was expected to occur and, should discrepancies be found, find out why the program was not executed as intended. In carrying out this phase of the work, the evaluation worker will function more like a private detective than a laboratory scientist, with even the most rigorously gathered quantitative data serving as clues.

The treatment of information relating to program costs, discussed at length in chapter seven, need not be repeated here. Some summarization of costs will undoubtedly be needed. One would hope that one or two tables would be sufficient to present this information, along with a few pages of narrative material describing and interpreting the cost information. The analysis and interpretation of supplemental information will also depend largely on the form of the data. Information in the form of responses to interview questions, testimonials, and reports of discussions will have to be dealt with qualitatively and summarized in narrative form. In contrast, information gathered from attitude and opinion measures can be analyzed and interpreted in much the same way as learner-performance information. Similarly, information about supplemental learnings, that is, competencies not included in a program's stated objectives but considered enough a part of the program domain as to be worthy of inquiry, can be treated like other learner-performance information, even to the point of using the same form of graphic presentation illustrated in Figure 11.1. One must, however, take care to report the results of such analyses in separate graphs, separate, that is, from those based on learner performance in terms of the stated objectives. Combining these data at this stage of the evaluation is clearly a disservice to the program and may be perceived as unfair by program personnel. In all other respects, the treatment of supplemental information can parallel the treatment of other kinds of information.

It is difficult to specify or even suggest how to treat information bearing on the side effects of programs. The reason for this is that it is not possible to anticipate what kind of information about side effects will be obtained. Likely, much of the information about side effects will come in the way of comments, observations, or casual reports. If this is the case, then the most one can do, after some attempt to verify this information, is to prepare a written summary. If quantitative data are available, conventional statistical procedures can be used.

Up to this point, the discussion has proceeded on a class-by-class presentation. That is, each major class of information is analyzed and interpreted separately. This is necessary. For some, it may not be sufficient. Sometimes one wishes to carry out analyses that involve several classes of information simultaneously. Powerful methods for performing such analyses have been developed in recent years and are becoming more widely used. Path analysis (Pedhazur, 1982) and structural equation models (Bentler and Woodward, 1979) are two such approaches to data analysis. Another is partial least squares (PLS) path analysis. However, while these approaches are powerful, they are extremely complex and require a sizable computing facility. Joreskog and Sorbom (1978) have developed LISREL, a highly versatile computer program to perform such analyses. Also, Sellin has developed a program to carry out PLS path analyses (Sellin, 1983). These programs are quite complex and an evaluation worker may need assistance in using them.

SUMMARY

Evaluation studies produce a wealth of information. This chapter has suggested strategies for the analysis and interpretation of such information. Stress was placed on the treatment of data in terms of the five major classes of information in the framework for evaluation used throughout this book. For ease and meaningfulness of analysis, however, the first two classes of information—initial and later performance of learners in terms of a program's objectives—have been combined. The use of statistical procedures was discussed. Distinctions between statistical significance and educational importance were made, and the importance of having results meet both criteria has been emphasized. Finally, the crucial role of judgment in interpreting results in evaluation studies was stressed.

The analysis and interpretation of qualitative information was examined and the need to verify results by checking with program personnel was noted. Whether information bears on the execution of the program or on supplemental information, such as opinions and reactions of persons associated with the program, the procedures to be used, were similar: narrative summarizations need to be prepared, then compared to program intentions, and judgments made about the adequacy of various aspects of the program.

References

Bentler, P. M. and Woodward, I. A., 1979. "Nonexperimental evaluation research." *Improving Evaluations,* edited by I. Datta and R. Perloff. Beverly Hills: Sage.

Berliner, D. and Cahen, I. 1973. "Trait-treatment Interaction and Learning." *Review of Research in Education,* vol. 1, edited by F. Kerlinger. Itascoe, Ill.: Peacock.

Bogatz, G. and Ball, S. 1971. *The Second Year of Sesame Street: A Continuing Look,* vol. 2. Princeton: Educational Testing Service.

Cohen, J. 1977. *Statistical Power Analysis for the Behavioral Sciences* (rev. ed.). New York: Academic Press.

Cronbach, L. and Snow, R. 1977. *Aptitudes and Instructional Methods.* New York: Irvington Publishers.

Glass, G. V. 1976. "Primary, secondary and meta-analysis of research." *Educational Researcher* 5:3–8.

Glass, G. V., McGaw, B., and Smith, M. I. 1981. *Meta-analysis in social research.* Beverly Hills: Sage.

Haggard, E. 1958. *Intraclass Correlation and the Analysis of Variance.* New York: Dryden Press.

Joresborg, K. G. and Sorbom, D. 1978. *LISREL IV.* Chicago: National Educational Resources.

Kennedy, J. J. 1983. *Analyzing Qualitative Data.* New York: Praeger.

Pace, C. R. 1969. *College and University Environment Scales.* Princeton: Educational Testing Service.

Pedhazur, E. J. 1982. *Multiple Regression in Behavioral Research,* 2nd edition. New York: Holt, Rinehart and Winston.

Sellin, N. 1983. *PLSPATH—Version A: Estimating latent variable path models by partial least squares.* Hamburg, FRG: University of Hamburg.

Additional Readings

Berk, R. A. 1981. *Educational Evaluation Methodology: The State of the Art.* Baltimore: The Johns Hopkins University Press.

Glass, G. and Stanley, J. 1970. *Statistical Methods in Education and Psychology.* Englewood Cliffs, N.J.: Prentice-Hall.

Guilford, I. and Fruchter, B. 1973. *Fundamental Statistics in Psychology and Education,* 5th edition. New York: McGraw-Hill.

Hays, W. 1963. *Statistics for Psychologists,* New York: Holt, Rinehart and Winston.

Tatsuoka, M. and Tiedeman, D. 1963. "Statistics as an Aspect of Scientific Method." In *Handbook of Research on Teaching,* edited by N. Gage. Chicago: Rand McNally.

Walker, D. 1976. *The IEA Six Subject Survey: An Empirical Study of Education in Twenty-One Countries.* New York: Halstead Press (John Wiley).

Walker, H. and Lev, J. 1953. *Statistical Inference.* New York: Holt and Co.

Wolf, R. 1974. "Data Analysis and Reporting Considerations in Evaluation." *Educational Evaluation: Current Application,* edited by W. J. Popham. Berkeley: McCutchan.

Wolf, R. 1981. "Selecting Appropriate Statistical Methods." *Educational Evaluation Methodology: The State of the Art,* edited by R. A. Berk. Baltimore: The Johns Hopkins University Press.

——— *12* ———

EVALUATION AND DECISION MAKING

INTRODUCTION

In the early sections of this book a distinction was drawn between judgments about the worth of an educational program and judgments about future action. In this chapter both kinds of judgments will be addressed. Specific questions to be discussed include: How does one make judgments about the overall worth of an educational treatment? What are the major considerations that enter into making such judgments? On what bases does one make judgments about the worth of an enterprise? How does one weigh different kinds of information in making judgments of worth? What is the evaluation worker's responsibility with regard to judgments about future action? These and other related questions take the evaluation worker into areas in which he or she may not feel comfortable. Having come so far in the evaluation process, however, it is necessary to take these last steps to complete the task. Otherwise, the time and effort expended in the design and conduct of an evaluation study will have been largely wasted.

The evaluation worker may be somewhat reluctant to make the judgments described above. There are two reasons for this. First, the kinds of judgments to be made will normally go somewhat beyond the evidence that has been gathered. Evaluation workers reared in a methodologically rigorous training environment may view judgments of the worth of educational programs as a violation of the norms of their essentially conservative training. Having been taught not to go beyond the data, they are now encouraged to do so. While research training is often valuable for evaluation work, the rather different nature of educational evaluation requires that judgments be made. If the evaluation worker does not make them, someone else will. It is necessary that the evaluation worker contribute to making such judgments.

194 / *Evaluation in Education*

A second reason for reluctance to make such judgments is that others may not accept them. This is a real possibility. While evaluation workers will typically feel comfortable in defending a finding that one group statistically outperformed another on a particular measure, the defense of a judgment about the overall worth of a program is much more difficult. This is because there are no agreed upon standards for making such judgments. Different individuals, examining the same body of evidence, could come to different conclusions. Rather than risk rejection of one's judgments, the evaluation worker may want to avoid making them. Again, the possible educational loss of not making such judgments would seem to be far greater than the risk that a particular judgment or set of judgments may be challenged.

It is interesting to note that evaluation workers whose background and training have been in curriculum and administration do not suffer from the same reluctance to make educational judgments. On the contrary, there is often a rush to judgment on the part of such workers. Such judgments are often made in spite of the evidence that has been gathered. What seems to happen in those cases is that such evaluation workers often hold strong views about what an educational enterprise should be like and how it should function, and these may override the evidence. This is indeed lamentable. Conclusions and judgments should not be inconsistent with the evidence.

The task for the evaluation worker is to draw conclusions and judgments about the worth of educational undertakings as carefully and as reasonably as possible. A major basis for doing this should be the evidence that has been systematically gathered and analyzed. This is not sufficient, however. The larger educational and social goals to be served by particular programs will also need to be considered. A specific course, program, or even curriculum will have been initiated to meet some perceived educational or social need. It will be necessary to determine how well the enterprise meets the need. Determining attainment of program objectives is important as part of this process, but a judgment of the importance of the objectives in terms of the educational need that gave rise to the program is needed for a comprehensive evaluation.

Since the evaluation worker will be going beyond the bounds of the kinds of conclusions that are made in conventional research studies, it is important that judgments of worth be clearly separated from the rest of the material in an evaluation report. There are two reasons for this. First, it is important to label the judgments being made in order to distinguish them from the more objective evidence. Second, if readers choose to reject such judgments, this can be done without jeopardizing the body of evidence on which they rest. A delightful example of how this can be done is furnished by Beeby in his classic evaluation of junior high schools in New Zealand (1938, pp. 204–5). The following note appears in Beeby's book just before his conclusions and recommendations.

It has become the practice for certain writers of detective fiction to interpose, just before the denouement, a page such as this, on which they state, "The reader now has all the facts necessary for the solution of the mystery, which he can, if he wishes, work out for himself. But, if for any reason he does not desire to do this, he can read on." Whilst harboring no illusions that the resemblance between this report and a "thriller" extends beyond the complexity of the plot and the multiplicity of the clues, I wish to adopt the same procedure.

At the risk of repeating what was said in the Introduction I must draw a sharp distinction between what has preceded and what is to follow. Up to this point I have confined myself as far as possible to objective facts. Admittedly, these facts are not objective in quite the sense that the detective novelist's heavy blunt instrument is objective. They are selected facts. Worse still, they are interspersed with my own personal judgments. Such judgments were necessary, sometimes because the facts themselves would have been meaningless to the reader without analysis, and sometimes because the complete segregation of fact and opinion would have meant an unjustifiable waste of time and space. If complete objectivity is denied to the facts, at least it will not be denied that up to now no constructive solution has been offered of the problems raised. Such judgments as have been made have not reflected any preconceived philosophy of intermediate education, but have been the naive reactions of an enquiring mind to the facts as they arose.

The reader now has almost all the facts that I have, the facts contained in Parts One to Four and in the Appendices. I have, perhaps, the advantage of having absorbed during three months in the schools a myriad to tabulate. Part Five contains my own solution, product of the objective facts and my philosophy of education. The reader may follow me if he wishes, or may construct a solution for himself from the same facts and his own philosophy. The main conclusions of Parts One to Four would, I believe, have been arrived at by almost any unbiased investigator, and have a value and an authority of their own that mere clash of opinions cannot affect. Every conclusion in Part Five is preceded by an implicit "I think that . . . "

Unfortunately, few evaluation workers possess Beeby's gift of language. Nevertheless, some statement that one is about to leave the relatively safe area of findings for the rather dangerous waters of judgments, conclusions, and recommendations is needed to alert the reader.

PROCEDURES IN JUDGING THE WORTH OF EDUCATIONAL PROGRAMS

Performance in Terms of Objectives

How does one go about making critical judgments about the worth of an educational enterprise? The question appears simple but is extraordinarily complex. In fact, there are no clear or definitive answers. One begins with the findings and low-level judgments in each of the five major classes of information emphasized throughout this book and discussed in some detail in the preceding chapter. This serves as the raw material from which comprehensive evaluative judgments will be fashioned. The initial questions to be addressed involve the extent to which the program succeeded in attaining its stated objectives. This involves a review of the judgments about the general objectives of the program, as well as a synthesis of these judgments into an overall statement of the extent of attainment of the program's objectives. Such a synthesis can be achieved in several ways. There is a sizable literature on the weighting of part scores (performance on objectives, in the case of evaluation studies) to obtain composite scores. Unfortunately, this literature is of little help, since most of the empirical procedures involve the use of an external criterion or, if judgmental procedures are used, every individual has been administered a full battery of instruments. Neither condition is likely to be met in an evaluation study. Thus, the evaluation worker will usually be forced to rely on judgmental procedures.

At the simplest level, one can employ equal weights to the percentage success for each general objective, if such information is available, to compute a grand average. More than likely, however, the judgments with regard to the general objectives will not be in numerical form (the Numbers Test total score in the "Sesame Street" study is an exception). The evaluation worker will thus be forced to employ a judgmental approach. Discussion with program personnel throughout the study should furnish some indication of the relative importance of various program objectives. Such information will be useful in deciding how much weight to accord each objective. While numerical weights would be highly desirable for aggregating information, they are not likely to exist. Also, attempts to obtain them from program personnel are likely to fail. Such failure is likely to be due to the fact that program personnel are probably not clear as to what the weights should be. The inclusion of a particular objective signifies that it has a nonzero weight. Usually, program personnel are in no position to say much more than that an objective is important.

In one way or another, the evaluation worker will have to review learner performance information and arrive at an initial judgment about how successful the program was in achieving its objectives. In making this judgment, the evaluation worker will, at least implicitly, be giving greater weight to some objectives than to others. Ideally, such weighting should be made explicit so that others can understand the bases used for judgment. For example, in an elementary school mathematics program, one may wish to give greater weight to objectives involving basic operations (addition, subtraction, etc.) than to, say, Roman numerals. However, how one weights basic operations in relation to solving word problems can be quite difficult. One could quite reasonably choose to give them equal weight. In any case, some scheme for weighting objectives and then judgmentally aggregating learner performance information is needed in order to arrive at an initial judgment of the extent to which the program's objectives were attained.

There are two important points to note here. First, rarely will a program achieve all objectives equally well. Some objectives will be achieved better than others. Nonetheless, an overall judgment is required. Later, particular objectives that have not been achieved as well as desired can be singled out for discussion and recommendations for future action can be made. The second point is that an overall judgment about how well a program has succeeded in achieving its objectives is not a judgment of the worth of a program. The latter will involve much more. For example, a secondary school vocational program may be highly successful in training students in developing certain technical skills, but if there is no market for such skills the program may be virtually worthless. The determination of a program's worth involves considerably more than achieving its objectives. The additional factors involved in determining program worth would include the other major classes of information in the framework followed throughout this book and the educational need that gave rise to the program.

Program Execution

Once an overall judgment about the effectiveness of a course, program, or curriculum in attaining its stated objectives has been made, it needs to be interpreted. If an enterprise has not succeeded very well in achieving its objectives, the question that must be immediately raised is whether the intended enterprise was, in fact, carried out. This will involve an examination of the information about program execution. Obviously, if the program was not carried out as intended, or did not actually get underway until close to the time when later status measures were obtained, one cannot make any judgment about the efficacy of the treatment. It remains, at best, an untested commodity. If the program had been carried out reasonably faithfully, then the failure to achieve the objectives is a matter of considerable concern. In most instances, however, things will not be so clear cut. On an overall basis, few programs will either be a howling success or an outright failure. Moderate degrees of success or failure are more likely. Some objectives will have been achieved rather well, others will be achieved with modest success, while still others are apt to show poor results.

While an overall judgment might indicate that the program was only moderately successful in reaching its goals, an analysis by general objectives may reveal that there is a relationship between program execution and learner performance. That is, learner performance may be higher on those aspects of a program that were carried out as intended and lower on those that were not. Such direct relationships, if found, would go a long way toward accounting for learner-performance results. In some instances things may work out this way; in other cases they may not. For example, instruction may not have been carried out as intended, but learner performance may be high because so much instructional time was devoted to achieving particular objectives. This is sometimes the case in mathematics education where educationally questionable procedures may be used to get learners to master the multiplication tables but enormous amounts of time are devoted to the task. In other cases, instruction may have been carried out as intended but learner performance is low because of the difficulty and/or complexity of the objectives. This frequently occurs in areas where the objectives stress higher mental processes or other complex kinds of performances (Bloom and Rakow, 1969).

The patterns described above are not exhaustive. Rather, they illustrate only a very few of the possible patterns that could be found in a single course, program, or curriculum. The evaluation worker will have to examine the information resulting from his or her own study, develop hypotheses as to why things are as they are, and attempt to check them out. This activity will necessarily be somewhat informal so it seems best not to dignify it by labeling it as hypothesis testing. The major classes of information that will enter into such analysis are initial and later performance of learners in terms of the objectives and execution of the treatment. The goal of this phase of the evaluation is to account for why the program did or did not succeed as a whole or in part.

Supplemental Information

Once the review of learner performance and treatment execution information has been completed, the evaluation worker will need to consider the class of supplemental information. The first type of information within this class that should be considered is supplemental learning information. It should be considered in conjunction with learner-performance information in terms of the stated objectives. The evaluation worker will need to determine how much supplemental learning has occurred. This will then have to be related to the stated objectives, as well as to the program as executed, and explanations sought. Certainly, it is noteworthy if a program that does not set out to accomplish certain objectives succeeds in doing so. Also, if a program eschews certain traditional objectives, say computational proficiency in an elementary school mathematics program, and it is found that students are not equipped to compute, this too should be noted. Comparative information on the performance of learners undergoing different treatments would be highly useful in making judgments about program effectiveness in a larger educational context, one going beyond the formal program objectives. Such judgments will be part of the comprehensive evaluation of the study.

After an examination of the supplemental learning information, consideration should be given to how the program was received. Opinions, views, and reactions of learners, teachers, administrators and others associated with the program, need to be considered. In viewing such information, major attention should be given to extreme results. That is, strong views or reactions, for or against the program, should be noted. For example, if a sizable percentage of parents feel strongly that a particular course is harmful, this is important to note regardless of the effects that it may be having on learner performance. Similarly, if teachers harbor hostile feelings toward a particular curriculum, this too is significant. The converse can also be true: considerable enthusiasm may exist for a program whose effects may be rather weak.

In many cases there are no strong reactions for or against a particular program. This, in fact, may be the typical finding of an examination of how a program was received. While some critics of education have reported a sense of joylessness in American education, the absence of strong positive affect should not be taken as necessarily indicating a deficiency. If the enterprise is characterized by hard work on the part of both learners and teachers, it seems unreasonable to expect participants to go around chortling about it. As long as they are not gnashing their teeth in fury, one can be reasonably satisfied. A lack of enthusiasm may not be laudatory; it need not be damning. If reactions are extreme, however, they may be of considerable import.

The last kind of information within this class to review involves unintended effects. Here, the evaluation worker may have little to go on. Information in this area is hard to obtain, since no one has a clear idea of what to look for. One hopes that observations of the program in action, conversations with persons associated with the program or, even better, follow-up information may furnish clues about possible unintended effects a course, program, or curriculum is having. Such effects may be beneficial or harmful. While one would hope to detect them early, it is possible that they will not emerge until the program has been in operation for some time. An inability to detect such effects in a program just launched need not be considered a deficiency of evaluation. What is important is that an effort is made to identify and record such effects.

After gathering the three kinds of evidence in the class of supplemental information, the evaluation worker should review the initial judgment of program effectiveness in terms of the stated objectives, with a view to formulating a revised judgment about the program. This revised judgment goes beyond effectiveness per se by explicitly taking into account supplemental learning (or lack of it), opinions and reactions of various parties, and whatever side effects may have been noted. This is not to say that the initial judgment is simply abandoned. Such a course would be imprudent. What needs to be done is to examine the evidence in the class of supplemental information to see whether there is any reason to modify one's initial judgment about the program and its effects. Even if initial judgments are not modified substantially, they may be qualified in ways that could prove valuable to program administrators and others associated with the program. For example, a program may be generally succeeding in its stated objectives but not be particularly well received by parents. Such information, incorporated into a judgment about the worth of the program, could be quite useful for program modification.

Costs

After completing this phase of the analysis, the matter of costs comes next. The estimation procedures recommended in chapter seven should produce a body of information bearing on program costs. If the program has been compared to one or more alternatives in terms of costs, the evaluation worker will be in a stronger position to make judgments about its worth.

In reviewing cost information, it is necessary to address the question of how well the program succeeded, given its expense. As noted in chapter seven, this judgment cannot be made in a vacuum. One has to have some notion, albeit crude, of the costs of alternative ways of meeting the educational need the program was intended to address. This may involve considerable guesswork if firm estimates are not available; it could, in fact, be virtually impossible to obtain. Note though, that in facing this larger set of issues, the evaluation worker is going beyond the stated objectives and is judging the program in terms of how well it fulfills a larger educational need. This judgment of worth is apt to take the evaluation worker into unfamiliar, and possibly uncomfortable territory. Yet it is critical that evaluation workers move to this higher level if they are to be more than technocrats.

A critical question that evaluation workers must address is whether there are less costly ways of meeting the educational need than the course, program, or curriculum under study. Such a judgment cannot be made hastily and will inevitably need to be qualified. After all, evaluation workers will have far less to go on about a decision alternative than they have about the program being evaluated; consequently, any judgments about alternative courses of action will need to be highly tentative. They should probably be regarded more as hypotheses than as conclusions. While no one advocates that judgments about educational enterprises be so highly qualified as to end up saying nothing, it must be recognized that the information base on which judgments about alternative ways of meeting an educational need are formulated may be so limited that very little can be said. On the other hand, when the available information permits a strong judgment, it should be made. In the 1960s, for example, there was considerable enthusiasm about the use of computers in the classroom. Only later did educators realize that the costs involved in using computers in the instructional process were so high and the payoff so little (compared to conventional instruction) that their continued use was unjustified. Careful analysis could have developed such a conclusion far earlier, and the conclusion could have been made with a high degree of confidence. Of course, things are rarely this simple. While one would like to make strong judgments, it may not be possible, given the limited knowledge base on which one has to build. Tentativeness, more often than not, will be the hallmark of the evaluation worker's judgments.

EVALUATIVE JUDGMENTS

An additional note about evaluative judgments is in order at this point. While no one deliberately sets out to be too tentative in one' judgments or to over-qualify them, the available evidence may not allow anything else. Few educational enterprises are such spectacular successes or dismal failures that unequivocal judgments can be made about them. The typical finding in research studies or instructional treatments is "no significant difference between treatments" on the outcome measures studied. It is quite likely the same finding will be present in evaluation studies that include a comparison with an alternative. This may be discouraging to program developers and teachers with a stake in a particular treatment; it should not be troublesome to the evaluation worker. The latter's task is to determine how well a program is working. Where it is working well and at reasonable cost, no further attention is needed; attention can then be devoted to where it is failing. Possible reasons why a program is not succeeding can then be identified, investigated, and suggestions for improvement made. As modifications are put into effect and further evaluations made, it should be possible to gradually but continually improve courses, programs, and curricula so that they eventually do succeed. The goal of evaluation work must be the improvement of education either by identifying programs that are so bad they must be immediately eliminated, recognizing outright successes that should be continued, or most likely through the incremental improvement of existing programs. Educational evaluation, if properly done, should result in programs that are doomed to *succeed*.

There is little room in education for the mentality of the media where things are judged as hits or flops. Most educational enterprises can safely be expected to fall somewhere in between. The evaluation worker must resist the temptation to make an extreme judgment, since available evidence will hardly ever warrant it. An evaluation study may show that learners in a new course do not perform significantly better than learners in an older one. They may, however, have better attitudes toward school and better attendance. Rather than conclude that the new course is no better than the old, one should recognize its benefits and seek to strengthen it so that it will be an improvement on the old one in other ways as well. Such a commitment requires continuous evaluation rather than the one-shot study that currently characterizes much evaluation. Unfortunately, while many writers advocate ongoing evaluation of the kind described here, there is correspondingly little commitment to actually doing it.

In judging the overall worth of an educational program, the larger educational need the program is intended to meet should serve as the major criterion. Neither the stated objectives, the operational program, nor even learner performance represent fully adequate bases for judgment. In order to determine if a program is pursuing worthless goals, there must be some basis for judgment. The educational need that the program is intended to fulfill seems to offer the most suitable basis. Any other is apt to be arbitrary and, perhaps, even capricious. The educational philosophy of the evaluation worker, for example, would seem highly inappropriate, and unscientific, as a standard for judgment, although it is apparently used more often than one would care to admit, especially by individuals who feel strongly that they can judge the adequacy of educational endeavors without evidence. Exposing programs to purely personal standards for judgment is extremely hazardous, since programs are thereby judged on subjective grounds rather than on their own merits. Thus, an evaluation worker, personally convinced that open education is the solution to most of education's ills, will tend to judge such programs highly, regardless of how bad or good they might actually be. One surely wishes to avoid such extremes.

If personal standards are not acceptable as a basis for judgment, the stated goals of the institution where a program is located are not much better. While there is a surface plausibility in judging educational endeavors in terms of institutional goals, there is often such a large gap between program objectives and broad institutional goals that it is impossible to make judgments of the former in terms of the latter. Institutional goals are usually stated at such a high level of abstraction that they are virtually useless as criteria for judgment. Furthermore, such goals are often so ambiguous that they are open to a variety of interpretations, many of them quite personal. Most schools, for example, espouse citizenship as one of their goals. Unfortunately, there are as many definitions of good citizenship as there are people to define it. A similar case can be made for most statements of institutional goals. They are, characteristically, vague and ambiguous statements representing aspirations and, as such, seem intended more to inspire allegiance to an institution than to serve as guides for action. For reasons such as these they usually cannot be used as criteria for judgment of operational programs.

Educational needs, on the other hand, have a much more practical quality. The improvement of reading proficiency and the training of qualified welders or capable nurses are examples of educational needs that can serve as reasonably clear, specific guides for judging the adequacy of programs, courses, and curricula. Furthermore, such judgments can be competently made by reasonably proficient evaluation workers. Neither an advanced degree in educational philosophy nor completion of a sequence of courses in multivariate statistics is needed to make evaluative judgments of the kind advocated here although, one hopes, such accomplishments would enhance the ability to make reasonable decisions.

POLITICAL CONSIDERATIONS

While educational considerations have been the chief concern throughout this book, they are not the exclusive concern. Political factors and considerations can and do intrude on the evaluation process, and any evaluation worker who ignores them does so at some peril. Sometimes, evaluation studies are undertaken for political reasons. For example, an administrator hopes to gather evidence that can be used to justify an existing program so as to ward off critics. This is perfectly normal. People undertake all kinds of actions for all kinds of reasons. An evaluation worker may never fully know why he or she has been engaged to evaluate a particular program. It is even possible that clients may not be fully aware of their reasons for requesting that a particular program be evaluated. Why a program, course, or curriculum has been singled out for evaluation is not particularly relevant. What is important is that the evaluation study be conducted as competently and as fairly as possible.

While there are tales of clients specifying in advance of a study what the conclusions should be, this is not of primary concern here. Political pressure, even dishonesty, exists in many places. To expect educational evaluation to be immune from this would be naive. Evaluation workers can and should expect to be subjected to various pressures that are political in nature. It is what they do about them that matters.

There are a number of courses of action open to evaluation workers subjected to political pressures. These can range from quiet (or not so quiet) withdrawal from the study to caving in and going along. Neither of these practices is recommended. Only as evaluation workers persist and do an honest job can their work be efficacious. Quitting or giving in is not likely to produce the results that evaluation workers aspire to achieve. It will probably be necessary to have a number of conversations with persons associated with the enterprise being evaluated. Much of this is intended to obtain information that is needed for the evaluation. This was discussed many times in previous chapters. In addition, it will be useful for workers to get ideas about the particular concerns program personnel and administrators have. How much pressure is on them? What would the likely effect of unfavorable judgments be? Are they committed to meeting the educational need that the program is addressing, or are they committed to the program per se? These are some of the major questions that need answers. They are not often directly talked about, but useful information bearing on them can usually be picked up while discussing various aspects of the evaluation.

If it appears that program personnel have a considerable stake in seeing that the results of an evaluation are favorable (a not uncommon situation), then it is important that the evaluation worker and program personnel develop together constructive and effective ways of dealing with information that is critical of a program. Two steps that have typically proven helpful are (1) early reporting and (2) oral reports. Early reporting involves the preparation and submission of reports at various times during the course of an evaluation study. In research studies it is common practice to prepare progress reports for funding agencies, reporting on the work to date. Such reports are also useful in evaluation studies, since they serve to keep administrators and program personnel informed about what is being done and what is being learned about the enterprise being studied. Such reporting serves two purposes. First, it reduces, if not eliminates, any element of surprise about the study's findings that, presented at a later time without preparation, could lead to attempts to discredit or dismiss the results of the study. Second, it affords program personnel time to consider the findings, conclusions, and even recommendations and to decide what to do about them. Thus, when a formal report is presented, administrators and program personnel are prepared to deal with any criticisms or weaknesses in the program and state what they plan to do about them. In contrast, if unprepared, they may end up disputing the findings. The former action is constructive, the latter is not only nonproductive but possibly hazardous to the institution and, even worse, the learners.

The second step that can be taken to deal with information that is likely to be critical of a program is to transmit it orally. There is a certain starkness and finality to information presented in written form that can produce resistance on the part of the recipient. Orally presented information, on the other hand, can be discussed, clarified, examined, and generally managed in such a way that its impact can be softened considerably. Such softening is not intended to result in a dismissal of negative findings but, rather, in an increased likelihood of their being accepted and a willingness to do something about them. Oral presentations and discussions with program personnel may be one of the most important aspects of an evaluation study, since it is here that the initial imparting of results will often take place, and the climate and context within which this takes place will determine whether program personnel move ahead in a constructive manner or dig in their heels and resist. The importance of oral communication has only recently begun to receive the attention it deserves. That the emerging field of policy research recognizes the need for such communication is made abundantly clear by Castleton and Poty (1974, pp. 10–11):

The typical and traditional way research findings are communicated is through publication. Papers read at professional conferences, articles, books, and even stenciled reports are the most widely used modes of communication.

Yet, policy researchers must expect some resistance to their conclusions, resistance on the part of the policy maker that is emotional (due to commitments to other policies), cognitive (due to lack of information and training), and self-interested (the recommended policies may serve some groups less well than the obsolete ones do). Formal means of communications, such as those listed above, are particularly ineffective in overcoming such resistance. Frequently repeated, face-to-face exchanges seem very necessary. Presocialization (preparing for the report) and follow-up (after it is handed in) are essential. The report itself often is not really necessary; it serves more to fulfill contractual obligations and to provide an opportunity for and legitimization of interaction with the policy makers than to communicate with them.

Put differently, policy researchers must be willing to invest a significant amount of their time and energy in communicating. They must learn how the world looks to the policy makers, how best the policy makers will absorb the new ideas, which means of documentation and presentation will be most successful, and in what sequences the findings should be offered. A policy researcher must be able to interact effectively with politicians, bureaucrats, housewives, and minority leaders. Direct contact with policy makers, with the questions they raise, is useful and necessary to policy researchers; it clarifies in their mind the constraints policy makers face and must live with and must be shown how to overcome. Frequently the policy researcher alone has the authority and knowledge to deal with the policy maker's questions.

While one may take issue with the last sentence, the general point is well taken. As evaluation workers begin to recognize the pressures and constraints that administrators and program personnel work under and take these into account, they can increase their effectivenss markedly. Unfortunately, evaluation workers have not always been noted for their sensitivity and tact. Oral presentation and discussion with program personnel and administrators may go a long way toward solving or, better yet, dissolving what have long been regarded as major communication problems.

This is not to say that political problems and considerations will not intrude on an evaluation study. Adequate recognition of such problems, however, and honest and sensitive efforts to deal with them, usually in an anticipatory way, can often lead to a satisfactory resolution without any sacrifice in the integrity of a professional evaluation study.

SUMMARY

This chapter addressed two critical issues: the first, how to formulate judgments about the worth of an educational endeavor; the second, how to handle political factors that can intrude on an evaluation study. While suggestions were made, no settled prescription was made with regard to either issue.

With regard to judging the worth of an educational program, the necessity to go beyond program objectives and actual attainments in evaluation was stressed. Some guides for doing this were presented. The many ambiguities found in them suggested the central importance of the educational need that a program was designed to meet. It was argued that the larger educational need would provide the soundest basis for judgments of value. The contribution of supplemental information in making judgments was also considered.

A discussion of some political factors that affect evaluation work was presented. That political factors can and do intrude on evaluation studies is an accepted fact and should be recognized as such. While recognition of a problem is an essential first step, the proposals for solving it are modest. Early reports and oral presentation could be of some help. Unfortunately, this area has not been subjected to adequate investigation. Greater attention should be devoted to it in the future.

References

Beeby, C. 1938. *The Intermediate Schools of New Zealand.* Wellington: New Zealand Council for Educational Research.
Bloom, B. and Rakow, E. 1969. "Higher Mental Processes." In *Encyclopedia of Educational Research*, edited by R. Abel. 4th edition. London: Macmillan.
Bogatz, G. and Ball, S. 1971. *The Second Year of Sesame Street: A Continuing Look*, vol. 2. Princeton: Educational Testing Service.
Castleman, N. and Poty, P. 1974. *Center for Policy Research: The First Five Years, 1968–1973.* New York: Center for Policy Research.

Additional Readings

Brickell, H. 1976. "The Influence of External Politics on the Role and Methodology of Evaluation." *Evaluation Comments*, no. 2: 1–6.
Cook, T. D. and Campbell, D. T. 1979. *Quasi-experimentation: Design and Analysis Issues for Field Settings.* Chicago: Rand McNally.
Popham, W. J. 1975. *Educational Evaluation.* Englewood Cliffs, N.J.: Prentice-Hall.
Wolf, R. 1974. "Data Analysis and Reporting Considerations in Evaluation." In *Educational Evaluation: Current Applications,* edited by W. J. Popham. Berkeley: McCutchan.

13

REPORTING THE RESULTS OF EVALUATION STUDIES

INTRODUCTION

The importance of continuous oral communication with program personnel was stressed in the last chapter. It will be stressed again here. Such communication, however, is no substitute for written reports. Written reports are necessary for at least three reasons. First, it is necessary for an organization to have a formal record of an evaluation enterprise. Changes in personnel in an organization can and do occur. An official written report furnishes a base for continuity. Second, written reports are often necessary to justify funding, meet legal or legislative requirements and, in general, satisfy a number of formal organizational demands. Third, an official report often furnishes a basis for the legitimization of various decisions about policy and practice. While such decisions will be made by professional personnel, administrators, and governing boards, the formal written report is very often seen as a necessary basis for such decision making. No evaluation worker should conduct a formal evaluation study and not prepare a written report of his or her activities, findings, conclusions, judgments, and recommendations.

Since formal written reports are routinely required in evaluation studies, it is necessary to consider what kinds of reports are necessary, the forms of such reports, how they might be prepared and disseminated, as well as which features of reporting should be followed and which should be avoided.

TYPES OF REPORTS

There are two general types of evaluation reports: progress reports and the final report. Progress reports usually include a relatively short summary of activities engaged in during a particular time period, a preview of upcoming activities, a statement of problems encountered and/or resolved and, possibly a brief statement of preliminary findings. They are intended to keep administrators and program personnel informed about the progress of evaluation work. Frequently, information presented in a progress report will necessitate or result in a meeting between evaluation workers and administrators, program personnel, or both. The purpose of such meetings is usually to plan and coordinate activities so that both the program and the evaluation can proceed on schedule and without difficulty.

Progress reports can sometimes be used as a vehicle for soliciting needed information. For example, considerable time and effort in the early stages of an evaluation study is directed at the identification of the general and specific objectives of a program, course, or curriculum, if these are not already available. An early progress report can report the objectives as specified by program personnel and request comments and reactions. Similarly, other progress reports can report preliminary results and solicit ideas about explanations for particular findings. The chief purpose of the progress report, however, is to keep all concerned informed about the progress of an evaluation.

The final report is a rather different document since, in addition to reporting the results of the study, it will contain conclusions, judgments of the worth of the program, and recommendations about future action. As such, a final report of an evaluation study is to a certain extent a political document. Failure to recognize this fundamental point is likely to lead to considerable difficulty. For example, if an evaluation worker were to conclude that a particular course or program contributes nothing to meeting an educational need and recommends immediate termination, it could result in either loss of jobs or reassignment for some people. It could result in the abolition of one or more administrative positions that were established to oversee the program. With potentially so much at stake, the evaluation worker needs to exercise considerable care in the preparation of a final report and in the dissemination of its findings, conclusions, and recommendations. Any failure to make sure that both the written final report and its presentation are handled with extreme delicacy could lead to rejection of part or all of the report. Since so much is at stake, it is vital that the evaluation worker take a number of steps to insure that the results of the evaluation effort will, at the very least, be given a fair hearing.

The steps required to insure a fair hearing for an evaluation effort begin long before the preparation of the final report. Initial contacts with administrative and program personnel should be used to define what the evaluation worker will and will not be doing. Agreements and understandings need to be reached about the scope of the evaluation study. Distinctions between findings, conclusions, judgments, and recommendations need to be clear to all involved. If administrative and program personnel do not want written recommendations as part of the final report, then this needs to be made clear. Parts of the final report can be transmitted orally, if this is desired. The important point is that such understandings and agreements be arrived at in concert and the sooner the better.

After initial contacts, it will be necessary for the evaluation worker to stay in touch with administrative and program personnel. Progress reports will help achieve this purpose. Face-to-face meetings to review progress and discuss other issues in connection with the evaluation are also essential. Such meetings are necessary to build and maintain a sense of trust, insure the cooperation necessary for the conduct of the study and, perhaps most important of all, minimize or even eliminate any element of surprise. Meetings are also necessary to review the work of the study and secure agreement on certain important points. It is critical, for example, that administrative and program personnel agree about the objectives of the enterprise being evaluated. Much of the evaluation specialist's initial work will be directed toward identifying and clarifying program objectives. This will be done on the basis of documents and discussions with various people. At some point, it will be necessary to secure agreement that a particular set of objectives does indeed represent the educational intentions of an enterprise. Such agreement is necessary before serious evidence-gathering efforts can commence. If such agreement is not formally obtained, the evaluation worker runs the risk of having his efforts rejected on the basis that the objectives set forth in the report were not the ones the program sought to attain. This occurrence, unfortunately, is not rare. In fact it happens with unsatisfactorily high frequency. If one wishes to discredit an evaluation study because the results are not palatable, the quickest and surest way to do so is to impugn the stated program objectives. Once they are disposed of, everything else can be easily dismissed. The evaluation worker will need to insure that agreements are reached at each stage of an evaluation study, that they are formally recorded, and that administrative and program personnel are continuously informed about the conduct and progress of the study.

If continuous contact is maintained with administrative and program personnel and they are apprised of the study's progress, possible problems with a final report will be considerably reduced. They will not be eliminated, however. The evaluation worker should take particular care with the organization, presentation, and discussion of results of an evaluation study.

Unfortunately, there is no ideal form for evaluation reports. In fact, there is not even a single form that is likely to satisfy the several audiences that will be its consumers. There are at least five forms an evaluation report can take. Each is appropriate for a somewhat different audience and for a rather different purpose. This is not to say that one will give different and even conflicting reports to different groups. Rather, it is that different groups have different informational needs, and a single reporting form is not likely to be satisfactory for all groups.

The most general form for reporting, and certainly the shortest, is the executive summary. It is normally between five and ten pages. It is succinctly written and presents the major findings, conclusions, and recommendations of the study. It contains a minimum of supporting data and only the sketchiest description of the design and conduct of the study. It is written in nontechnical language and is intended for administrators and governing board members. It may be written in outline form and include only as much reasoning and evidence as is absolutely necessary for a busy, and presumably, impatient reader who can give only the briefest time to reviewing an evaluation. While educational evaluation workers would typically wish that others were as interested in what they are doing as they are, the readers for whom executive summaries are intended are apt to be interested only in the results, conclusions, and recommendations and not be concerned with procedures, designs, and analyses. The preparation of an executive summary requires considerable discipline and restraint.

In contrast to the executive summary, a full evaluation report is a more leisurely document. A full evaluation report will be the major source of information for most readers about the program, what it set out to accomplish, how it actually operated and with what results. There will also be a separate section on conclusions and recommendations for future action, if this has been agreed upon earlier.

While the full evaluation report will normally be the major document produced from an evaluation, it will differ from a formal research report in a number of ways. Some of these differences are worth noting. First, an evaluation report should be written as simply as possible. Technical terms should be avoided wherever possible. Sentence structure should be simple, the writing direct. Sections of the report should be tried out on uninvolved readers as soon as they have been written for a check on comprehensibility. Second, an evaluation report should generally attempt to avoid tabular presentations and, instead, rely on graphical displays as much as possible. Many persons may be apprehensive about numbers (this includes teachers and administrators), and inclusion of tabular presentations may get in the way of their reading of the report. The results of tests of statistical significance, F and t ratios as well as ω^2 for example, are likely not to be understood or misunderstood. They may just as well not be reported but rather presented expositorily in the text of the report. Third, as mentioned previously, there should be a clear distinction between the results of the study and conclusions, judgments, and recommendations. The more these sections of a report can be separated, the greater the likelihood that they will not be challenged. The device used by Beeby, reported in chapter twelve, is an excellent way of separating the two. It can even be argued that readers be invited to draw their own conclusions, judgments, and recommendations—should they wish to do so. That is, the evaluation worker's judgments, conclusions, and recommendations are not the only ones that are possible. In contrast, the results and findings are less subject to challenge. They should represent what any qualified evaluation worker would have found, assuming the work was carried out with reasonable care and precision.

A third form of report, often used in connection with other forms, is the technical appendix. A technical appendix usually consists of a number of tables and the detailed results of statistical analyses. It sometimes contains discussions of various technical issues encountered in the conduct of the study and data analysis, along with a description and rationale for how they were resolved. Such technical material is apt to be of little interest to most readers of the other reports but is included as part of the formal record for archival purposes and possibly for later reanalysis by others. In general, however, technical appendixes supply the detailed information that underlies many of the procedures used in the conduct of the study and the analysis of the data. Examples of exemplary technical appendixes can be found in the Sesame Street Evaluation (Bogatz and Ball, 1971), the Equality of Educational Opportunity Survey (Coleman et al., 1966), the between schools analyses of the Equality of Educational Opportunity Survey (Mayeske et al., 1971), and the International Educational Achievement Studies (Peaker, 1975).

An evaluation worker preparing a report on a study is continually confronted with the problems of deciding what findings and results to include in an executive summary, what to include in a main report, and what material to relegate to a technical appendix. While no hard and fast rules can be given, it seems that only those findings that are absolutely vital to judging the overall worth of the program should be presented in an executive summary, while results and findings which, if omitted, would result in a serious gap, should be included in a main report. Whenever possible, detailed findings and results of data analyses should be placed in a technical appendix. There are two reasons for this. First, the inclusion of detailed quantitative material, in either an executive summary or main report, is apt to interrupt the flow of the narrative. Such interruptions should be kept to a minimum. Second, the people for whom the report is intended are apt to have a rather limited technical background. Inclusion of technical material in either an executive summary or the main report will detract from the evaluation worker's main goal of effective communication. The technical appendix, on the other hand, may consist entirely of tabular material and extensive technical footnotes and commentary. An introductory section should inform the reader of the nature of the material included, and a note to the effect that assistance may be needed in reading and understanding the material should be included.

A fourth reporting form for an evaluation study would be a document written for teachers and other program personnel. Such a document would contain a brief summary of the study, possibly an extract from the executive summary, and a somewhat detailed presentation of findings bearing on the execution of the program and learner performance, along with recommendations about ways that the program might be altered. The object of such a report is to bring those findings and issues that are of direct and immediate concern to teachers to their attention. It can serve as a basis for discussion and planning for improvement of the educational enterprise, especially if the document is presented in a sensitive and responsible way. This would involve, at a minimum, an oral presentation of the report to teachers by the evaluation worker and an invitation to review and discuss its contents. Such a presentation and discussion poses many potential problems. If the evaluation worker adopts the posture of an expert who is grading the efforts of teachers, resistance and rejection are apt to be the most likely responses to such a presentation. This is perhaps one reason why such presentations do not occur with much frequency. On the other hand, if evaluation workers present their findings and recommendations in a modest and tentative manner and not as revealed truth, if they invite teachers to focus on how the course, program, or curriculum under study could be strengthened, then such meetings can be highly constructive affairs that can contribute to improvements in the educational enterprise. They must be handled with extreme delicacy, however. The manner in which information is presented can have a far greater effect on the outcome of such meetings than the nature of the information presented.

Teachers can and do admit weaknesses in courses, programs, and curricula. They are most apt to do so in a nonthreatening environment. As long as the goal of such meetings is program improvement and everyone understands that judgments about professional competence and personal effectiveness are not at issue, then it is likely that teachers will approach and participate in such meetings in a constructive manner. It may also be judicious to arrange to have no administrators present so as to further reduce the likelihood of any feelings of threat. If the conditions described here are met, the evaluation worker may find that such meetings are one of the most professionally rewarding aspects of his or her work, since they offer the prospect of a very direct contribution to the improvement of an educational enterprise.

A fifth form of report is one that is addressed to a lay audience. Parents and the general community not only have a right to know what is going on but need such information if they are to make intelligent judgments about the job schools are doing. Periodic reporting is necessary if the groups that are called on to support educational institutions are to intelligently discharge their responsibilities. Reporting the results of an evaluation study to a lay audience is an extremely delicate undertaking, one in which the evaluation worker will need to work closely with administrative and program personnel and, most likely, public information specialists in the institution. Typically, reports to lay audiences will be prepared by someone other than the evaluation worker. A school district, for example, may publish a regular newsletter for the community: the editor and writers for such a publication will undoubtedly be in the best position to determine the general level at which reportorial articles should be written. The role of the evaluation worker would generally be confined to supplying the information for such reports and reviewing drafts for accuracy. The executive summary and the full final report will probably provide sufficient information about the results for developing reports to lay audiences. It is expected that the evaluation worker will meet with those who will actually be writing the report for the lay audience to explain some of the technical aspects of the report and to identify important results that will be of particular interest to the intended audience. After that, the evaluation worker's major responsibility is to check for the accuracy of statements in the final report, whether it be a single article, a series of articles, or a separate publication. If a public presentation to a lay audience is scheduled, it is highly desirable that the evaluation worker be present to answer questions of a technical nature and to clarify various points and issues that might be misunderstood or misinterpreted.

THE PRESENTATION OF EVALUATION REPORTS

Just as there are no fixed rules for the forms of reporting the results of evaluation studies, there are no strictures either about the manner or timing of the presentation of such reports. Nor can one say very much about how many different forms of reporting should be used. All of these matters will have to be determined in consultation with persons who are knowledgeable about the local educational scene. In general, an executive summary, a full final report, and a technical appendix will be required. The executive summary might be an abstract of the final report, and the technical appendix may be only an extra section of the final report. Local conditions and the magnitude of the program being evaluated will be important determiners of the extent of formal reporting. An individualized spelling program, undertaken in only a few classrooms in a single school, will require less reporting than a comprehensive mathematics program carried out at a number of grade levels in an entire school district.

Some of the problems of timing in the presentation of written reports can be reduced if written and oral progress reports have kept all who are concerned with a program well informed. In addition, it is wise to submit drafts of sections of various reports to members of the various audiences for which they are intended for their review. There are several purposes for doing this. First, it will minimize, if not eliminate, any element or surprise for the intended readers. This should reduce the likelihood of later resistance or, at least, anticipate it. Second, having various persons review drafts of sections of an evaluation report permits the evaluation worker to find out if what has been written is clear and comprehensible. If it is, fine; if it is not, then it will have to be rewritten and reviewed again. An evaluation report must communicate. If it fails to do so for any significant number of people, it must be redone. Of course, the evaluation worker will have to be alert to distinguish between legitimate objections and objections based on other grounds, often unstated. For example, if a section of an evaluation report contains results that are clearly unflattering, they may be challenged by administrators and program personnel on various grounds, even clarity and comprehensibility. It is the responsibility of the evaluation worker to assess comments about the various sections of an evaluation report and decide what to do about them. A third reason for having various people read sections of an evaluation report in draft form is that the accuracy of statements about a program, course, or curriculum can be checked. The evaluation worker is not infallible, and honest mistakes may have been made in describing or reporting on a particular enterprise. By having those with the largest stake in a program read drafts of an evaluation report, any inaccuracies or mistakes are almost certain to be detected. The evaluation worker should be grateful for such exposure and take immediate steps to correct anything that is wrong. This will save the evaluation worker from embarrassment when the final report is officially submitted and (more important) reduce the likelihood that it will be challenged or discredited on the basis of technicalities.

The circulation of sections of drafts of evaluation reports is a practice that is strongly recommended for reasons presented above. It is not without drawbacks, some of which have been suggested. An evaluation report is not merely an educational document; it more often than not has political consequences. Jobs and positions may be at stake; financial considerations are involved; careers can be affected. Circulation of drafts of an evaluation report's sections telegraphs what is coming and affords interested groups the opportunity to mobilize their forces for or against the study. This is not unusual, and the larger the enterprise is, in terms of money and personnel, the greater the political cross-currents are likely to be. If the evaluation worker recognizes this at the outset, he or she is less likely to be surprised by the reactions the report produces. But beyond that, it offers the evaluation worker an opportunity to gauge the kinds of reactions that are likely to be encountered later and the strength of those reactions. If reactions are positive, there is no problem. The vital question is how one deals with negative and even hostile reactions.

There are a number of steps an evaluation worker can take to forestall negative criticism. The first and obvious one is to make sure that every finding likely to be challenged is reported fully and accurately and supported by the evidence. Drawing from reactions to initial drafts, the evaluation worker may choose to add material that will anticipate and counter some of the likely criticisms. A second step would be to play down findings that arouse the strongest reactions *if such findings are not central to the study*. This strategy requires tact and fine judgment; peripheral issues should be played down. For example, if the teachers in a program have not given much time or effort to explaining the goals of a program to parents and other teachers, some resentment may have developed toward the program. There would probably be little to gain by making much of this point in a written report. Rather, the information should be transmitted orally to those concerned and appropriate action taken, especially if the rest of the program seems to be doing reasonably well.

Findings that are likely to be controversial must be handled with great care but that does not mean that they should be suppressed. In some cases, they may be given considerable prominence, if they are central to the evaluation of the program. In other cases, they may be omitted from the written report, if they are only peripheral. (They would, of course, need to be reported orally.) How various findings are presented depends, to some extent, on their central-

ity to the evaluation of the program and the nature and extent of the antici-
pated reaction. No one argues that unflattering results should be suppressed;
that would be unethical. The evaluation worker does, however, have some latitude in deciding how various kinds of information will be reported. The important consideration is to obtain a fair and full hearing for the full report of
the evaluation. If the reporting of one finding or group of findings threatens
this overall goal, the evaluation worker will have to consider carefully how
such material should be presented. Inclusion in a written report may result in
a stiffening of resistance on the part of program personnel and even administrators; the presentation of the same material in oral form may be more acceptable.

The above discussion applies primarily to the findings and results of an evaluation study. Judgments, conclusions, and recommendations constitute a different matter. Judgments and conclusions are, to some extent, personal statements about an educational enterprise; the same holds for recommendations
about future action. While it is expected that such statements will be based on
the results of the evaluation study, it is equally true that they will also go considerably beyond them and probably contain a fair dose of the evaluation
worker's own views of the larger educational context in which the particular
enterprise takes place, the educational needs to be met, and the weight to be
accorded to the various classes of information. In properly preparing the
reader of the evaluation report, the evaluation worker should point out the
somewhat personal nature of the various judgments, conclusions, and recommendations. It is important that the evaluation worker inform policymakers,
administrators, and teachers in advance about those judgments, conclusions,
and recommendations that may come as a surprise. Informing people about
what to expect does not mean that one is obliged to modify them on the basis
of informal reaction. The evaluation worker may choose to ignore initial reactions to this part of the report if he or she chooses to do so. The sole obligation is to inform about what is to come. The evaluation worker may decide
to remove any judgments, conclusions, or recommendations from the final
written report and transmit them orally instead. One may choose to do this
for strategic or other reasons but is under less obligation to do so than in the
case of findings or results because of the more objective nature of the former.

EVALUATION AND ACTION

The relationship between the results of an evaluation and the subsequent action taken is extremely complex and unfortunately still only dimly understood. A number of evaluation workers have had the experience of conducting
a study of a particular course, program, or curriculum and producing a report
only to see that decisions made about the enterprise are nearly opposite to
what was recommended. Such events are frustrating, at times demoralizing,

and, in some cases, a cause for cynicism. What should be the relationship between the outcomes of an evaluation study and educational decision making?

As previously suggested, no definitive answers can be given to this question. Certain points are worth noting, however. First, decisions about educational ventures are the prerogative of governing boards and administrators. In some cases this power may be shared with teachers and other program personnel but, if this is done, it is done so because of a decision by a governing board or administration. The evaluation worker, especially if he or she is an outsider, has no decision-making authority with regard to educational policy or practice. Even if the evaluation worker is an employee of the institution, he or she is apt to have little or no authority in the area of decision policy or practice. Further, until philosophers become kings, no one is likely to advocate that evaluation workers be granted such powers. While they have considerable knowledge about the programs they are called upon to evaluate, this does not mean that they are in the very best position to decide about the future course of educational programs.

There are several reasons why decisions about educational programs may be at variance with evaluation workers' recommendations. This raises a second point about the relationship between the outcomes of an evaluation study and decision making. An evaluative judgment about a particular educational enterprise involves a weighting, either implicit or explicit, of various kinds of information. In the framework emphasized throughout this book, five classes of information have been repeatedly stressed. Synthesizing this information into an overall judgment of the worth of an educational enterprise involves a weighting process. This is the evaluation worker's prerogative and responsibility. It is also true that other individuals, using the same information, can arrive at different conclusions and judgments and, furthermore, do so legitimately and reasonably. By applying a different set of weights to the same body of information, different conclusions can be drawn. A good example is when policymakers and administrators decide to terminate a successful but costly program. No one can say that such a decision is right or wrong. It reflects a different weighting of the same set of information.

The fact that other people, namely, governing boards and administrators, apply different weights to the same information is no reflection on the integrity or competence of the evaluation worker. In fact, it is the evaluation worker's responsibility to point out that such differential weighting is not only possible but legitimate. The preface to the section on conclusions and recommendations should indicate this clearly. Thus, if the decisions that are eventually made do not accord with those that the evaluation worker advocates, this does not reflect poorly on the quality of work. It may have been an excellent study. Rather, the values of the decision makers, as reflected in the weighting of various classes of information, do not accord with those of the evaluation worker. Since decision makers have the ultimate responsibility for the management of an institution, they must have the authority to decide what will be done. The evaluation worker fulfills his or her professional function by conducting a study as best as can be done with the given resources and seeing to it that all relevant information, including conclusions and recommendations, are transmitted to the appropriate decision makers and program personnel.

Another reason for a difference between the evaluation worker's conclusions and the eventual decision with regard to future action may arise from the fact that decision makers deal with a larger set of considerations than does the evaluation worker. While the evaluation worker may be concerned with whether a particular educational program is effective in meeting a particular educational need, the decision maker is generally concerned with a set of needs. Given limited resources, the decision maker must decide which needs will receive highest priority. Should a high school, for example, hire more guidance counselors or remedial reading teachers? Should an additional position be used to provide enrichment for gifted students or assistance for disadvantaged ones? These are policy questions that the evaluation worker is not likely to have much to say about. Decisions about which of a number of different needs shall be addressed is beyond the scope of the evaluation worker.

On some occasions, when decisions about a course, program, or curriculum run counter to what was recommended by an evaluation worker, the reason may be because there were segments of the community that were so opposed to it that continuation would have caused more problems than it would have resolved. This has happened on occasion where sex education programs have been introduced into communities with highly conservative segments, or when textbooks that contained material considered to be particularly offensive were adopted for use (only to be removed later). Such events have sometimes taken evaluation workers by surprise.

It is difficult to generate much sympathy for evaluation workers in these cases. The framework for evaluation emphasized in this book has stressed the importance of gathering a wide range of information bearing on an educational program. This includes not only performance data but other data as well. If evaluation workers have failed to gather critical information, then it is perhaps fitting that their recommendations be rejected. The evaluation worker must insure that a body of information as comprehensive as possible is obtained in connection with the evaluation of a specific program. Nothing less will do.

The issue of evaluation and action has taken on heightened importance recently as a result of a series of articles by Patton (1988a and 1988b) and Weiss (1988a and 1988b). The issue debated by these writers was utilization, namely, the extent to which information resulting from evaluation studies, especially recommendations, were adopted. Patton's position, based on his own experiences and the work of others, was that a very high proportion of recommendations in evaluation studies were adopted. Weiss, on the other hand, reported a very different view. Her experience and that of others she knew was that there was a very low acceptance of recommendations. Furthermore, Weiss contended, even when the proportion of recommendations that were accepted was high, the accepted recommendations tended to be minor ones and that major recommendations that would require real adjustments were ignored. Smith and Chircop (1989) tried to resolve a number of the differences between Patton and Weiss in a review of the issue. While some of their statements are plausible, a full resolution of the issue was not effected. Much work remains to be done to estimate the effects that evaluation has on practice.

References

Bogatz, G. and Ball, S. 1971. *The Second Year of Sesame Street: A Continuing Evaluation,* vols. I and II. Princeton: Educational Testing Service.

Coleman, J., et al. 1966. *Equality of Educational Opportunity.* Washington: U.S. Government Printing Office.

Mayeske, G., et al. 1969. *A Study of Our Nation's Schools.* Washington: U.S. Government Printing Office.

Patton, M. 1988a. "The Evaluator's Responsibility for Utilization." *Evaluation Practice,* 9 (no. 2): 5–24.

Patton, M. 1988b. "How Primary Is Your Identity as an Evaluator?" *Evaluation Practice,* 9 (no. 2): 87–92.

Peaker, G. 1975. *An Empirical Study of Education in Twenty-One Countries: A Technical Report.* New York: Halstaad Press (John Wiley).

Smith, N. and Chircop, S. 1989. "The Weiss-Patton Debate: Illumination of the Fundamental Concerns." *Evaluation Practice,* 10 (no. 1): 5–13.

Walker, D. 1976. *The IEA Six Subject Survey: An Empirical Study of Education in Twenty-One Countries.* New York: Halstaad Press (John Wiley).

Weiss, C. 1988a. "Evaluation for Decisions: Is Anybody There? Does Anybody Care?" *Evaluation Practice,* 9 (no. 1): 5–19.

Weiss, C. 1988b. "If Program Decisions Hinged Only on Information: A Response to Patton" *Evaluation Practice,* 9 (no. 3): 15–28.

Additional Readings

Passow, H. 1987. "Reporting the Results of Evaluation Studies." *International Journal of Educational Research,* 11 (no. 1): 115–23.

Popham, W. J. 1975. *Educational Evaluation.* Englewood Cliffs, N.J.: Prentice-Hall.

Wolf, R. 1974. "Data Analysis and Reporting Considerations in Evaluation." In *Educational Evaluation: Current Applications,* edited by W. J. Popham. Berkeley: McCutchan.

─── 14 ───

CONTEMPORARY EDUCATIONAL EVALUATION

The development of the educational evaluation field over the past twenty-five years has been notable. What was once a miniscule field has grown into a sizable enterprise within the field of education. It is likely that few people could have predicted the size and character of the evaluation field in 1965.

THE DEVELOPMENT OF EVALUATION

Evaluation has acquired the trappings of a developed field. In 1986, the American Evaluation Association was formed through the merging of the Evaluation Research Society and the Evaluation Network. The association currently boasts over two thousand members. Besides holding an annual meeting, the organization issues two quarterly publications. *Evaluation Practice* contains articles, reviews, and news of the field. It is a general journal for the membership. *New Directions for Program Evaluation* is a publication in which each issue contains a number of articles written around a central theme. Recent themes for this publication include "International Innovations," "Evaluation and the Federal Decision Maker," and "Evaluating Program Environments." To date, the American Evaluation Association has shown a high degree of responsiveness to the needs of its members and a strong service orientation. It is clearly a thriving organization with a core of dedicated and hard-working members occupying the key leadership positions.

The other major journal in the field of evaluation is *Educational Evaluation and Policy Analysis*. This journal was started in 1979 by the American Educational Research Association (AERA). This organization, with over fourteen thousand members, is the largest organization in the United States for educational researchers. Recognizing that many of its members were engaged in evaluation work, AERA launched *Educational Evaluation and Policy Analysis* as a journal that would be responsive to the needs of that segment of the membership. The journal contains articles on a variety of matters, often methodological, that are of interest to evaluation workers. AERA also has a quite active division on evaluation. It sponsors a number of sessions at the AERA annual meeting, bestows awards of various kinds, and issues a newsletter to its members.

Publications are one of the most visible signs of the existence of a field. Less visible, but no less important, is the existence of standards to guide and judge the work of practitioners. The field of testing has long had a series of standards for educational and psychological tests and manuals. Standards were first issued in 1954 by a joint committee of people representing the American Psychological Association, the American Educational Research Association, and the National Council on Measurement in Education. Subsequent editions of this publication were issued in 1966, 1974, 1978, and 1985. One outcome of the 1974 edition of the *Standards* was a recognition of the need for a set of standards to guide the work and products of evaluation workers. Accordingly, a joint committee was formed in 1976 that consisted of members from twelve organizations who were considered to have an interest in evaluation and something to contribute to such an enterprise. The chair of the joint committee was Daniel Stufflebeam, a recognized specialist in the field, from Western Michigan University. Under Stufflebeam's leadership, the joint committee produced a comprehensive set of standards that were issued in 1981 (Stufflebeam, 1981). The standards that were developed were organized into four broad categories: utility, feasibility, propriety, and accuracy. In each category, the number of specific standards ranges from three to eleven for a total of thirty standards.

The standards are eclectic: no single view of evaluation predominates. This could be expected since the standards had to be approved by twelve rather diffe: nt organizations, for example, the American Psychological Association and the American Federation of Teachers.

A cursory reading of the standards suggests that the identified standards are rather benign. Consider the following two standards:

A1 Audiences involved in or affected by the evaluation should be identified, so that their needs can be addressed.

and

D7 The data collected, processed, and reported in an evaluation should be reviewed and corrected, so that the results of the evaluation will not be flawed.

The benignness of the standards is illusory. Each standard represents an important area of consideration in the planning and conduct of an evaluation. It may be hard to imagine how such apparently self-evident and desirable features of an evaluation are not met, but, the fact is that the frequency with which they are not is far higher than one would want. Material presented to elaborate each standard shows how the standards are often not met.

While the standards have been generally accepted, there is not much evidence to suggest that they are being used. There is no solid evidence to suggest, for example, that the evaluation standards, unlike the standards for tests and manuals, have been used in court cases. Also, it is not clear which individuals or groups would apply the standards in a particular setting. Those responsible for the conduct of an evaluation are usually too busy doing the work to step back and judge their own efforts. Also, it is questionable whether they could even do so. Some degree of detachment from the actual conduct of an evaluation seems necessary in order to apply the standards. Evaluation workers can be expected to be knowledgeable about the standards and even to take them into account in the planning and conduct of an evaluation. However, it seems unrealistic to expect such workers to systematically apply them during or at the conclusion of an evaluation.

Clients are also not likely to use the standards for several reasons. First, they are usually not proficient enough to use them. Second, they are more likely to be interested in the results of an evaluation than in the application of a set of standards to judge the evaluation. Third, the clients are likely to have many responsibilities that are more pressing than applying the standards to judge an evaluation.

This does not mean that the clients do not have a strong interest in seeing that an evaluation is planned and carried out properly. They certainly do. Their interest in judging the adequacy of the evaluation would seem to be at its highest when receiving reports of the evaluation. If the reports of an evaluation produce results that are dissonant with their own views, they are likely to question the evaluation. This is perfectly normal since the clients can learn the basis for various results, conclusions, and recommendations. If such examination of evaluation reports reveals that there is little or no basis for particular results, conclusions, and recommendations, then the clients will simply dismiss them. In either case, there is no need for the standards per se. Rather, it is the normal critical judgment of the clients that is involved.

If evaluation workers and clients are not likely to use the standards, then who is? There does not seem to be a clear-cut answer to this question. Education is not like the business world where there is a need for external auditors who apply accounting standards to a company's financial records and issue opinions about the fiscal state of a company. The lack of a clearly identified group who would apply the standards along with the absence of a defined audience for such information leads one to suspect that the evaluation standards are likely to be a guide but not a force in the field of evaluation. However, the mere existence of a set of standards for the planning and conduct of evaluations is important in two ways. First, it serves as a guide to the conduct of evaluation work. Second, it helps to legitimize the field of evaluation by showing people both within and outside of the field that it is governed by a set of standards.

There can be little doubt that the field of education has developed enormously in the past quarter of a century. Evidence of this development abounds. There is a thriving association for evaluation workers. There are several high quality publications that serve the evaluation community. Evaluation requirements are codified in various pieces of legislation and administrative policies and regulations. Finally, there is a set of standards to guide the conduct of evaluation studies and by which their results can be judged.

CONVERGENCE AND DIVERGENCE IN VIEWS ABOUT EVALUATION

These are the outward manifestations of the field's development. It is also possible to inquire how much the field of evaluation has coalesced intellectually. To what extent do evaluation workers share a common view of what evaluation is and should be? What do recognized leaders in the field think? Have the views of major theorists in the field come closer together over the years or are there major differences?

Some answers to these questions are provided in a set of papers that were presented at a symposium at the 1988 annual meeting of the American Educational Research Association. The symposium was organized by Marvin Alkin of UCLA and the papers were presented by three of his students. The students attempted to determine whether evaluation theories have converged over time. The paper by Sarah J. Stanley set out to compare early and later positions of Michael Scriven, Robert Stake, and Michael J. Patton. This was done through a comparison of their early with their later writings. Stanley found that differences between these writers continued to exist, but they had moved toward similar positions with regard to attention to multiple audiences and utilization of results. Stanley concluded her paper on an optimistic note. Her feeling was that if three individuals start at very different positions and end up evincing the same kinds of concerns, there was considerable hope for convergence in the field of evaluation.

The paper by Gretchen W. Guiton was similar to that of Stanley's. Guiton selected William Cooley, Lee Cronbach, and Peter Rossi as the three leaders whose works were to be compared. All three had a list of publications stretching over at least fifteen years so a tracing of their views was possible. Guiton reported mixed results. She recognized that each writer's concern is with a somewhat different part of the field of evaluation, for example, Rossi's involvement with large-scale evaluations in contrast to Cooley's exclusive concern for local situations. Despite these differences, Guiton felt that the three writers shared some common concerns, namely, that evaluations should be useful to decision makers and that an evaluation's effectiveness is to be judged, at least in part, by its utilization. Guiton concluded her paper on a hopeful note.

The last paper in the set was by Janice E. Williams. Her paper is different from Stanley's and Guiton's in that she actually sought out a dozen leaders in the field of evaluation and asked them to respond to a specially developed questionnaire that probed their views on a number of issues. In responding to the items, each individual was asked to rate the similarity of his own theoretical position to the positions of each of the other eleven theorists. In the second part of the questionnaire, each individual was asked to relate the degree to which they emphasized particular approaches in actual evaluations both currently and in the past. This was deemed the "evaluation practice" section of the instruments.

The questionnaire information was analyzed using a multidimensional scaling procedure that resulted in the identification of four dimensions of theory and two dimensions of practice. They are as follows:

Theory Dimensions

1. Formal Approach vs. Informal Approach
2. Value-oriented vs. Value-free Judgment
3. Immediate Orientation vs. Future Orientation
4. Economic Structure vs. Political Structure

Practice Dimensions

1. Causal vs. Descriptive Claims
2. Specified vs. General Audience

The largest difference between the respondents was in the theoretical dimension, but two important practice dimensions were also identified. Williams concluded that no convergence had taken place in the positions espoused by the individuals she studied during the period 1978 to 1988. This was definitely true in the area of theory but also seemed to hold for the area of practice as well.

The lack of convergence in a field is neither good nor bad. In the particular case of evaluation, it is probably a reflection of the youth of the field. Modern educational evaluation is barely twenty-five years old. It has had heavy burdens placed on it during its youth and, on the whole, has generally met these challenges with success. The fact that the field has not fully crystallized hardly seems a matter for great concern.

QUALITATIVE VS. QUANTITATIVE APPROACHES TO EVALUATION

What is emerging as the major area of controversy in the field of evaluation as well as research is the qualitative vs. quantitative debate that has been building over the past ten to fifteen years.

On the face of it, there seems to be little reason for qualitative and quantitative approaches to be in opposition. In fact, the two approaches can be regarded as complementary. For example, even a highly rigorous experimental study with large amounts of quantitative data could profit from the use of anecdotal material gathered through the use of observational procedures or interviews. Such information can put "flesh on the bones" of a study. Not only can it enliven the presentation of results, but it can also convey important information to an audience.

The view taken throughout this book, although not explicitly stated, is that quantitative and qualitative procedures and techniques *both* have a place in evaluation studies. The choice of technique depends on the purpose to be served. In the framework presented in chapter two and elaborated in chapters four through eight, both quantitative and qualitative techniques and procedures are presented and discussed. This is especially evident in Table 4.1. The sole criterion guiding the use of a particular evaluation procedure, it was emphasized, was appropriateness.

At this level, any debate between quantitative and qualitative approaches is as meaningless as the question, "which is a better tool—a saw or a hammer?" The question is meaningless because it fails to identify the purpose for which a tool is to be used. Similarly, some of the current debate between quantitative and qualitative approaches is equally meaningless because it fails to identify the purpose of a procedure. Once the matter of purpose is cleared up, debate often fizzles out.

If the debate were over techniques and procedures, it would hardly draw attention. In fact, it would be downright silly. The field of evaluation can only benefit from having as large an arsenal of techniques and procedures as possible. To eliminate broad classes of these on some sort of doctrinnaire grounds would be foolish. But, the debate is not just about techniques and procedures, it is primarily about paradigms. This is a more serious matter, arousing passions usually not characteristic of a scientific community.

The general tradition out of which evaluation developed was positivistic in nature. Among its many characteristics, positivism stresses the existence of an objective reality that scholars investigate with the goal of determining its nature. In evaluation terms, this means studying programs to find out what effects they are having on people. However this was done, scholars working within a positivistic framework held to the notion that there was an objective reality "out there," and that it was the investigator's job to describe and empirically verify it.

Positivism has many other attributes, well described by Phillips (1987). However, a philosophical treatise is not the aim of this section. A gradual erosion of logical positivism's credibility occurred over a number of years. One work that accelerated this erosion was Kuhn's highly influential work, *The Structure of Scientific Revolution* (1962). By the mid-1970s, Phillips (1987) notes that, "the 'rationality of science' had become a major issue" in the philosophy of science. Some investigators turned away from any form of positivism and sought refuge in other paradigms.

One type of paradigm that has had considerable appeal is phenomenological in nature and is sometimes referred to as "postpositivistic." Lincoln and Guba (1985) stress such an approach. They list the "axioms" of this position as follows:

Realities are multiple, constructed, and holistic.

Knower and known are interactive, inseparable.

Only time- and context-bound working hypotheses (ideographic statements) are possible.

All entities are in a state of mutual simultaneous shaping so that it is impossible to distinguish cause from effects.

Inquiry is value-bound.

The emergence of a phenomenological paradigm, with various embellishments, has been taken up by a number of individuals. Such a paradigm draws heavily on the use of various qualitative methods and techniques ably described by Fetterman (1988a). The term "qualitative research" is often used to describe the approaches of such investigators although Fetterman carefully points out that one should not think it is a monolithic entity: "qualitative approaches are varied and manifold" (Fetterman, 1988b).

In contrast, evaluation workers who are more allied with a positivistic approach are more inclined to use quantitative methods and procedures. The use of various tests and scales, questionnaires, and other formal instruments are characteristic of a positivistic paradigm. Such investigators may make use of qualitative techniques such as interviews, observations, and case studies but if they do, they do so because that is the best technique for gathering the requisite information. Qualitative investigators, on the other hand, are not likely to use quantitative techniques and procedures.

At the level of paradigms, there are deep differences between qualitative and quantitative investigators. Fetterman (1988b) describes the general explosion of the credibility of positivism and the ascendance of a phenomenological approach as a "silent scientific revolution." It is, "like a quiet storm. There are no ominous clouds hovering overhead, but the power of the storm threatens to tear through the intellectual landscape like a tornado" (Fetterman, 1988b, p. 22).

These are strong words indeed. Are they justified? Unfortunately, there is no easy answer to the question. Many qualitative researchers would agree with Fetterman's position. Lincoln, for example, used the term "revolution" in one of her works (Lincoln, 1986). Other qualitative researchers such as Patton (1988) and Miles and Huberman (1984) do not take such an extreme position. Quantitatively oriented investigators often simply dismiss such talk as being excessive and unwarranted.

The position taken throughout this book is eclectic. Both qualitative and quantitative techniques and procedures are stressed. The demands of a particular evaluation study are considered more important determiners of what one does than an ideological position. While this does nothing to resolve the intellectual debate, it does enable one to get on with the job of evaluating educational programs.

The debate between qualitative and quantitative approaches in evaluation is just one outcropping of a larger debate that is going on in the philosophy of science. It is a serious debate and the outcome is not likely to be known for some time. A number of able scholars are identifying and addressing exceedingly complex issues. It is interesting to note that, besides the epistemological issues that are involved, there also seems to be a clash of temperaments. Phillips (1987) notes that the debate also involves temperament in such issues as tough-mindedness vs. tender-mindedness, and formalism vs. antiformalism. Separating out the emotional from the intellectual issues and dealing with each is an enormous challenge. Until some resolution is achieved, evaluation work will have to proceed as best it can. It is felt that the eclectic approach offered here will be serviceable until the philosophical issues are resolved.

THE ROLE OF TEACHERS IN EVALUATION

An implicit view in this book is that teachers are partners in an evaluation enterprise. Not only is their cooperation needed if an evaluation study is to be successfully carried out, but their expertise is vital to the planning and conduct of a study. The purpose of this section is to explicitly set forth the various roles that teachers play in an evaluation study.

1. *Formulation and review of objectives.* Teachers have a vital role in the formulation and review of objectives. It is quite common for evaluation workers to be asked to conduct studies of programs that have no written objectives, or objectives that are so vague and general that they are virtually useless. In such situations, teachers are invariably the best source of information about program objectives since they are the ones in closest contact with the program. The evaluation worker is thus heavily dependent on the teacher to be a major source of information about a program's objectives. Teachers are similarly in the best position to review objectives once they have been identified.

2. *Review prototype items.* Once objectives are identified and evaluation procedures selected, prototype items are developed for the various objectives. Teachers are the logical choice to review these items for the same reasons noted above, namely, they are the ones who are closest to the instructional situation.

3. *Data collection.* It should be self-evident that teachers are central to the collection of information. All evaluation workers, regardless of their philosophical orientation, acknowledge this. Unfortunately, some evaluation workers see this as the only role teachers have in an evaluation study. When teachers are used only as data collectors, they are not apt to like it. On the other hand, if data collection is just one of a number of functions that teachers are asked

to assume in connection with an evaluation study, they are more likely to accept it.

4. *Interpretation of results.* Teachers can play a vital role in interpreting the results of an evaluation study. What may strike an evaluation worker as puzzling results are often self-evident to teachers. Evaluators need to draw on teacher expertise in interpreting the results of evaluation studies. Not only can teachers help explain discrepancies between intended and implemented programs, but are invariably useful in interpreting achievement and attitudinal results.

5. *Review drafts of evaluation reports.* Teachers can be one's most thoughtful critics. It would be wise to share the initial drafts of reports with teachers for several reasons. First, teachers are closest to the instructional situation and can often provide the most penetrating review and analysis of an evaluation report. Second, they are often in the best position to judge how realistic the evaluation worker's recommendations are. Third, teachers appreciate finding out about matters likely to affect their professional life earlier rather than later. By working closely and continuously in partnership with teachers, the chances for a successful evaluation study are improved considerably.

The inclusion of teachers in an evaluation enterprise will undoubtedly contribute to its likelihood of success. This does not mean that an evaluation worker has to succumb to teacher dictates if a difference of views develops, especially in the areas of interpretation of results and recommendations. The evaluation worker has a unique function to perform and must do this in an honest way. If others do not agree with particular recommendations, it is important that this is discovered as early as possible. It does not mean that recommendations need to be changed. The statements about the independence and integrity of the evaluation worker that were made in chapter twelve still hold.

References

American Educational Research Association, American Psychological Association, and National Council on Measurement in Education. 1974. *Standards for Educational and Psychological Tests and Manuals.* Washington, DC: American Psychological Association.

Fetterman, D. M. (ed.) 1988a. *Qualitative Approaches to Evaluation in Education: The Silent Scientific Revolution.* New York: Praeger.

Fetterman, D. M. 1988b. "Qualitative Approaches to Evaluating Education." *Educational Researcher* 17(8): 17–23.

Guiton, G. W. 1988. "The Evolution of Three Evaluation Theories: Do They Suggest Convergence?" Paper presented at the annual meeting of the American Educational Research Association, New Orleans.

Joint Committee on Standards for Educational Evaluation. 1981. *Standards for Evaluations of Educational Programs, Projects, and Materials.* New York: McGraw-Hill.

Kuhn, T. S. 1962. *The Structure of Scientific Revolutions*. Chicago: University of Chicago Press.

Lincoln, Y. S. (ed.) 1986. *Organizational Theory and Inquiry: The Paradigm Revolution*. Newbury Park, CA: Sage.

Lincoln, Y. S. and Guba, E. G. 1985. *Naturalistic Inquiry*. Newbury Park, CA: Sage.

Miles, M. and Huberman, A. M. 1984. "Drawing Valid Meaning From Qualitative Data: Toward a Shared Craft." *Educational Researcher* 13(5): 22–30.

Patton, M. Q. 1988. Paradigms and Pragmatism. In D. M. Fetterman (ed.), *Qualitative Approaches to Evaluation: The Silent Scientific Revolution*. New York: Praeger.

Phillips, D. C. 1987. *Philosophy, Science, and Social Inquiry*. Oxford: Pergamon Press.

Stanley, S. J. 1988. "A Convergence or Divergence? The Evolving Evaluation Advice of Scriven, Stake and Patton." Paper presented at the annual meeting of the American Educational Research Association, New Orleans.

Williams, J. E. 1988. "Mapping Evaluation Theory: Overlap and Convergence." Paper presented at the annual meeting of the American Psychological Association, New Orleans.

INDEX

ABOUT THE AUTHOR

RICHARD M. WOLF is Professor of Psychology and Education and Chairman of the Department of Measurement, Evaluation, and Statistics at Teachers College, Columbia University in New York. Previously, he taught at the University of Southern California and the University of Chicago.

Dr. Wolf has published widely in the areas of evaluation and measurement. His previous books are *Achievement in America* (1977) and *Crucial Issues in Testing* (1974), the latter coauthored with Ralph W. Tyler. His articles have appeared in the *Journal of Educational Measurement, International Journal of Educational Research, Comparative Education Review, International Review of Education, International Encyclopedia of Education, Encyclopedia of Educational Research* and *World Book Encyclopedia*. In 1975, he was a Fulbright Lecturer in New Zealand and in 1981 served as a UNESCO consultant in Singapore. Dr. Wolf is the United States General Assembly Member to the International Association for the Evaluation of Educational Achievement (IEA).

Dr. Wolf holds a B.A. degree from Antioch College, an Ed.M. from the University of Buffalo, and a Ph.D. from the University of Chicago.